D0554114

Why Canada Is
As Close to Utopia As It Gets

The
Efficient
Society

Why Canada Is
As Close to Utopia As It Gets

The
Efficient
Society

Joseph Heath

PENGUIN

VIKING

Viking
Published by the Penguin Group
Penguin Books Canada Ltd, 10 Alcorn Avenue, Toronto, Ontario, Canada M4V 3B2
Penguin Books Ltd, 27 Wrights Lane, London w8 5TZ, England
Penguin Putnam Inc., 375 Hudson Street, New York, New York 10014, U.S.A.
Penguin Books Australia Ltd, Ringwood, Victoria, Australia
Penguin Books (NZ) Ltd, cnr Rosedale and Airborne Roads, Albany,
Auckland 1310, New Zealand

Penguin Books Ltd, Registered Offices: Harmondsworth, Middlesex, England

First published 2001

1 3 5 7 9 10 8 6 4 2

Grateful acknowledgement is made for permission to reprint excerpts
from the following copyrighted works:

Better Living: In Pursuit of Happiness from Plato to Prozac by Mark Kingwell, copyright
1998 Mark Kingwell. Reprinted by permission of Penguin Books Canada Ltd.

The One Best Way: Frederick Winslow Taylor by Robert Kanigel,
copyright © 1997 by Robert Kanigel. Used by permission of Viking Penguin,
a division of Penguin Putnam Inc.

Printed and bound in Canada on acid free paper ⊗
Text design and typesetting by Ruthe Swern

CANADIAN CATALOGUING IN PUBLICATION DATA
Heath, Joseph, 1967–
The efficient society: why Canada is as close to utopia as it gets

ISBN 0-670-89149-5

1. Canada — Social conditions — 1991– . 2. Canada — Politics and government
— 1993– .* 3. Canada — Economic conditions — 1991– . I. Title.

HN103.5.H42 2001   971.064'8   C00-932632-4

Visit Penguin Canada's website at **www.penguin.ca**.

for
Alice

Contents

Acknowledgements

First and foremost, I would like to thank my colleague at the University of Toronto, Mark Kingwell, along with Jackie Kaiser of Penguin Canada. Without their advice, encouragement, and assistance, this book would never have been written, much less published. Andrew Potter provided invaluable research assistance, along with very helpful comments on the manuscript. I would also like to thank my friends and colleagues who read the work at various stages of development: Peter Nixon, Marian MacNair, Donald Ainslie, Kevin Olson, Joel Anderson, and Terrence Heath. Special thanks to Jim Preston and Troy Young for helping me to refine these ideas over the course of countless conversations. I would also like acknowledge the contribution of two former teachers of mine: Jürgen Habermas and James Johnson. They may not recognize it, but their ideas continue to provide an important inspiration for my work. Thanks also to David Kilgour for his judicious editing of the manuscript and Mary Adachi for copy-editing.

Introduction

Canadians currently enjoy the highest quality of life on the planet. Year after year, the United Nations Human Development Index ranks Canada as the best country on earth in which to live. How have we managed to achieve the highest level of "human development" in the world? Why do we rank number one?

Is it because we're rich? No. Being rich helps, but there are lots of countries where people are richer than we are. In terms of dollars-and-cents income, the average American is significantly richer than the average Canadian. And yet they enjoy a lower quality of life.

Is it because we have so many natural resources? No. We certainly do have an abundance of resources, but there are other countries in the world that have even more. Russia comes to mind. And the Russian quality of life is nothing to envy.

Is it because we live in a just society? Hardly. Canada has very good government, but it also suffers from considerable inequality in the distribution of income. Income inequality is greater in Canada than in most European nations.

So why is life in Canada so good? The answer is actually quite simple. It's because Canada is an efficient society, perhaps the most efficient on earth. We run a tight ship. We get maximum results while minimizing effort and waste.

Simple question, simple answer. Unfortunately, it's an answer that most people will have a hard time believing. Canada doesn't feel very efficient. It *feels* kind of sluggish, laid-back. The Japanese seem to organize things much better than we do, the Americans certainly out-gun us when it comes to business, and the Germans—let's not even get started on the subject of German efficiency.

But much of this is an illusion. The American economy seems efficient, but fundamentally the United States is not a land dedicated to the pursuit of efficiency. When given a choice between liberty and efficiency, Americans consistently choose liberty, even when it makes life more difficult for them.

Reasonable people all agree, for example, that the most efficient way to provide health care is through the public sector. In 1995, the Canadian government spent approximately 6.9 per cent of the Canadian GDP (gross domestic product) on health care. With that money, it provided health services to all Canadians. In the same year, the American government spent 6.6 per cent of the American GDP on health care. With that money, it provided health services to *less than* 30 *per cent* of Americans. And yet in spite of lower total health care spending, Canadians are, on average, healthier than Americans. Part of the reason may be that the Canadian health care system actually delivers a greater quantity of physician services per capita than the American.

One of the major reasons that Americans get so little bang for the buck is that private health insurance generates massive overhead costs. Approximately half of the difference in health care spending between Canada and the United States can be attributed to the giant bureaucracy that is required to keep track of and process all the different claims in the United States. As a result, every year Americans throw away more than 2 per cent of their GDP on useless health care bureaucracy. An estimated 1.4 million Americans are employed doing completely unnecessary administrative jobs in the health care sector. These people could be doing something a lot more useful.

Why do Americans tolerate this sort of inefficiency? Mainly it is because they feel that having government deliver health care would infringe on their liberties by denying them the freedom to purchase whatever type of health services they want. So they are willing to make the sacrifice. Canadians, on the other hand, are more pragmatic. If the government can deliver health insurance more efficiently than the private sector, we are happy to let government do it. This is why even the political right in Canada presents itself as committed to defending medicare.

Of course, if one thinks of efficiency only in the most narrow economic terms, the American way may look efficient. All those bureaucrats pushing paper around, sending out bills, and processing insurance claims are making a substantial contribution to the American economy. The GDP measures the total value of goods and services bought and sold every year in a given country. It doesn't draw any distinction between useful and useless expenditures. Thus the fact that much of the paperwork in the private health care system is unnecessary doesn't show up in the economic statistics. But just think what those 1.4 million people *could* be producing if they didn't have to spend their days managing a hopelessly inefficient medical system.

In Germany, the situation is quite the opposite. While Americans worship free markets and insist on using them to organize their affairs even when other types of institutional arrangements would be more efficient, Germans suffer from chronic distrust of the private sector. Part of this stems from a greater commitment to promoting equality in the distribution of wealth, but much of it stems from a straightforward control fallacy. Germans tend to believe that the only way to guarantee socially optimal outcomes is through central administration. So they have trouble letting go. As a result, they chronically underestimate the power of decentralized systems, such as markets.

The most powerful effects of this are felt in the labour market. Between government, unions, and corporations, the number of rules and regulations governing employment in Germany make Canada look like the Wild West. Germans pay for this in the form of unemployment, which is chronically stuck in the double digits. On any given day, at least four million able-bodied Germans are sitting around, willing to work but with nothing to do. This is a huge waste of human resources.

In Japan, the problems are similar. One of the reasons that market economies promote efficiency is that they are very good at rewarding success. But the flip side of the coin is just as important. An efficient market economy must also *penalize failure*. In Canada, for instance, 25 per cent of small businesses go bankrupt in the first year of operations, 80 per cent within ten years. That's pretty ruthless correction.

Japanese corporations are very efficient in part because they are able to command strong loyalties among both employees and business partners. When times are good, this works out quite well. But when the economic tide turns, these loyalties turn out to be a huge hindrance. Businesses that should be allowed to go bankrupt are kept on life-support by other firms, just as employees who are no longer doing useful work are kept on the company payroll. No one ever pulls the plug.

All of this helps to protect Japanese culture and society from destabilizing social changes. But the country takes a huge hit on the efficiency front. The Japanese economy has been completely stalled for the past ten years. As a society, the Japanese have been highly reluctant to take the steps necessary to correct the situation. So while the Japanese economy is very good at generating exports and capturing market share in foreign countries, it is not very good at improving the quality of life of the average Japanese citizen.

Canada has few of these problems. The old joke about Canadians being merely unarmed Americans with health insurance has a lot of truth to it. Our economy resembles the economy of the United States more than that of any other country. The central difference is that the majority of Canadians have no ideological opposition to government. We do not love the state, but neither do we fear it. Thus we get all the benefits of a loosely regulated economy while also enjoying the massive improvements in social welfare that can be organized and delivered only by government. This has proven to be a winning formula.

But what sort of values underlie this Canadian success story? If Americans value liberty, Germans equality, and the Japanese loyalty, what do Canadians value? The easy answer would be "nothing." We're just pragmatists, willing to move whichever way the wind blows.

There may be a grain of truth in this, but it is uncharitable. I would argue that we *are* committed—to efficiency. The problem is that we often mistake this commitment to efficiency for an absence of values. And because we are not quite clear about the nature of this commitment, we are also not entirely clear about why Canadian society works so well. Sometimes we don't even realize *that* it works well. In fact, every year when the United Nations releases its human development ranking, Canadians tend to react with a mixture of confusion and dismissiveness. Most of us have no idea why we are being ranked so high. As a result, we run the risk of inadvertently destroying what we have built. Unless we figure out how we got to be so efficient, it is unlikely that we will remain so.

Ironically, it is the agenda of the right in Canada that poses the greatest threat to the efficiency of our economy. This is largely because the unreasoned hostility to government that prevails south of the border has had a greater influence on the right here. Nothing could illustrate the danger more clearly than the infamous tainted-water scandal in Walkerton, Ontario. One of the big differences between living in a First World country and living in a Third World country is that in the First World it's supposed to be safe to drink the tap water. In Ontario, as in many other jurisdictions, maintaining the quality of the water supply is the responsibility of the Ministry of the Environment. The Conservative government of Ontario, however, didn't care much for environmentalists. In its view, the Ministry of the Environment was staffed by meddling bureaucrats who spent their days harassing industry and generating mountains of red tape. And so it cut the ministry's budget by 40 per cent, leading to staff reductions of 30 per cent.

It's hard to imagine a more clear-cut example of a false economy. As it turned out, many of the staff at the ministry were actually doing very useful work. One of the useful little things they were doing was making sure that people didn't get poisoned by their tap water. When the staff monitoring water quality was cut, the ministry lost its ability to adequately supervise municipal water supplies. In June 2000, an outbreak of bacterial contamination in the town of Walkerton left thousands of people sick and at least six dead. Many of those who fell sick were left with weakened kidneys, and some worry about spending the rest of their lives on dialysis.

What the Conservatives forgot was the cardinal rule of common sense: if it ain't broke, don't fix it. There was nothing wrong with the job that the Ministry of the Environment was doing in monitoring water quality, and there was certainly no reason to cut back its funding. It's obviously more efficient to spend a bit of money on environmental protection than to let people get sick and then spend a fortune paying for their medical care. The problem is that the benefits that come from environmental regulation are very difficult to quantify. And so it may *look* like an efficiency gain when the government lays off a mass of bureaucrats.

This is the most basic problem with the way that efficiency is understood by the right and one of the reasons that efficiency has been given a bad name. There is a strong tendency to think of efficiency only in very narrow terms—to judge it by looking at the total value of goods produced by the market. This is deeply wrongheaded. Our economy is not efficient because it produces a lot of stuff. It's efficient because it satisfies our needs. But life is very complex, and humans have a lot of very different needs. Markets are efficient when it comes to satisfying *some* of these needs, but they are quite inefficient at satisfying others. Our need for clean air, beautiful surroundings, knowledge, and even protection against risk is generally ignored by markets, but can often be satisfied by government.

One of the reasons that the United Nations began the Human Development Index was precisely to correct this bias in our understanding of efficiency. Standard economic indicators such as the GDP present a very lopsided picture of what life is like in a particular country. Natural disasters, for example, provide a huge boost to the economy. If your house is swept away in a flood, nobody is going to subtract the value of the building from the GDP. But if you hire someone to rebuild it, the value of this new house *will* be added to the GDP. So even though the flood resulted in a net loss of time, energy, and resources, the economic statistics make it look as though it made everyone richer. Thus the nation's central economic indicator "works like a calculating machine that adds but cannot subtract."

This is completely perverse. It becomes even worse when impact on GDP is used to evaluate government policy. The best way to deal with a flood is to prevent it from occurring. But a government that levies taxes in order to invest in flood control will be punished with a less robust economy. A foolish government that ignores the problem until disaster strikes will be rewarded with a burst of economic growth.

The solution is certainly not to ignore the economy or to set aside the question of how efficiently we use our resources. After all, the primary reason for government to invest in flood control is precisely because it is the most *efficient* way to protect people's homes. The solution is to articulate a broader conception of what makes a society efficient, one that gives due consideration to all the various components of human welfare, one that does not place undue emphasis on the narrow range of goods that are produced and exchanged in private markets. This is what the Human Development Index attempts to do.

When we talk about efficiency, we need to keep the big picture in mind. Canada does not have huge per capita GDP. What the Canadian system succeeds at doing is delivering a broad range of goods, services, and benefits that people want—not only cars and houses, but also personal security and freedom from crime, a clean environment, and liveable cities. The reason we're able to deliver a balanced package of this sort is that we use a combination of organizational forms—not only markets, but also large corporations and governments. Each type of organization makes its own contribution to our overall quality of life.

Unfortunately, when it comes to defending this arrangement, the traditional left in Canada has proven to be almost as unhelpful as the right. In its defence of the role of the public sector, the left consistently appeals to the principle of fairness or equality—rather than efficiency—as the underlying rationale. This is fine as far as it goes, but it tends to perpetuate the myth that government acts as a drag on the economy. In fact, government is the source of huge gains in efficiency. Much of the quality of life enjoyed by rich and poor alike in this country is provided by government. The much-vaunted "social safety net," for instance, can just as easily be defended by appealing to the principle of efficiency as it can by appealing to fairness.

As a result, efficiency is something of a political orphan. Even though our quality of life is largely a product of the efficiency of our social institutions, very few people explicitly defend these institutions in such terms. In fact, many people don't even think of efficiency as a value, much less recognize the central role that it plays in the organization of Canadian society.

Throughout the interminable debates over Quebec secession, federalists were routinely accused of having failed to "make the case" for Canada. While Quebec nationalists can appeal to strong values—preservation of language, community, and solidarity—federalists are more likely to point out the economic benefits that Quebec gets from membership in Canada—equalization payments, unemployment insurance, or membership in NAFTA. These things may not sound as exciting, but it would be wrong to say that, in pointing to these considerations, federalists are failing to articulate any shared Canadian values. Values are precisely what are being expressed. Federalists are arguing, in effect, that we function more *efficiently* as a single country than we would as two partially conjoined nation states. And Quebecers, by and large, have bought this argument. This is part of the reason that despite a sentimental attachment to the idea of an independent Quebec, they have twice rejected the sovereigntist option.

Efficiency is a value. And whether we realize it or not, it is the central value in Canadian society. It has largely displaced religion, ethnicity, and language as a source of public loyalty. There is a lot to be said for this development. In fact, our increased commitment to efficiency is a sign of progress. Efficiency is not necessarily a cold, calculating virtue nor is it merely a mask for self-interest. Efficiency is a noble, humanistic value intimately related to a number of other values that we hold dear, such as cultural diversity, respect for individual rights, and the alleviation of suffering. Rather than trying to conceal our commitment to efficiency, we should pin it to our sleeves.

Or so I will attempt to argue.

The word "efficiency" gets bandied about a great deal, but the meaning of the term is often far from clear. Most importantly, economists and social scientists use the term "efficiency" in a special sense that seems to bear no relationship to our everyday understanding of the idea. So the first step is to get clear on this concept of efficiency, and to understand how social institutions in general serve to promote this ideal. Once this is done, it will be much easier to see how welfare state arrangements of the type that prevail in Canada serve to promote economic efficiency. Only from this perspective is it then possible to understand the major challenges that we face, challenges that threaten our ability to rely upon efficiency as the central organizing principle of our society.

Part I. Culture

Efficiency is our best friend and our worst enemy. When the price of gas goes up, I love my fuel-efficient car. While sitting through another interminable meeting, I wonder whether there isn't a more efficient way to make decisions. When I get all my errands done with time to spare, I take pride in how efficiently I have organized my affairs. On such days, I think that efficiency is a great thing. Other days, I'm less sanguine. I pick up the newspaper and read about another huge round of layoffs at another big company looking to improve efficiency. At work I hear about administration plans to eliminate summer break so that facilities will be used more efficiently. I listen to people arguing that Canada needs to scale back its social programs in order to promote economic efficiency. On these days, I think our obsession with efficiency is sometimes not worth the sacrifice.

This ambivalence is not uncommon. Efficiency, as a value, has penetrated every nook and cranny of our culture. Some of the consequences of this we like. It makes things, as a whole, run a lot more smoothly. It helps us to go about our business with a minimum of hassle. But some of the consequences are less attractive. It makes things more homogeneous and impersonal. Everyone complains about fast-food chains such as McDonald's that serve up exactly the same food in exactly the same setting everywhere in the world. But who hasn't had the experience of wandering around some foreign city, tired and hungry, desperately needing to go to the washroom. Suddenly, turning the corner, you spy a McDonald's. A feeling of enormous relief suddenly dawns. As every seasoned traveller knows, no matter where you are in the world, McDonald's washrooms are always free, functional, and reasonably clean.

Experiences like this capture our attitude towards efficiency in a nutshell. We fret a lot about how this commitment makes us shallow, superficial, and materialistic. But we cannot deny that, on some days, it is also extremely useful.

Welcome to the culture of efficiency. It's not perfect, but it's not so bad either.

This is the compromise at the heart of our society. The world we live in clearly fails to satisfy many of our deeper needs and impulses. And yet any serious attempt to change it seems to entail even greater sacrifice. We may be as close to utopia as we can get. The big question then becomes, how did we wind up here and not someplace else?

What Is an Efficient Society?

1 A *couple of summers of ago* I learned how to sail. On the very first
night of lessons at a local club, I discovered that I would need to
find more appropriate shoes. As part of an affectation common
among members of my generation, leather boots were the only
sort of footwear I had owned for most of my adult life. Leather
boots are not the best thing to be wearing when your chances of
being dumped into the lake are a near certainty.

Naturally, there are plenty of retailers around willing to take a
shocking amount of your money in return for "specialty" sailing
footwear. Members of my club assured me, however, that a simple pair
of canvas sneakers would be more than adequate. With this in mind, I
set out looking for a bargain. An older member of the club had directed
me to a famous retailer in downtown Toronto (which he referred to,
somewhat oddly, as "Edward's on Bloor"), a place that could best be
described as a "bargain emporium." There I found the perfect
sneaker—lightweight, navy blue, and only $7.59. I left feeling quite
pleased with myself.

My pleasure was slightly diminished the next day when several other
members of my class showed up wearing exactly the same shoes. But my
pleasure dissipated entirely when I made the mistake of asking one

woman where she got hers. "Wal-Mart," she said. "They were a great deal, only two dollars." Two dollars, I had to admit, was a great deal.

This little episode put a lot of things into perspective for me. Wal-Mart stores are a relatively recent addition to the Canadian retail scene, and they caused a certain amount of anxiety when they first appeared. Much of this is due to the impact that Wal-Mart stores have on communities in which they set up shop—putting "mom-and-pop" stores out of business, desolating the main streets of small towns, and so on. There's a reason why they call chains like Wal-Mart "category killers." In the United States, the stores are subjected to constant criticism. In Canada, the same concerns have been significantly amplified by knee-jerk anti-Americanism.

But if Wal-Mart stores have been putting their competitors out of business, it is primarily because people are choosing to shop there. And they are not simply brainwashed—Wal-Mart spends less on advertising than most of its rivals. The episode with the shoes gave me some insight into what's going on. The shoes weren't a little bit cheaper there; they were a lot cheaper. When a store is able to sell goods at less than one-third the price of its nearest competitors, it's very hard to make a case against it.

How does Wal-Mart manage this? Setting aside the accusations of "dirty tricks"—since the same sorts of accusations could be made against any of its competitors—Wal-Mart is simply the most efficient operation around. During its major period of expansion, Wal-Mart had overhead costs that were approximately half that of its major rival, Sears. At the heart of the Wal-Mart empire (and despite the firm's folksy image), there is an extraordinarily sophisticated computer system that is linked to every Wal-Mart store through the largest privately owned satellite communications system in the world. This gives the company superior inventory control: whenever a product passes through the checkout at any Wal-Mart store anywhere in the world, the central computer database is automatically updated. As a result, Wal-Mart stores have the seemingly magical ability to remain stocked with precisely the goods their customers want to buy.

Apart from inventory control, Wal-Mart is also the largest user of what we now refer to as "e-commerce" technology. As far back as 1990, Wal-Mart had arranged for paperless financial transactions with more than one-third of its suppliers. This is part of the reason that Wal-Mart was able to instantly double the productivity of the Woolco stores that it bought when entering the Canadian market.

Perhaps because Wal-Mart's success stems ultimately from its superior efficiency, a note of fatalism colours much of the popular discussion of the chain. Words such as "inevitable," "irresistible," and "unstoppable" always seem to crop up in these discussions. When analysts announced, in 1999, that Wal-Mart controlled about 40 per cent of the Canadian discount retail market, it only confirmed the inevitable. When Eaton's declared bankruptcy shortly thereafter, there was much disappointment but little surprise. The ultimate triumph of Wal-Mart seemed to be part of the natural order.

But this impression is misleading. There is nothing natural about the fact that companies such as Wal-Mart are able to take over. As a society, we have arranged things so that they can. Our primary economic and social institutions have been specifically *designed* so that the most efficient organizations prosper, while others are destroyed. Once these basic institutions are in place, the dynamics of business success and failure play out in a quasi-natural manner. But the fundamental character of these institutions reflects a choice that we have made as a society. And the choices that we make reflect our values. Our institutions reward efficient organizations because efficiency is the paramount value in our culture.

This is why, despite a lot of complaining and hand-wringing about the Wal-Marts of the world, no one actually contemplates *doing* anything to stop them (short of low-level, and generally ineffectual, consumer boycotts). We all recognize, in one way or another, that our society is unlikely to take back its fundamental commitment to efficiency. While we may complain about many of the side-effects of this decision—such as the blighted urban landscape or the homogenizing influence that franchising exerts on popular culture—the values that are compromised are ultimately of lesser significance.

Many people will be sceptical of this claim. If you ask some friends to make up short lists of their core values, "efficiency" will probably not show up on many lists. Tell someone that their house or car is "efficient," and you may well be suspected of damning with faint praise. A running storyline on *Star Trek: Voyager* features a cyborg crew member who constantly strives for "perfection" but, failing that, is willing to settle for "efficiency." The fact that she is half machine is no accident. Efficiency makes us think of machines—cold, inflexible, unfeeling. Generally speaking, this is not the way we want our society to be.

This does not show, however, that efficiency is not a core value in our society. It only shows that we don't like to admit just how deep our commitment to efficiency runs. The term carries with it a certain amount of baggage, which often leads us to disavow it.

Let me give just one example.

Despite a certain amount of grumbling, most people think that our society has made considerable moral progress in the last hundred years. Whatever the remaining flaws, the fact is that women can now vote, the state does not officially discriminate against citizens whose parents weren't British, child labour has been abolished, and so on. One of the most significant of these achievements is a substantial improvement in the welfare of the working classes. Workers in turn-of-the-century factories routinely used to toil for upwards of eighty hours per week in return for wages that would barely keep them alive. It was quite common for an entire family to live in a single room without running water or (needless to say) electricity.

Since then, the condition of the average worker has improved dramatically. But how exactly did this improvement come about? Did the world somehow become more *fair*? The answer is clearly "no." The major difference between now and then is that our economy is more efficient—we can produce more with less. In the twentieth century, total world economic output exceeded that of all previous centuries *combined*. At the same time, the overall level of social inequality *increased*. Our economic system is just as unfair as it always has been.

The amount of wealth that actually gets redistributed from rich to poor in our society has been, and remains, puny. We rely on efficiency—not brotherly love—to do the work of making our economic system even halfway tolerable for those at the bottom of the heap.

Given a choice between doing something efficiently and doing it inefficiently, it just seems natural to do it efficiently. It doesn't appear to require any special value judgement to make that kind of decision.

Or does it?

The fact that efficiency seems so "natural" to us, that we find it easy to choose the efficient over the inefficient, does not mean that efficiency is not a value. It simply reveals the centrality of efficiency in our culture. For a medieval Christian, the choice between serving God or rejecting him was just as easy. It was perfectly natural that one should choose to serve God (regardless, I might add, of how efficiently one did so).

People sometimes think that efficiency is not a value because questions of efficiency are ultimately decided by experts. Economists, engineers, and managers are in the business of deciding what is efficient and what isn't. Most people are happy just to go along with their decisions. But again, this is nothing new. For the medieval Christian, the details of how one should serve God were also decided by experts. Priests and monks were in the business of determining the will of God, and most people were happy to go along with their decisions.

Thus the mere fact that we find efficiency obviously preferable to inefficiency does not mean that we are not making a value judgement when we rank things that way, any less than the medieval Christian was following a particular set of values in deciding to serve God.

So what is it that makes efficiency a value? Fundamentally, a value is just a criterion that we use to decide what is good and what is bad. Those of us in the business of professional philosophy sometimes say that a value determines what is "choiceworthy." Efficiency is a value because it tells us how we *should* do things. In particular, it is a principle that we use to decide how we ought to organize our co-operative activities.

Of course, values have gotten a lot of bad press in the last century. Values are often thought to be inherently unscientific, irrational, or subjective. If so, then efficiency doesn't sound like much of a value. Whether or not something is efficient seems more a scientific question—either it is or it isn't. Values, on the other hand, are like "rival gods and demons." People do not discuss them calmly; they fight over them. That's why it's considered impolite to discuss religion or politics at dinner parties (unless you already know what everyone is going to say). We can imagine going to war to defend our values, but how much is anyone willing to sacrifice in the name of efficiency?

Quite a lot, it turns out. It is important not to forget that much of the twentieth century was dominated by a war in which one of the central issues was precisely this commitment to efficiency. The major feature of the Cold War was a contest between two economic systems—capitalism and communism. One of the central merits of capitalism has always been its superior efficiency. The architects of communism, on the other hand, thought that equality was more important than efficiency. (Although many thought they could have their cake and eat it too—that communism could be just as efficient as capitalism but with less social inequality. Certainly during the 1950s, it was far from obvious that capitalism was more efficient. Nevertheless, the big draw for communism was always the promise of equality, not efficiency.) The Cold War was a protracted struggle to determine which set of ideas could ultimately capture the hearts and minds of people throughout the world. Capitalism won.

But the victory of capitalism did bring to light one peculiar characteristic of our commitment to efficiency. One couldn't help but notice a distinct lack of enthusiasm among the citizens of the victorious capitalist nations. Watching excited East Germans flooding into West German malls and supermarkets, anxiously snapping up blue jeans and cases of Coca-Cola, it was hard to resist the impression that they had been sold a bill of goods in more ways than one. Many in the West felt that even though we had won, we didn't really *deserve* to win. The values in whose name the war had been waged were ultimately hollow.

This lack of enthusiasm reflects the fact that many people in our society are alienated from its core system of values—radical counter-cultural movements are a permanent feature of our social landscape. Many more recognize the importance of efficiency in our culture, but feel that it is overrated. While we can see that capitalism is more efficient than its rivals, the level of social inequality generated by the system is a source of ongoing anxiety. And for those who do earn a decent salary, the pressure to increase productivity seems to generate a constant increase in the pace and intensity of life. As a result, most people's attitude towards efficiency is characterized by profound ambivalence. We are a society that values efficiency above all else, but we are not necessarily comfortable with all the consequences of this commitment.

One of the reasons that efficiency can remain so central despite this ambivalence is that our commitment to it does not stand alone. Efficiency is intimately connected with a number of other values that are very important to us (even those of us who downplay or oppose the role that efficiency plays in our culture). It is no accident that our society, which values efficiency, is also one which values personal autonomy, democracy, and diversity. This is because efficiency is a type of value that allows individuals who have fundamentally different goals and aspirations to engage in mutually beneficial co-operation.

Efficiency is all about creating (in contemporary management jargon) "win-win" scenarios. When everyone's a winner, no one has any reason to object to the way things are being done. So even people who are deeply divided by language, religion, or culture can usually get along when it comes to promoting efficiency. This is why it has gradually won out over many traditional value systems. It is tempting to say that efficiency is the new religion of our society. This is not quite true. Efficiency has *replaced* religion as the primary source of value in our culture. This is because striving for efficiency is one of the few ways that we have to achieve social order in the context of a pluralistic society.

In order to see why this is so, it is necessary to dig back a bit, and figure out what efficiency is and what it means to organize a society "efficiently."

❧

The idea that a *society* could be more or less efficient is almost brand-new. This is surprising when one considers how often the word turns up in the average newspaper, office memo, or political party platform. People began to use the word "efficient" in something like the modern sense only in the early nineteenth century. At the time, it was used only to describe certain properties of machines. Shortly before the First World War, it became popular to apply the same idea to workers and corporations. The idea that a society as a whole could be efficient did not develop until the 1950s. This use of the term originated among economists as the central concept in what we now call the "new welfare economics." The full story of how this came about is a bit complicated, involving Aristotle, the steam engine, a steel mill in Philadelphia, and a reclusive Italian fascist.

The fact that the word "efficiency" makes most people think of machines is not an accident. My washer and dryer have huge stickers on them telling me precisely how "efficient" they are. But the connection runs much deeper than that. Efficiency, in the modern sense of the term, was originally a technical notion, adopted by engineers to describe a certain property of water wheels. The subsequent invention of the steam engine led to the generalization of the concept and brought it into everyday usage.

Prior to the machine age, the word "efficient" was nothing but a loose synonym for "effective," or "efficacious." In order for something to be efficient, it simply had to be active in producing an effect. The idea underlying this use of the term is very old, dating all the way back to Aristotle.

In the fourth century B.C., Aristotle suggested that there were four different ways to explain pretty much anything. Suppose, for example, that one afternoon you are sitting out in the backyard watching the grass grow. "Why is that happening?" you ask yourself. The answer you give will depend upon exactly what you mean by the question. One way of thinking about it is in terms of "final causes." Everything in the world exists to fulfil some purpose. In the Christianized version of Aristotle, one would say that when God created the earth, he must have had something in mind when he decided to include grass. If you can guess what that is, then you have found one way of answering your question. You might decide, for example, that the grass is growing so that sheep will have something to eat tomorrow.

But that is not the only type of explanation available. While God was primarily an ideas man, he also had to implement his grand designs. His plan to keep the sheep fed was good, but he needed some way to carry it out. In order to get the whole thing going, he had to design a little mechanism that would make the grass get longer and longer. So he put on his engineering hat and came up with cell division, photosynthesis, etc.

Because God's plans are executed through this physical mechanism, when you ask why the grass is growing, you may not be inquiring about the final cause, but rather about the operations of the mechanism. You may want to know how it actually comes about that the grass grows. This was known as the "efficient cause." The inclusion of the word "efficient" is due to Aristotle's Roman translators, who called this type of cause the *causa efficiens*, or the cause that "makes it happen." The choice of words is appropriate since the efficient cause, in Aristotle's view, is simply the cause that accomplishes the physical task of bringing about an observed effect.

One thing to note about the "efficient cause" is that it corresponds to what nowadays we would just call "the cause." When we ask what the "cause'" of a fire was, we are not wondering about what purpose it served in God's overall plan for the universe. We want to know what sparked it off. Thus we tend to think of all causes as efficient causes. This is also not an accident. The two other types of causes in the Aristotelian system were the "formal" and the "material." To make a long story very short, the Newtonian revolution in physics effectively collapsed the formal and material causes into the efficient cause. And the "final cause" came to be seen as superfluous, or largely speculative (who knows what God was thinking?). As a result, modern science developed an exclusive interest in efficient causes. All the others fell by the wayside.

So with the steady march of science, the term "efficient cause" became increasingly pleonastic. At the beginning of the nineteenth century, saying that something was efficient, or that it "had efficiency," was not saying very much. It simply meant that the object brought about some effect in the material realm. A particular lever or gear was "efficient" just because it *did* something.

It was the growing popularity of engines that ultimately changed this. An engine is a mechanism that converts energy into some kind of useful motion. A water wheel, for instance, takes the energy found in water as it flows downhill and uses it to turn a crank. A steam engine, on the other hand, turns a crank by transforming some of the heat released by burning coal or wood. An internal combustion engine does it by harnessing the force of the explosion that occurs when gasoline fumes are ignited.

In the old sense of the term, the efficiency of an engine is simply its capacity to generate motion. But the technology of machine design leads inevitably to the question of just how *much* motion it generates, or how much of the energy pumped into it gets transformed into useful motion. An engine takes useless energy and transforms it into useful energy. But no machine is perfect—not all the useless energy present can be converted, nor can it all be turned into a useful form. Inevitably some of it escapes, or remains useless. A water wheel, for instance, doesn't entirely transform the force of the water into crank-turning. There is friction along all the gears and shafts, which means that some of the energy will be "lost" in the form of heat.

Since energy is always conserved (whatever goes in has to come out), we can think of an engine as an input-output device in which useless energy goes in and some combination of useful and useless energy comes out. One way to improve an engine is therefore to reduce the amount of useless energy produced, or equivalently, to increase the ratio of useful energy on the output side to useless energy on the input side. Engineers began to use the term "efficiency" to refer to this ratio. Improving a machine in this sense means making it more efficient.

With all this talk of engines and physics, it is important not to lose sight of one key aspect of this new use of the term "efficiency." According to one prominent nineteenth-century definition, the efficiency of an engine is "the ratio of useful work performed to the total energy expended or heat taken in." This sounds very scientific, except for one little detail. Notice the persistence of the word "useful." An engine is efficient only if it does something useful. But what counts as useful is not a fact about the machine, it is a function of how we, as human beings, choose to use the machine. If our needs and desires change, then what counts as "useful" and "useless" may change along with them. A machine that was once praised as highly efficient may then turn out to be quite inefficient.

The point is that even when we are dealing with machines, the concept of efficiency already involves an explicit value judgement. To say that a machine is efficient is to say that it is good at satisfying a particular need that we have. Take, for example, the lightbulb and the toaster. Both work on the same principle. If you take electricity and run it through a coil that offers it resistance, some of the energy will dissipate in the form of light, some in the form of heat. A lightbulb produces both heat and light, but it is designed to produce as much light as possible. The filaments in the toaster are designed in just the opposite way, to shed more heat than light. A lightbulb is therefore very efficient if you want to read at night, but not particularly efficient if you want to make toast.

So even though the modern sense of the term efficiency arose among engineers talking about machines, it is nevertheless used to pick out a human property of these machines. It is used to describe how well these machines work *for us*.

For the sort of person who likes to tinker around with machinery out in the backyard toolshed, the nineteenth century was a great time to be alive. The mechanical geniuses of the world, the people with a knack for working with gears, pulleys, cranks, and levers, suddenly found themselves in a land of opportunity. In part, this was due to the creation of patents. This nineteenth-century legal innovation led to an explosion of creativity, since it helped guarantee, for the first time, that inventors would be financially rewarded for their work. But the other reason that invention flourished had more to do with the simple progress of industry and trade. When engines were first developed, people were happy just to get one that worked at all. Engines were so much more powerful than human labour, and so much cheaper, that it didn't really matter just *how* powerful or cheap they were. It takes approximately thirty men to generate one horsepower of energy. At the end of the nineteenth century, according to one contemporary estimate, the same amount of energy could be generated by as little as one pound of coal per hour. This meant that the first shop to mechanize could easily outperform all of its rivals.

Things began to change, however, when *every* shop became mechanized. Under these circumstances, just having an engine was not enough. The competitive advantage now flowed to the shop with the most efficient machine—the one that consumed the least fuel or generated the most horsepower. So people who could improve the performance of machines found themselves in high demand. In those days, there was some truth to the saying "Build a better mousetrap, and the world will beat a path to your door."

But with all this attention focused on improving the efficiency of machines, it was not long before someone started to look a bit more closely at the workers who were slaving away next to them. Industrial production at the end of the nineteenth century was still dominated by what has been called the "craft" mentality. Workers and supervisors had certain traditional routines, which had been handed down, more or less intact, across generations. People seldom stopped to wonder whether these methods were the best possible ones.

The man who changed all this was a mechanical engineer named Frederick Winslow Taylor. His idea, quite simply, was to take the same methods used to assess and improve the efficiency of machines and apply them to workers. In 1910, Taylor became one of the founding members of the "efficiency movement," which would eventually revolutionize the way that the United States, and then the rest of the world, thought about industrial production. He was the original "efficiency expert," wandering around the shop floor with a stopwatch, timing the workers as they performed various tasks, then reorganizing the workplace in order to eliminate waste and delay.

One of the easiest ways of generalizing the concept of efficiency from machines to workers involves the use of cost-benefit analysis. The efficiency of a machine is determined by the ratio of useful work it performs to the energy it consumes. One way of calculating this is by figuring out the monetary value of what the machine produces and subtracting the cost of the fuel it consumes. If prices remain the same, then an increase in the balance of benefits over costs represents an increase in the efficiency of the machine. The same logic can be applied to workers—in this case subtracting the amount of their wages from the value of what they produce.

Much of this seems obvious to us now, so it is hard to imagine the furor that Taylor's methods generated when they were first introduced. In part, this is because we live in a world that has been completely revolutionized by his ideas. It is because of the efficiency movement and the religious zeal with which its adherents promoted its virtues that "efficiency" was transformed from a piece of technical engineering jargon into a household word.

If there is one thing that the efficiency movement is best remembered for it is the "motion studies" conducted by Frank Gilbreth, one of Taylor's men. Like Taylor, Gilbreth treated efficiency as something of a religion, not just at work but at home too. His memoir, in which he recounts his exploits at fathering twelve children, was aptly titled *Cheaper by the Dozen* (which some may remember as a movie from the '50s). A former bricklayer, Gilbreth had as his highest ambition the goal to eliminate unnecessary movements from industrial processes. He claimed to have found a way of reducing the number of discrete movements needed to lay a brick from eighteen to five, thereby allowing a skilled bricklayer to double his hourly output.

These motion studies quickly captured the popular imagination. It seemed to many that "science" had found a way to improve every aspect of daily life. One excited author made the following recommendation, quite typical at the time: "The user of an ordinary make of safety razor may try the simple experiment in shaving of recording his motions over a given time, with the aid of a watch, and he will find that usually he makes nearly 250 motions to get a perfect shave—when by a close study of movement and the instrument these motions can be reduced to 60."

(It's not exactly clear what the watch contributes here, other than lending an aura of scientific exactitude to the proceedings.)

The idea that one could increase one's personal efficiency by eliminating unnecessary movement was a huge fad at the beginning of the 1910s. The inevitable backlash followed quickly on its heels. One magazine cartoon from 1913 shows an efficiency expert catching a young couple engaged in a bit of office romance. "Young man," he says, "are you aware that you employed fifteen unnecessary motions in delivering that kiss?"

On a more serious note, the efficiency movement got a major boost from a Boston lawyer named Louis Brandeis, who would later be appointed to the American Supreme Court. In 1910, state-regulated railroads in the United States had appealed to Congress for an increase in the rates they could charge their customers. Brandeis argued against the rate hike on the grounds that the railroads were being run inefficiently. Rather than passing along increased costs to the consumer, he claimed, the railroads should reduce their own overhead and streamline their operations. This may seem like an obvious point now, but at the time it was unprecedented. Railroad executives were completely blindsided by Brandeis's argument. They came to the hearings unprepared to discuss even basic features of the cost structure of their operations.

The public was both drawn to and repelled by Brandeis's position. Efficiency seemed to promise something very much like a free lunch. Instead of paying more for transportation, the public could simply demand that the railroads operate more efficiently. But many suspected that there would be a catch. Ultimately, it would be the workers who paid the price. Greater efficiency, it was suspected, could be achieved only by speeding up the work process or increasing its intensity.

But beneath this concern was an even more fundamental set of moral qualms. The efficiency movement, quite simply, treated workers like machines, objects to be manipulated instead of persons engaged in a co-operative work process. This might have been just a source of minor anxiety were it not for Taylor's extraordinarily blunt mode of expression. He had a tendency to spice up his treatises on scientific management by including little snippets of stylized conversation between himself and his workers. In the best known of these exchanges, Taylor recounts his interactions with a worker at the Bethlehem Steel Company in Philadelphia, where Taylor first applied his management theories. "Schmidt," he asks, "are you a high-priced man?—Vell, I don't know vat you mean. —Oh, you're aggravating me . . . If you are a high-priced man, you will do exactly as this man tells you tomorrow, from morning till night. When he tells you to pick up a [piece of iron] and walk, you pick it up and you walk, and when he tells you to sit down and rest, you sit down. You do that straight through the day. And what's more, no back talk."

Taylor grants that this "seems to be rather rough talk." But "with a man of the mentally sluggish type of Schmidt it is appropriate and not unkind, since it is effective in fixing his attention on the high wages which he wants and away from what, if it were called to his attention, he would probably consider impossibly hard work."

There is something refreshing about a management theorist who simply admits that his goal is to trick workers into accepting "impossibly hard work." But partly as a consequence of this frankness, a substantial anti-Taylor backlash developed within a few years of the efficiency movement's first appearance on the public stage. Looking back, this is not surprising. It is impossible to read Taylor's writing today without being offended by many of his attitudes. But the fact that we are more easily offended than many of Taylor's contemporaries is itself part of his legacy. Heightened moral sensitivity is just one of the many luxuries that our material prosperity affords us. In order to see why Taylor's work was once so attractive, why it was able to generate such quasi-religious fervour, it is important to keep in mind just how much the world has changed since his time. As one of Taylor's biographers, Robert Kanigel, reminds us:

> The world into which Taylor was born enjoyed nothing like
> the material prosperity of ours, where ballpoint pens are
> made so inexpensively that they're handed out for free;
> where a color television goes for a day's wages; where all but

a small aggrieved underclass, oppressed by cruel historical circumstances, enjoy a material bounty unknown in any previous epoch. Taylor's world was one where making pumps, sewing machines, books, steam engines, springs, stoves, and shirts was hard; where cutting things, shaping them, fitting them, assembling them, and carrying them across rivers, mountains, and plains roused the imagination and intelligence of the nation's most energetic citizens. Taylor promised the chance to do all these things faster and cheaper.

Once it became common to talk about people as more or less efficient, a number of important new refinements of the concept arose. After all, people and machines are not quite the same.

The most important difference involves the way that goals are set. The efficiency of a machine is assessed in terms of the amount of useful output it generates. But who decides what is useful and what isn't? Presumably the user of the machine. People, on the other hand, have the capacity to set their own goals, to determine for themselves what is useful and what isn't. This means that in order to assess the efficiency of a person, there is no need to have someone else standing outside, determining whether or not that person's actions are useful. People can decide for themselves.

One of the reasons the efficiency movement was thought to dehumanize workers was that the concept of efficiency it promoted ignored the goals that workers might set for themselves. Workers were assessed in terms of how many tons of iron they could move, how quickly they could lay a brick, or how accurately they could type. The goals being served here were ultimately those of their employers, not the workers themselves. An entirely "external" standard was used to judge their efficiency.

An interesting feature of Gilbreth's motion studies, however, is that they showed how much more widely the concept of efficiency could be applied. By shaving more efficiently, cooking more efficiently, or walking to work more efficiently, people could improve every aspect of their lives. And increased efficiency would benefit not just the boss. Everyone who applied these methods to their own life would be rewarded, because they would be better able to achieve their *own* goals. This suggested that efficiency could be much more than a technique for boosting profits. It could be a general source of increased welfare.

According to this view of efficiency, people should be judged according to "internal" standards. Whether or not someone is acting efficiently is to be determined by how well they achieve their own goals. And their own goals need not necessarily coincide with those of their employer. Take, for example, the work strategy known as "slacking." The goal of the slacker is to do the absolute minimum level of work necessary to avoid being fired. This is a highly efficient job strategy when judged by the internal standards of someone whose work is intrinsically unrewarding and who just wants to bring home a paycheque. Naturally, this person is unlikely to be named employee of the month, because he is not an "efficient" worker from the standpoint of the firm. The internal and the external standards for judging efficiency need not coincide.

What struck many people as interesting about the internal concept of efficiency was that it seemed to provide a very general theory of how people act. Isn't there a sense in which we're all just self-contained efficiency machines? We set goals and then try to realize them as best as we can. For example, when driving to work, I attempt to do so efficiently—by choosing the shortest, least-congested route. If someone shows me a shortcut, I will quickly adopt it, automatically adjusting my behaviour to incorporate the more efficient driving strategy. It seems to be a general feature of human nature that we strive to achieve our goals as efficiently as we can.

This observation set the stage for one of the biggest intellectual revolutions of the twentieth century. The most popular "scientific" theory about human action prior to this century was hedonism. According to this view, our basic desire is to seek pleasure and avoid pain. We are like little machines that are wired up to chase after pleasure, just as a moth is drawn to the light. But there have always been problems with this view.

No one has ever denied that some people are like this—we all probably know a few. And there have always been enough people like this around to make hedonism a popular theory; it was widely held in ancient Greece and has been debated ever since. The central problem with hedonism is that there are all sorts of clear exceptions to the rule.

The most obvious exception is altruistic behaviour—when people sacrifice some of their own pleasure or happiness in order to benefit someone else. While some people like to explain away this kind of conduct by seeking out hidden motives ("that Mother Teresa was just after publicity . . ."), examples of altruistic behaviour can be found in most animal species, not just in humans. The evolutionary benefits of altruism are such that it is quite difficult to explain how a species of creatures interested only in their own pleasure could have developed or survived.

The new concept of efficiency promised to provide a much better theory of human action, one that would avoid all the classic problems with hedonism. Hedonism assumed that people have just one goal—to secure pleasure—and that they try to maximize their attainment of this goal. Efficiency theory, on the other hand, can remain neutral on the question of what goals people have. It just says that people set goals and then try to achieve them as efficiently as possible. If your goal is to seek pleasure, then you will try to do so as efficiently as possible. If your goal is to assist the poor and downtrodden, then you will also try to do so as efficiently as possible.

Harrington Emerson, one of the more humanistic members of the efficiency movement, realized this early on. In a subtle jab at Taylor, he wrote: "In tabulating inefficiencies it is not assumed that it is a human ideal to work hard all the time and spend nothing. The unit is the man. If he elects and can manage it, he can live in a tub, bask in the sun, and curtail his efforts and wants to a minimum. If he elects, he can work hard for days, weeks, or months, and in short and riotous extravagance spend all he has accumulated."

The general picture that emerges with this new theory is as follows: People start off with a "wish list" of things that they would like to see happen—a set of "preferences." Anything that they are able to bring about can be called an "achievement." Anything that they are forced to give up can be called a "sacrifice." Every choice will involve some combination of achievement and sacrifice (e.g., going to the coffee shop means that you can't go to the zoo). Efficiency is achieved when one maximizes the balance of achievement over sacrifice (in the same way that one tries to maximize the balance of benefits over costs).

A theory of action like this is obviously much more robust than hedonism. But it also deploys a concept of efficiency that is much more palatable, more humanistic, than the version propounded by Taylor. This new theory of efficiency does not treat people as automata, there to be ordered about by expert supervisors and efficiency experts. Industrial organization, according to this view, does not involve imposing efficient work routines on workers. The corporation exists, as Emerson put it, "to promote the efficiency of the individual worker."

The efficiency movement always aspired to be more than just a campaign to reform management practices. Its proponents hoped to create an entirely new set of ideals for all of society. This ambition was most obvious in Emerson's writings. Although he was a great fan of Taylor's work, Emerson was regarded by Taylor as something of a windbag, and the two men were never close. Educated in Germany and France, Emerson clearly had philosophical pretensions that set him apart from many of the engineers in the efficiency movement. He referred to his own work unselfconsciously as "the Gospel of Efficiency," and regarded himself as the harbinger of a "new morality" for all of society.

But despite these ambitions, Emerson never quite got it right. The efficiency movement was successful at popularizing the term, but it never succeeded in formulating a vision of the efficient society that could capture the public imagination. The man who did succeed at this task was, ironically, someone who did not use the term "efficiency," had nothing to do with the movement, and would have had very little sympathy for it anyhow. This man was Vilfredo Pareto, a professor of political economy at the University of Lausanne, Switzerland.

Perhaps unsurprisingly, Pareto was also an engineer. Although he was born in Paris, his father was an expatriate Italian who sent his son off to study in Italy at the age of ten. The young Pareto completed an engineering degree at the Polytechnic Institute of Torino and eventually became the general manager of the Italian Iron Works. He dabbled in mathematical economics on the side until deciding, at the age of forty-five, to become a full-time academic.

When he died in 1923, Pareto was best known for two ideas, both of which had nothing to do with efficiency. First, he claimed that the level of inequality in the distribution of incomes was the same in every society and could be expressed in a simple formula (which became known as "Pareto's law"). Second, he developed a protofascist theory of élite rule, articulated in his sociological writings. (In fairness, Pareto supported Italian fascism not because he was a racist or a xenophobe, but because he thought that someone needed to bring order to Italian society. He died before the full consequences of this commitment became apparent.)

By the end of the twentieth century, both these ideas had been consigned to the dustbin of history. What established Pareto's claim to fame was his strategy for applying the concept of efficiency to social institutions. Although it is often referred to as "Pareto efficiency," or "Pareto optimality," Pareto's definition has acquired such currency among economists and social scientists that it is now regarded as the standard definition of the term "efficiency" in social and political contexts.

What was so new about this concept of "Pareto efficiency"? Earlier economists had tended to proceed from hedonistic assumptions. They regarded society as something like a big machine designed to produce pleasure. An efficient society was one that produced as much pleasure as possible, given its available resources. This view had many problems, the most obvious being that it rested on controversial assumptions about what people want. But it also had some funny consequences.

Suppose you are given the task of handing out candy to a bunch of kids at a birthday party, and imagine that you want to execute this task so that the most "efficient" arrangement is achieved. According to the

hedonistic view, you should try to distribute the candy so that it produces as much pleasure as possible. Obviously, the way to do this is to
find the kid with the biggest "sweet tooth," the one who gets the most
pleasure from eating candy, and give it all to him. If the other kids complain, just tell them that they are "inefficient" at converting candy into
pleasure, and that it would be a waste of perfectly good candy to give
them any.

This sort of absurd scenario makes the concept of "efficiency" seem
like an unsuitable social ideal. Pareto managed to rescue it, however,
by shifting from the hedonistic to a "preference"-based theory of
action. Each individual, in his view, sets his or her own goals. The efficiency of society as a whole is determined by whether or not it helps
individuals to achieve these goals. The most efficient organization of
society is the one in which each member of that society is able to act
most efficiently. Thus the efficiency of society is to be judged by the
internal criteria of individuals, not by some external standard such as
how much pleasure it produces.

Pareto used the somewhat strange term "ophilemity" to refer to the
satisfaction people get when their goals are satisfied. The state of "maximum social ophilemity" is reached when it is impossible to increase one
person's ophilemity without decreasing someone else's. This is what eventually became known as Pareto efficiency. A society becomes more efficient when the condition of at least one person is improved without
worsening the condition of anyone else. Maximum efficiency has been
achieved when it is impossible to improve anyone's condition without
harming someone else.

If we return to the candy example, we can see how the consequences of the Pareto definition play out. In order to achieve a distribution of candy that is efficient in Pareto's sense, the goal must now be
to ensure that the candy given out is well suited to the tastes of the
children who receive it. If you give chocolate to a kid who likes gum,
and gum to a kid who likes chocolate, then the resulting distribution is
inefficient. By switching around the allocation of chocolate and gum,
you could make both children happier, without making anyone else

unhappier. It is a "win-win" transformation. A perfectly efficient allocation of candy has been achieved when it is impossible to make any more "win-win" changes.

When economists and business leaders talk about capitalism being efficient, they are using the term in this Pareto sense. The economy is not considered efficient simply because it produces a lot of stuff. If people didn't *want* all the stuff our economy produces, then it wouldn't be considered very efficient. If our economy produced millions of left shoes and no right ones, then this would not count as a sign of efficiency. It would count as a gross waste of resources. Our economy works efficiently when it produces the right sort of stuff and delivers it to the right place at the right time, allowing each individual to satisfy his or her own particular needs and desires.

So, unlike an efficient machine, an efficient society is not itself efficient. Society does not exist in order to produce any one thing, and so it cannot do so efficiently or inefficiently. Our society is efficient because it enables us, its members, to act efficiently. It *facilitates* efficiency. It allows us to go about our business with a minimum of hassle. It is more like a traffic light than a steam engine. This is the ideal of efficiency that eventually captured the popular imagination and became the central value in our society. It is an image of a society that is without waste, where the resources available are used in such a way that each individual has the best possible opportunity to realize his or her own life's project.

So in what sense is Wal-Mart an efficient retail operation? It's no accident that people want to buy the stuff that Wal-Mart sells. Wal-Mart is efficient precisely *because* it gives people what they want (or because, given the same resources as its competitors, it is able to give more people more of what they want). This is ultimately why our economy is designed to let companies such as Wal-Mart flourish.

It May Not Be Perfect, But It Is Efficient

The softening of public attitudes towards homosexuality is one of the most dramatic social changes to have occurred over the course of my lifetime. In the summer of 1999, more than 750,000 people attended the annual Gay and Lesbian Pride Parade in Toronto. Politicians and corporate sponsors jostled with each other for the most prominent positions at the front of the parade—a bit hard to believe when compared to the climate of opinion I grew up in.

When I was a kid in Saskatoon in the 1970s, homosexuality was so deeply taboo that most people couldn't quite bring themselves to believe that it existed. It was treated like something of an urban myth. At my high school—I swear this is true—no one had the faintest idea that the Village People were gay. (I remember quite clearly some years later, after having lived in Montreal for a while, suddenly putting the pieces together: "So *that's* why they were so into hanging out at the YMCA . . .")

Conservative critics have done a lot of hand-wringing about the consequences of these changes, and in particular their impact on the family. But while there may be some merit in their concerns about the future of the family, these are invariably expressed in a highly misleading vocabulary.

The standard complaint is that traditional family *values* are under attack, and that some other alien set of values is going to replace them.

The mistake is to think that values are what is at stake in the cultural politics of homosexuality. While there has clearly been an enormous change in popular *attitudes*, it is not clear that there has been any change in our underlying system of values. If anything, the increased acceptance of homosexuality is an obvious consequence of the values that have been central to our civilization for the last two hundred years.

One of the core principles of a capitalist economy is that society has no business interfering in private exchanges when these transactions are entered into voluntarily and do not violate the rights of any third parties. The reason is quite simple: exchanges like these represent "winwin" transformations. They create a more efficient allocation of resources.

It is not hard to see how these principles can be applied to the case of homosexuality. When two adults freely consent to a sexual relationship—especially one that will not be procreative—the result will be another "win-win" transformation. Both of the individuals involved will be happier, and no third parties will be harmed. Thus homosexual unions permit a more efficient allocation of sexual partners. The acceptance of homosexuality is simply one more consequence of our commitment, as a society, to the value of efficiency.

Many people today find the idea that society should tolerate homosexuality so natural that they have difficulty imagining what those who disagree with them were ever thinking. The repression of homosexuality is often regarded as something that belongs to the dark ages of civilization, when people were held captive by mysterious phobias and obsessions loosely stitched together into the form of religious doctrine. But while there is more than a grain of truth in this view, it is simplistic. The repression of homosexuality was also a consequence of a very sophisticated theory about how societies function, and what sorts of rules were needed to keep them from breaking down. It was only when this theory lost its appeal that we could begin to think that consent was an important factor in determining the admissibility of sexual relations.

Those of us in the business of professional philosophy describe this change as a shift from a "perfectionist" to a "contractual" view of society. This is why so much time in political philosophy classes is spent studying Thomas Hobbes, John Locke, and other "social contract" theorists. These are the men responsible for burying perfectionism. All of our ideas about human rights, democracy, gender equality, and multiculturalism ultimately stem from the intellectual revolution that the social contract theorists initiated.

The history of popular attitudes towards homosexuality provides an excellent device to track this shift and dramatize its consequences. But in the end it is just a way to illustrate the story. The important point involves our attitudes towards efficiency. The reason that we attach such significance to this value—I will attempt to show—is that it captures the central idea of the social contract. Improvements in the efficiency of our society are improvements that everyone can freely accept. This is why we have such difficulty saying no to them.

The history of perfectionism, like all good stories, starts with Aristotle. Most of the great ancient Greek philosophers, Aristotle included, thought that the most important question for humankind was how to lead a *good* life. Aristotle claimed that the ultimate aim of human existence should be to achieve perfect happiness or fulfillment. He also thought that there was a specific set of virtues common to all of us as humans, and that our goal should be to cultivate these virtues to the highest degree. We can call this ultimate goal, following Aristotle, "the good."

So far so good. Things become a bit more controversial when Aristotle starts to apply these ideas to politics. It is impossible to achieve the good, he reasoned, all by yourself. People were obviously not designed to live in solitude. Someone who has no friends can hardly be accused of having lived a good life. Many of our virtues are social in character, involving the way that we interact with others. So people must form political communities—cities, in the case of ancient Greece—in order to engage in a shared pursuit of the good.

This framework makes it very easy to decide what the laws of the city should be. Since cities are formed so that individuals can achieve the good, the law should be there to punish those whose behaviour frustrates this goal. Since the good that people are trying to achieve is simply the cultivation of human virtue to its highest degree, the law should therefore punish vice and reward virtue. All that legislators have to do is make up a list of virtues and vices, and the basic work will be done.

This view of politics is called "perfectionist" because it is grounded in the idea that the purpose of political association is to achieve "the perfection of man." It starts with an ideal of the best human life and then organizes all of society to assist individuals in the pursuit of this ideal.

The perfectionist view of politics had enormous historical influence in both the Islamic and Christian variants of the Western philosophical tradition (and it still shows up now and then on the right wing of contemporary politics, where traditional religious views continue to hold some sway). Aristotle took his claim about the nature of the good life quite literally. He spent an inordinate amount of time trying to draw up the definitive list of virtues and vices. More than a thousand years later, Christian theologians were still working over the same ground. The familiar list of "seven deadly sins" arose from this attempt to develop a catalogue of vice.

But the fact that one thousand, even two thousand, years after Aristotle's death people were still engaged in heated debate over the precise nature of the virtues reveals the central weakness in this conception of politics. The organization of the political community presupposes an antecedent consensus over the nature of the good life. As long as everyone agrees about what is good and what is bad, the city will run smoothly. But what happens when they start to disagree?

This is a problem that many great minds studiously ignored for as long as possible. Aristotle was able to think that his own list of virtues was definitive because he took it for granted that his own culture was superior to everyone else's. This allowed him to ignore the fact that women, slaves, and "barbarians," if asked, would probably have produced very different lists. Slaves, for example, have had a tendency to put "mercy" quite high on their list of virtues—an idea that would never have crossed Aristotle's mind.

As states grew larger and more diverse, it became increasingly difficult to ignore the enormous differences of opinion that people tend to have on such questions. This is partly why religion eventually became so important to politics—with the conversion of the Roman empire and later the spread of Islam. These religious movements, by canonizing a set of texts as the "official" word of God, were able to secure a reasonable level of agreement about the proper conception of the good life, which could in turn provide the foundations for a political order.

Agreement was, however, secured at a price. With a set of full-time professionals dedicating their lives to the organization and reproduction of religious doctrine, it was possible to achieve a fairly impressive level of uniformity in belief. But this agreement was always accompanied by severe intolerance towards people who refused to go along with the program. Heretics had to be suppressed and infidels conquered. Within the perfectionist world view, killing or oppressing those who disagree with your community's conception of the good is an extremely natural thing to do. In Aristotle's view, the function of law is to enforce the pursuit of virtue and punish those who stray from the path. By doing so, the state is helping those who have lost their way return to the natural or true course. But what could do more to undermine a given virtue than someone who denies the importance of that virtue? So the whole logic of the legal system seems to favour punishing dissidents.

When the perfectionist view is applied to sex, it is easy to see how homosexuality could wind up being prohibited. Setting aside unconfirmed reports about life on certain Polynesian islands, the fact is that every society needs to have some rules to dampen sexual enthusiasm.

Apart from the fact that sex has a tendency to produce children, and someone needs to be held responsible for the care and upbringing of these children, there is also the more straightforward problem of sexual competition. A lot of fighting breaks out over sexual possession (most of it is men fighting with each other over their preferred object of desire). In our own, highly sublimated environment, it is easy to forget how much violence this sort of competition can generate. In order to recall the full magnitude of the problem, it is helpful to think back to more barbaric times—like high school.

No society can tolerate having people run around acting on every sexual impulse that comes their way. Sex causes too much trouble. Just watch a few episodes of the *Jerry Springer* show. But which acts should be prohibited? The perfectionist begins to answer this question by asking what the purpose of sex is. What good does the activity serve? Once the purpose is known, then virtuous action can be defined as that which helps us to achieve this purpose. Of course, the most common answer to this question has been procreation. God gave us sexual organs so that we could make babies.

Once this is settled, it is fairly easy to distinguish good sex from bad sex. Good sex is whatever leads to the production of babies. Any sexual activity that deviates from this purpose is bad. Good sex is "natural" because it fulfils the purpose that God had when he created us. (Note that this is not "nature" as the scientist understands it, but the older view of nature as packed full of divine intentions. Procreation is the "final cause" of sex.) This way of thinking is still reflected in our vocabulary when people talk about sexual "deviants" or "unnatural" acts.

Perfectionist thinking is what generates the classic catalogue of sexual vices: sodomy, fellatio, pedophilia, etc. All of these are forms of sexual activity that do not generate babies and therefore fail to achieve their rightful purpose. So it is hardly surprising that homosexuality got banned. It is for the same reason that contraception was banned. Our ancestors were not acting arbitrarily when they instituted these taboos. They were acting in a way that was consistent with

the perfectionist view of the universe. Our attitudes towards homosexuality began to change only after the perfectionist view as a whole
began to collapse.

The central weakness of a perfectionist political system is that it
requires agreement about a particular conception of the good. The law
enforces this agreement. When people come along who disagree, the
state has little choice but to punish them. Most often killing them is the
easiest way. This is why the two major world religions that incorporated
perfectionist ideals—Christianity and Islam—have traditionally been
so nasty, primarily to each other, but also to non-Westerners.

Of course, the fact that a political system has a weakness does not
mean that it is doomed. In particular, societies that are dedicated to
killing everyone who disagrees with them can get along tolerably well, as
long as they aren't very good at killing. Significant portions of the Christian and Muslim civilizations were wholeheartedly committed to either
converting or exterminating each other for more than a thousand years.
But this was very hard to do with just swords and horses. As a result, they
contented themselves for the most part with indecisive and interminable
border wars.

What ultimately changed all this—what finally exposed the fatal
weakness of perfectionism—is that Europeans got extremely good at
killing. If there is one thing that characterizes European civilization
above all, it is a peculiar genius for inventing and improving weapons.
Of course, everyone knows the apocryphal story about how the Chinese
invented gunpowder for use in fireworks, and the Europeans converted it
for use in cannons. (In actual fact, the Chinese invented cannons, and
Europeans probably first encountered them when they were used against
them by Muslim armies at the time of the Crusades. Europeans were
simply *better* at making cannons once they started, because all their technology for making church bells could easily be converted to the production of cannon barrels.) But setting aside these embellishments of the
historical record, the fact remains that Europeans have traditionally

been masters at the art of applying deadly force. Looking through the arsenal of a modern military force, it is hard to find anything that was not invented by a European or Euro-American.

The story of how Europeans brought these talents to bear on the rest of the world is a familiar one. What is often forgotten is the fact that Europeans used their weapons against each other far more often, and to much more deadly effect, than they did against outsiders.

Partly because of the geography of Europe, and partly because Christianity is a somewhat internally disorganized religion, the church always had a hard time securing uniformity of belief. Officials were always having to run around burning heretics and squelching reform movements. It was only a matter of time before one got away.

Finally in 1517, one man did slip through the cracks. The man was Martin Luther, and the set of events that he set in motion is now known as the Protestant Reformation. The most important aspect of Luther's revolt is not that he rejected official church doctrine, but that he secured military and political protection for his movement. Once properly armed, the movement became effectively impossible to put down. Heretics with pitchforks are one thing. Heretics with guns are quite another.

The Reformation triggered over two centuries of religious warfare and, perhaps more importantly, generated civil wars in every major European nation. Looking back, it is hard to see why Protestants and Catholics had such trouble getting along with one another. This is because we no longer subscribe to perfectionist ideals. Back then, the world looked very different.

One of the major aspects of Protestantism is that it rejected key elements in the older Christian conception of the good life. Early medieval Christians had adopted from ancient Greece the idea that an ideal life was one of quiet contemplation, removed from the pressures and concerns of daily life. As a result, Christianity was sustained for centuries primarily as a monastic religion. In order to lead a truly good life, one had to become a monk or a nun and retreat from the world. Luther rejected all this, perhaps most symbolically by dissolving the local nunnery and marrying one of the sisters. Protestantism was to be popular religion. No more religious professionals! People could read the Bible and make up their own minds about what it meant. And the best life was no longer one of quiet seclusion, but one of good works performed in the world.

We might now regard this as a perfectly reasonable disagreement about the ultimate aims in life. But at the time, the church was far too closely integrated with the state to tolerate dissent. The role of the state was to promote the perfection of man. For the traditional church, this meant providing conditions under which monasteries could flourish (through tax exemptions, political representation, and so forth). For Protestants, it came to mean dissolving the monasteries and selling off their lands to the highest bidder. In both cases, the state was regarded as being perfectly within its rights using force to achieve these ends.

The predictable outcome was bloodshed on an unprecedented scale.

One of the most idiosyncratic and entertaining figures in early modern philosophy is Michel de Montaigne. A retired country gentleman, Montaigne spent much of his later life writing melancholy essays and scratching graffiti on the wooden beams of his study. During this time, he also decided to try his hand at politics. From 1581 to 1585, he served as mayor of his hometown of Bordeaux. During his second term of office, one-half of the town's population was exterminated through a combination of religious warfare and plague.

That must count, by anyone's standards, as an unsuccessful foray into politics.

These events naturally led Montaigne to think about religion and intolerance. His solution to the problem of religious warfare was inspired by ancient scepticism. Since we can't really know whose God is the real God, he argued, perhaps we should all just try to get along. Our own ignorance is grounds for tolerating the contrary opinions of others. (This argument for tolerance is still quite popular, finding expression, for example, in the hippie claim that we shouldn't make "value judgements," since values are all subjective.)

Unfortunately, people are not very good at confessing their own ignorance, and it is impossible to get through a single day without making at least a dozen value judgements. As a result, Montaigne's solution never really took hold. Instead, the wars of religion found their ultimate philosophical response in the more pragmatic suggestions of Thomas Hobbes, the grandfather of social contract theory.

Hobbes saw clearly that the problems of intolerance and civil war had their origins in the fact that the Christian state was committed to promoting a particular conception of the good. Since people have a tendency to disagree about the nature of the good, this means that the actions of the state inevitably generate both winners and losers. The winners are those who happen to agree with the conception of the good that the state decides to promote, while the losers are those who happen to disagree. Problems arise from the fact that this arrangement gives the losers an incentive to resist the actions of the state, or to replace those in power.

The solution, Hobbes argued, was for the state to confine itself to actions that bring about only winners, or win-win transformations. For instance, everybody, no matter what conception of the good they endorse, has a need for physical security in order to pursue their goals. Thus the state, by guaranteeing peace and order, can make everyone happier, regardless of what these goals are. Similarly, when the state enforces contracts, it is helping to bring about an outcome that all parties to the contract desire, each for his or her own private reasons. If the state limits itself to exercising powers that generate mutually beneficial outcomes, people who disagree about the ultimate aims in life should nevertheless be able to peacefully co-exist within a unified political order.

The device that Hobbes chose to represent this view was a giant contract, which every member of society could agree to sign. The idea that the power of the state stems ultimately from the people is a very old one. Hobbes updated it by arguing that the only powers the state should have are those that everyone can agree to surrender. Because there is disagreement about what constitutes the good life, people would never surrender to the state their power to pursue their own particular vision.

On the other hand, everyone's interests are damaged by the climate of insecurity that is created when people use violence to achieve their objectives. Thus everyone could reasonably agree to surrender to the state their right to the private use of force, in return for a promise of state protection.

What Hobbes is providing here is the blueprint for an efficient society. According to Pareto's definition, the efficiency of a social arrangement can be increased whenever the welfare of at least one person can be increased *without* decreasing the welfare of anyone else. The concept of welfare here is subjective: a person's welfare is increased if that person is better able to achieve his or her own particular goals. Thus any suggestion to improve the efficiency of society should be able to secure universal agreement. Those who benefit from the change will vote for it, and those who are unaffected will at the very worst abstain. Since no one is harmed, there is no one with an incentive to resist the proposal. Thus any proposal that could be agreed upon in a social contract is one that will improve the efficiency of society, and any change that improves the efficiency of society is one that everyone should be able to accept.

What emerges from this is a radically different view of how political society is supposed to function. Hobbes effectively takes government out of the business of deciding what kinds of lives people should lead. According to the contract view, one's conception of the good life is a private matter, to be decided by one's own particular cultural traditions and personal experiences. There will inevitably be considerable disagreement in this domain. But despite such disagreement, there will be ample room for mutually beneficial co-operation among individuals. Our major social institutions are designed to facilitate these forms of co-operation. The authority of these institutions stems from the fact that we all agree to respect the powers that they exercise. And we all agree because when these institutions work correctly, they generate benefits that we all enjoy.

Thus the major reason for the success of a society committed to efficiency is that it is able to sustain an unprecedented level of pluralism. Efficiency is the kind of value that allows people to get along without shared values. This shows to what extent we are all complicit in the culture of efficiency, and how deeply embedded this value is in our political consciousness. We like efficient social institutions because they do not tell us how to lead our lives. They provide a neutral framework within which we can go out and decide for ourselves how we want to live.

An efficient society is like a good car. It doesn't select your destination, but it helps you get there with a minimum of hassles.

Back to sex. The contractualist view of society had obvious consequences for our understanding of sexual morality. The first consequence is that it drives a wedge between private morality and legal regulation. In the perfectionist view of politics, the law did little more than enforce morality. The fact that sodomy or fellatio (and also, significantly, abortion) were considered immoral was sufficient grounds for making them illegal. But in the contractual view, the state has the power to enforce a particular rule only if everyone can agree to give the state that particular power. The mere fact that a particular sexual practice is regarded as immoral by the majority of the population is therefore no longer sufficient to make it a legitimate object of legal regulation. A clear separation develops between what people should do and what the state can legitimately force people to do. Pierre Trudeau's famous suggestion that the state has no place in the bedrooms of the nation is a familiar expression of this view.

So what kind of sexual regulations are appropriate to this new contractual perspective on society? People may disagree about the relative merits of particular amorous manoeuvres or the desirability of certain partners, but the one thing that everyone can agree to is that sex must be *consensual*. It is fine to have people satisfy their potentially odd sexual desires ("If it makes you happy . . ."), but it is very important that no one be able to impose his or her particular desires on another. Sexual relations, like every other form of social relationship, are to be established on the basis of agreement. Whenever this consent is lacking, a violation of the person has taken place in which the state may take a legitimate interest.

Thus consent becomes the most important component of sexual morality in the contractual age. This is why we now consider rape to be the most serious sex crime. According to the old perfectionist view, a woman's consent to sex was considered absolutely inessential. There was nothing wrong with forcing a woman to have sex *per se*. As long as this occurred within marriage, then it served the overall goal of procreation, and so it was thought to be acceptable. (If the forced sex occurred outside of marriage, then it was generally regarded as a crime against the woman's father or her husband.) This is why there was no legal category of "marital rape" until recently.

The important point is that a woman's consent to sex was considered unimportant for exactly the same reason that a peasant's consent to the rule of a particular monarch was considered unimportant. All social institutions existed to promote a particular good. Whether or not the people involved fully understood what this good was, or agreed to pursue it, was irrelevant. If people didn't consent, then the problem was with the people.

This helps to clear up one of the most common misunderstandings about homosexuality. Many social conservatives have a tendency to lump together homosexuality and pedophilia and argue that if society begins to tolerate homosexual lifestyles, it will have taken the first step on the road to toleration of pedophilia, etc. This argument is one that baffles a lot of people, who don't see any reason we can't tolerate homosexuality and punish pedophilia.

The confusion stems from the fact that many conservatives still inhabit the old perfectionist world view, according to which anything other than straight sex among married couples is a perversion of the "natural" order. If you start tolerating one sexual perversion, they fear, then consistency requires that you tolerate all perversions. But for the rest of society, the concept of sexual "perversion" is almost meaningless. Everyone has his or her own sexual preferences. Live and let live. The difference between homosexuality and pedophilia is that the former is consensual, while the latter is not. Pedophilia is understood now as sex with someone *below the age of consent* and is therefore illegal for exactly the same reason that rape is illegal. Thus there is no danger that toleration of homosexuality will lead to toleration of pedophilia; the difference between the two is black and white.

In fact, while our society has become increasingly tolerant of homosexuality, it has become extremely skittish about any sexual activity involving young people. The old perfectionist view was considerably more relaxed when it came to pedophilia. Having sex with children was considered dubious, not because of its psychological effects on the child, but because it was generally not procreative. Nobody thought there was anything strange about twelve-year-old girls being married off as long as they had reached puberty. The idea that there is a magic age of consent, at which point it is suddenly okay to have sex or star in porno films, is a thoroughly modern one. It is closely related to the idea that there is a magic age at which people can be allowed to vote or get drunk in public.

While many people profess to being bewildered by the social changes going on around them, the underlying logic of these developments is not really so mysterious. Our ideas about morality and politics have been fundamentally altered by social contract theory. We regard agreement, or consent, as the ultimate court of appeal in deciding whether or not a particular social relationship is acceptable. We are strongly inclined to give people the benefit of the doubt when they freely choose to participate in any sort of activity. This is why there is so much less zeal for punishing the perpetrators of "victimless crimes"—recreational drug use, sadomasochism, prostitution, etc. It is for this same reason that efficiency is so highly valued. Improvements in the efficiency of our institutions benefit everyone, and so should be improvements that everyone can freely accept.

All of this is quite familiar to people who follow *Star Trek*. As I mentioned earlier, the *Voyager* spin-off features a cyborg crew member who would like to strive for perfection but must ultimately settle for efficiency. The full story is a little bit more involved. Our favourite cyborg, it turns out, used to belong to a galactic cyborg civilization known somewhat unimaginatively as the Borg. Within the Borg collective, all individuals are linked up like subprocessors into one collective "hive mind." As a result, their individuality is entirely submerged into the group consciousness. Individual drones simply receive and execute instructions from the core.

Much of the drama involving the cyborg (whose name, incidentally, is "7 of 9, tertiary adjunct to unamatrix 1") emerges as she is severed from the collective and must face the various challenges of integrating into human society. She soon realizes that it is only because of their collective thought structure that the Borg are able to have a society organized around the pursuit of perfection. Because they think as one, they are able to agree about what perfection consists of. Unfortunately, humans are unable to achieve this. Everybody has his own ideas about what kind of life is best, and so society as a whole cannot be organized around the pursuit of any one ideal. This is how 7 of 9 comes to the realization that efficiency is the highest value that human society can hope to realize. The best we can do is facilitate each individual's pursuit of his or her own goals.

This plot line provides a quick synopsis of what amounts to the major political insight to have arisen from the last five centuries of Western civilization. As 7 of 9 cautions, "The lure of perfection is great" but must ultimately be resisted. Perfectionism represents an extremely natural way of thinking about the organization of society, but it is ultimately incompatible with cultural and individual pluralism. This flaw has been driven home to us only gradually, through a series of hard lessons. So we are left settling for efficiency. This may not satisfy all of our deeper impulses. But there is very deep wisdom in the realization that we are unlikely to do any better.

These ideas find their most influential academic articulation in the writings of John Rawls, perhaps the most important political philosopher of the twentieth century. The cornerstone of Rawls's defence of liberalism is summarized in one line, which to paraphrase somewhat, reads as follows: The exercise of human reason, under conditions of freedom and equality, tends to generate more—not less—disagreement about the ultimate aims of life.

This should be engraved on a plaque somewhere and pressed into service as the official motto of the efficient society.

Perverse Outcomes

3 *Bob Summers spends most* of his day staring at a video screen. He's not a couch potato; he's the morning traffic specialist at ChumFM/CityTV in Toronto. Every day, it's his job to keep an eye on more than one hundred cameras that monitor the flow of vehicles coming in and out of the city. Highway 401 is the jewel in the crown of the Toronto system—the highest-volume expressway in the world. More than 350,000 vehicles pass through the Toronto segment every day. But on any given afternoon, it more closely resembles a parking lot.

You can learn some surprising things about efficiency by watching traffic. Obviously, the more efficient the road system, the more vehicles it can accommodate in a given period of time. Now, if the goal is to get cars through quickly, one might be tempted to assume that everyone should just drive as quickly as possible. That way as many cars as possible will be able to get through. Unfortunately, this is wishful thinking. As it turns out, when everyone tries to get through as quickly as possible, it can cause delays that will result in everyone getting through much more slowly.

Most of us assume that traffic jams are caused entirely by excessive volume—too many people want to get to the same place that you're going. But according to Summers, traffic is often just as slow when the volume is light. More open space on the road leads to higher speed, more aggressive lane changes, more collisions, and more cars in the ditch. "Light traffic just gives people more room to get into trouble, to show what bad drivers they are. They'll be flying along at 110 km per hour and suddenly decide they need to exit, so they swing across three lanes of traffic. That's when the trouble starts." Perversely, when a rain or snow storm slows things down, there are often not as many accidents, and so the traffic ultimately moves more quickly.

This illustrates a very general principle: when individuals act in the most efficient manner possible, it does not necessarily produce a collective outcome that is efficient. A set of actions that makes each individual in a group better off can also make the group as a whole much worse off. This is often called a perverse outcome.

In the end, the *way* people drive is just as much to blame for traffic jams as the number of people who are driving. Many of the laws governing traffic are intended to stop drivers from doing this to themselves. While building more roads and increasing public transit would both help ease traffic congestion, the fastest way to improve traffic flow, according to Summers, would be simply to get more police out there to enforce the rules.

What does this mean for a society that is committed to promoting efficiency? It means that, paradoxically, we sometimes have to stop people from doing what comes naturally to them in order to promote their own interests. More bluntly, we must sometimes use the force of law in order to allow people to obtain the goals that they themselves want to obtain.

Unfortunately, the inefficiencies that occur as a consequence of our actions are so perverse we often don't even realize we're responsible for them. As a result, we sometimes have difficulty seeing why it is that our society and our laws are organized the way they are.

Anyone who drives on a major road with any frequency has undoubtedly had the experience of being scared witless by an insane or aggressive trucker. Part of this is just because truckers can afford to drive more reck-lessly. If there's an accident, they won't be the first ones hurt. (Personally, I've noticed that drivers of minivans—the ones with airbags on every square inch of the interior—are even worse.) In any case, we are all fa-miliar with the standard litany of complaints about these sorts of drivers.

In Holland, the government decided to get serious about it. It is common knowledge that trucks pose the greatest danger to other vehi-cles while overtaking and passing. This is why, in many parts of North America, trucks are prohibited from entering the third lane on a high-way with more than two lanes. The Dutch decided to take it up a notch. They enacted a law that prevented trucks from entering the *sec-ond* lane as well, even on two-lane highways. This made it illegal for trucks to pass on more than 70 per cent of highways in the country.

The truckers, predictably, went ballistic. They claimed that the law would paralyze the economy. No more fresh vegetables! No more just-in-time manufacturing! All transactions and trade would take longer and cost more. International competitiveness would be crippled! The government ignored them.

A couple of weeks after the law came into effect, truckers began to notice something strange. They discovered that it was starting to take them *less* time, not more, to reach their destinations. A study was com-missioned. Sure enough, the average capacity of affected roads had increased by 36 per cent. Furthermore, the average speed had increased in *both* lanes. Even the truckers were forced to admit that the new regu-lation was an improvement. By preventing the truckers from passing slower vehicles, the law had the unintended consequence of actually speeding up all the traffic, including the truckers themselves.

How is this possible?

Passing is not a problem when one car is moving very slowly, hold-ing everyone else back. The problems arise when people try to beat the average speed of traffic on the road. If traffic on a highway is mov-ing just over the usual speed limit, it will be zipping along at about thirty metres per second. Drivers are also instructed to maintain a three-second following distance (although in practice they usually stay closer to two). In any case, with these following distances, at these speeds, there is plenty of room between vehicles to fit a third one in—even a large truck. This makes passing quite easy (whereas on a city street, it is often the case that someone must "let you in").

But while there is usually enough physical space to move in between vehicles without hitting either one, there is often not enough "time" space between them to do so without causing disruption. When you zip in between two cars, you often force the motorist behind you to hit the brakes in order to maintain proper following distance. This may cause a chain reaction back through all the other motorists behind. Each must slow down in order to adjust his following distance. So while the pass may shave a few seconds off your commuting time, it adds a few seconds to the commute time of maybe a dozen cars behind you.

Suppose that after making the pass, you are able to travel 10 km per hour faster. However, the pass has the effect of slowing down twelve cars behind you. In order for the pass to generate a net increase in the average travel time on the road, you would have to maintain the increased speed for quite a while. Chances are, however, that you will not have an unobstructed road in front of you. Within a few minutes, you will encounter another vehicle moving slower than you, forcing you to decelerate or, worse, execute another pass. If you choose to pass, it may again slow down the traffic behind you. As a result, your passes will speed up your trip, but they will slow down all the vehicles behind you, and thus reduce the average speed of vehicles on the road.

Of course, if you were the only one passing, you would not suffer any negative consequences. But just as your passing slows down everyone behind you, the people passing in front of you slow you down. In effect, commuters all slow each other down, even though not one of them slows him or herself down. Each motorist who speeds through, trying to maintain a velocity higher than the average for the road, generates a wake of disruption and delay, like the ripples emanating from the back of a boat.

The Dutch truckers, of course, had no idea that they were doing this to one another. It seems logical to suppose that if everyone drives as fast as possible, the traffic as a whole will move as fast as possible. But this turns out to be false. It is in fact a paradigm case of individual efficiency generating collective *inefficiency*.

What makes these inefficient outcomes especially perverse is that even if everyone recognizes the problem and sees how his or her own behaviour is contributing to it, this may have absolutely no effect. Having learned from the Dutch example, we now know that passing slows down traffic. Does this mean that we will all stop passing? Absolutely not—because we have no individual incentive to stop. After all, passing still helps you to get where you're going faster; it only slows down the people behind you. As economists say, the costs of your behaviour are *externalized*. So why not do it?

It should be noted that some of the passing that goes on is based on misperception. Studies have shown that many drivers have the impression that the "other lane" is moving faster, even when it isn't. The effect is a sort of optical illusion generated by the experience of sitting in traffic flow. As a result, drivers often make gratuitous lane changes, which has the effect of exacerbating the existing traffic flow problems. But it is important to see how different this case is from the one of passing a slower vehicle. Once the illusion that the other lane is faster has been exposed, it removes the incentive to switch. But when passing a slower vehicle, there is no comparable illusion. Passing does actually move you through faster. It only slows down others. As a result, simply becoming aware of the social consequences of the action does not necessarily make anyone less likely to do it.

Anyone who doesn't believe this should drive around downtown Manhattan. The first time I did this, I was somewhat alarmed to see large squares painted in the middle of many intersections, along with the message that any vehicle caught in the square when the light changed would be subject to a fine of up to $500. This struck me as being quite extreme.

The goal of this regulation, I was later told, was to prevent gridlock. Gridlock occurs when cars enter an intersection on a green light, but traffic congestion ahead makes them unable to "clear" the intersection. When the light changes, they remain stuck in the middle of the intersection, blocking traffic flow from the other direction. (The term "gridlock" has since come to be used much more loosely. Technically, it refers to the situation that develops when the intersections on all four corners of at least one city block get jammed up this way. These jams become mutually reinforcing, so that no one will be able to move forward until someone actually *backs out* of one intersection.)

In any case, gridlock is a natural consequence of drivers trying to get to where they are going as quickly as possible. After all, it is always in your interest to enter an intersection on green, regardless of whether you will be able to clear it by the time the light changes. At most you will cause inconvenience to the people trying to go the other way. (And if you wait for the next light, you may get blocked by someone going the other direction.) But when everyone does this (or even when lots of people do it), traffic will become completely paralyzed. This is, of course, in no one's interest. But just knowing it doesn't change things. The city of New York found it necessary to impose fines—not little fines, *massive* fines—in order to stop people from doing it, despite the fact that it is in their interest, as a group, not to do it.

These traffic examples are helpful because they illustrate a very general principle. Gridlock is an example of collectively self-defeating behaviour. Each one of the drivers is acting in a way that is efficient, given that driver's own particular goals, but the outcome is Pareto-inefficient. If *everyone* changed his or her course of action, then *everyone's* welfare could be improved without harming anyone else. But no one has an incentive to do so, and so the potential efficiency gain remains unrealized.

Those of us in the philosophy business sometimes describe the situation that drivers are in as a prisoner's dilemma. This is a somewhat odd expression, which has its origins in an influential piece of academic folklore that was circulated extensively in the 1950s. The story goes something as follows: Imagine that you and an accomplice were involved in a major crime—say, robbing a bank. The police do not have enough evidence to convict either one of you, but they happen to catch the two of you engaged in some minor offence—say, drug possession. They have enough evidence to convict both of you on the minor charge, but they will not be able to get a conviction on the major charge unless one of you agrees to testify against the other.

The police bring the pair of you down to the station and put each one in a separate interrogation room. After a brief delay, they make you the following offer: "If you refuse to co-operate, we will prosecute you on the minor charge, and you will go to jail for two years. If your partner implicates you, we will also be able to convict you on the major charge. That would add another eight years to your sentence. However, if you choose to co-operate with us and testify against your partner, we will drop the minor charge. Think it over, and we'll get back to you in a few minutes."

Let us assume that your goal is to minimize your own jail time, and that you don't especially care about what happens to your partner. Grabbing a notepad, which has been conveniently left behind, you sketch out the possible scenarios (in descending order of desirability):

1. I implicate my partner; he says nothing. My sentence: zero.
2. Neither of us says anything. My sentence: two years.
3. We both implicate each other. My sentence: eight years.
4. I say nothing; my partner implicates me. My sentence: ten years.

It is clearly in your interest to implicate your partner. Whether or not your partner confesses is beyond your control. If he is going to implicate you, then you are better off implicating him as well, so that you can at least get the minor charge dismissed. But if he is not going to implicate you, then you are still better off implicating him, again so that you can get the minor charge dismissed. As a result, you are always better off choosing to testify against your partner.

So far so good. Unfortunately, the police also happen to mention that they are going to make the same offer to your partner. The reason that your situation is called a dilemma is now starting to become clear. It is also in your partner's interest to implicate you. As a result, if both of you share the overriding goal of minimizing your own jail time, you will each turn each other in and will each serve eight years in jail. If you both keep your mouths shut, you will wind up with only two years. Thus acting on your desire to minimize jail time seems to be increasing, not decreasing, the amount of jail time that you are likely to serve.

How is this happening? Looking back at the list above, you can see that scenario number two is better for both of you than scenario three. Unfortunately, you don't have any control over what your partner does. Your choice will determine only whether you get scenario number one or two, or whether you get scenario three or four. Since one is better than two, and three is better than four, you will choose to implicate. Your partner will do the same, and so the two of you will wind up with scenario three, even though two is better for both of you. This is a Pareto-inefficient outcome. Your behaviour may be individually rational, but it is collectively self-defeating.

(Word has it that the police use this tactic quite often, and that it apparently works quite well. It certainly works all the time on *Law and Order* and *NYPD Blue*. Enthusiasts should take note, however. The assumption above was that the two suspects were actually guilty. In fact, it's in their interest to implicate each other *regardless of whether either of them has actually committed the crime*. Thus the prisoner's dilemma can be used just as effectively to extract confessions from the innocent as from the guilty.)

What does all this have to do with traffic jams? The two types of interactions have exactly the same structure. Imagine that knowing how much passing slows down traffic, you are trying to decide how you should drive. You might think of the choice as a sort of "dilemma" faced by you and the other drivers on the road.

1. I pass; the rest do not. My travel time: very fast.
2. None of us passes. My travel time: medium fast.
3. We all pass. My travel time: medium slow.
4. I do not pass; the rest do. My travel time: very slow.

Your reasoning here is just the same. If no one else is passing, then that certainly helps you out. But you will get through even faster if you make a few passes (scenario one is better than two). In any case, if other people are passing, then you would be doubly crazy to sit there and let them zoom by—you are still better off passing (three is better than four). If everyone thinks this way, then the overall outcome will be three, even though two is better for everyone. Thus, as drivers, you are stuck in a type of prisoner's dilemma.

It is easy to think of the prisoner's dilemma as a mere curiosity, a harmless little philosophical puzzle. This temptation should be resisted. The prisoner's dilemma actually reveals one of the deepest facts about human society. Life would be a complete disaster if each of us simply did what it was in our own best interest to do. If society didn't impose any constraints on the pursuit of self-interest, we would all be better off crawling back into the woods and living as hermits.

The first philosopher to make heavy weather of this fact was Thomas Hobbes. Hobbes noticed—as many of us have—that when left to their own devices, people have a tendency to make a mess of things. His genius lay in the discovery that we do not necessarily make these messes because we set out to harm one another. Often the mess occurs simply because our attempts to secure our own self-interest are collectively self-defeating. So if our "natural" inclination is to mind our own business and look after our own interests, then life in a "state of nature" would be unbearable. Our existence would be, as he so famously put it, "solitary, poor, nasty, brutish and short."

Hobbes's argument is, unfortunately, frequently misunderstood. It is commonly thought that his characterization of our "natural condition" is so unflattering because he assumes that people have evil motives. This is absolutely untrue. Hobbes does not claim that people's goals are corrupt or bad. His point is that even people who have perfectly reasonable goals—whether they be altruists or egoists—will fail to achieve these goals if they try to achieve them using whatever means are available.

In Hobbes's view, the core problem—the one that gets us into so much trouble—is that we have a natural tendency to get stuck in prisoner's dilemmas. To see why this is so, take a typically Hobbesian example. Imagine a situation in which there are no police or security guards, and no official rules to prevent you from doing what you want. Everyone will therefore be responsible for his or her own protection. In order to guarantee your personal security, you might reasonably decide to carry a weapon. Let's say (to modernize the example a bit) you have a choice between carrying a knife and carrying a gun. Your potential assailant will have the same choice. So if you do get attacked and need to defend yourself, the set of possible scenarios looks something like the following (in descending order of desirability):

1. You have a gun; your opponent has a knife.
2. You both have knives.
3. You both have guns.
4. You have a knife; your opponent has a gun.

Again, this interaction has the structure of a classic prisoner's dilemma. Both of you will try to get your own number one, and as a result, you will both get number three. Everyone will carry a gun. Thus the desire to achieve greater personal security has the effect of *increasing* the deadliness of any eventual conflict (and thus the overall level of insecurity). And it doesn't really matter who is the potential assailant and who is the potential victim. Both individuals reason in exactly the same way, and so both of them contribute equally to the climate of insecurity.

It may seem funny to think of examples like these as involving efficiency, but this is fundamentally what is at stake. The outcome in which everyone has a gun is inefficient in Pareto's sense. If everyone had a knife instead of a gun, then everyone would be better off, because everyone would be less likely to be killed in the event of a conflict. Thus outcome two is more efficient than three (outcome one, on the other hand, is not more efficient, because it makes only one person better off, and the other worse off).

One way of thinking about interactions of this type is in terms of the benefits and costs that your actions generate for others. When you carry a gun, it generates certain benefits for you (increased ability to defend yourself), but imposes costs on others (increased chances that you will kill them). By contrast, if you carry a knife, it generates a cost for you (decreased ability to defend yourself) and a benefit for others (decreased chances that you will kill them).

When everyone is carrying a knife, everyone is happier, because the benefits they receive from others (in the form of decreased chances of being killed) outweigh the personal costs (decreased ability to defend oneself). The prisoner's dilemma arises because this situation creates a *free-rider incentive*. By switching from a knife to a gun, you will continue to receive all the benefits from the others who are carrying only knives, but you will also get the personal benefit of an increased ability to defend yourself. Of course, when you switch to a gun, you will cease to provide any benefit to others. As a result, they are now *suckers*. They are providing a benefit to you, while you are not reciprocating. (In the list of scenarios above, anyone who winds up with scenario one is a free-rider; anyone who winds up with four is a sucker. If everyone tries to free-ride or tries to *avoid* being suckered, everyone will wind up with three, the inefficient outcome.)

None of this should be terribly surprising to anyone. We all know that conflict has a tendency to escalate, and that it is very difficult to "call off" an arms race once it has begun. Hobbes's more subtle observation is that the vast majority of economic activities also have a prisoner's dilemma–like structure. Life in the state of nature, he claimed, would be not only "short" but also "poor." This is because production almost always involves co-operation, and co-operation generates free-rider problems.

Building a house, planting a garden, setting a trap—all these activities are potential prisoner's dilemmas. Given a choice between growing your own vegetables and stealing someone else's, it is much easier to steal someone else's. As a result, unless there are rules to prevent stealing, no one will plant any vegetables. Thus the problem with the state of nature is not that that there will be a lot of stealing. In fact, there will be no stealing, because there will be nothing *to* steal. People won't bother to grow anything, because they have no guarantee that they will be able to enjoy the fruits of their labour. The natural condition of humanity is one of extreme economic inefficiency. People will refuse to apply themselves for fear of being suckered.

Not only will people be unwilling to engage in productive activities, but trade will also be close to impossible. Adam Smith claimed, famously, that humans have a "natural propensity" to "truck and barter." Some people take this to be obvious. For Hobbes it would have been wishful thinking. He took as a far more fundamental fact about humanity the propensity towards "force and fraud." Every exchange is facilitated by either an implicit or an explicit *promise* to pay. And it is always in one's interest to make such a promise. At the same time, it is almost never in one's interest to actually *keep* such a promise.

Again, the options can be sketched out in the familiar way. Suppose you agree to buy something from your neighbour. You face four possible outcomes:

1. He delivers the goods; you avoid payment.
2. He delivers; you pay.
3. He doesn't deliver; you don't pay.
4. He doesn't deliver; you pay.

Even though your desire to enter into an exchange is motivated by self-interest, self-interest alone will not let you actually carry out the exchange. Unless the exchange is carried out simultaneously (like a hostage exchange), you will each try to free-ride (the old "cheque's in the mail" strategy). You will try to avoid paying, and he will try to avoid delivering. As a result, you will wind up with outcome three. In short, our natural propensity to free-ride *undermines* whatever natural propensity we may have to truck and barter. This means that economic exchange, when it does occur, must involve more than just self-interest; it must also involve some form of moral or legal constraint.

What does all this mean? According to Hobbes, it means that some-times the best way to secure liberty is to give it up. Freedom is not always a good thing. Freedom is good when its consequences are good. When the consequences of freedom are not good, then people are bet-ter off without some of that freedom.

As we have seen, the mere fact that people realize they're in a pris-oner's dilemma, and realize that their own behaviour is contributing to the misery, does not mean that they have any incentive to change what they are doing. For example, just knowing that it's a "bad thing" for every-one to be running around with guns does not mean that individuals don't have an incentive to own a gun (and especially not if everyone else is going to be running around with a gun, regardless of what you do). In order to actually change the pattern of behaviour, people must be given some kind of incentive.

(These incentives actually come in two flavours: internal and exter-nal. The internal controls are what we normally think of as morality, and these can be quite effective under certain circumstances. But this is complicated, and so I will set it aside until the next chapter. For now I will focus, following Hobbes, on the set of external incentives.)

According to Hobbes, the rules and institutions of society are designed to prevent our interactions from degenerating into prisoner's dilemmas. They lift us out of the "state of nature." Since our "natural liberty" includes the right to free-ride, the exercise of this liberty undermines all forms of economic and social co-operation. And so we should be willing to give up this right in order that we might all prosper. Similarly, our "natural liberty" includes the right to the private use of force when settling disputes. But if everyone exercises this right, the result will be a state of generalized violence. So our self-interest dictates that we all agree to give up this right and grant the state a monopoly on the use of force.

Of course this argument sounds paradoxical. And some people still refuse to get the point. The debate over gun control provides many examples. "If you don't want to exercise your rights, that's fine," say the opponents of gun control. "Just don't buy a gun. Why should all the rest of us give up our right to bear arms just because you don't see the need for guns?" This argument may sound persuasive, but it misses the point. The benefits of gun control don't come from not owning a gun; they come from eliminating the possibility of a certain type of free-rider strategy. The benefits come from knowing that *other people* don't have guns. Thus the outcome that everyone wants—a safer society—cannot be achieved through the exercise of individual rights. It can be achieved only if everyone is denied certain rights.

Gun control is perhaps too controversial an example. A more home-grown case involves the so-called "hockey helmet paradox." In 1979, the NHL made it mandatory for all new players to wear helmets. A significant number of players supported the change. The strange thing is, *not one of those players had previously worn a helmet*, even though they all had the option of doing so. So what was the point of the rule? If the players wanted to wear helmets, why didn't they just start wearing them?

The answer is simple. Nobody wanted to be the only one on the ice with a helmet. Why not? A helmet makes you look like a dork, especially if others are not wearing them. (Even now, players refuse to wear face-masks on the grounds that it makes them less recognizable, thereby diminishing the value of their commercial endorsements.) Players also complained that helmets interfered with their hearing and vision. So having the option of either wearing a helmet or not wearing a helmet created a free-rider incentive. And as long as there could be free-riders, the vast majority of players were unwilling to be suckered. They were, however, happy to comply once a law was introduced that eliminated the free-riders.

This is in fact why a lot of "common-sense" safety regulations nevertheless need to be enforced—from helmet laws to seatbelt legislation. No one wants to look cowardly or overly risk-averse. As a result, people are often happy to put on their seatbelts; they just don't want to be the only ones to do so, or they don't want to appear to be *choosing* to do so. They are more than happy to give up the freedom to choose, because the outcome is ultimately one that benefits them.

Not only is individual efficiency not always compatible with collective efficiency, but individual freedom does not always lead to collective efficiency either. An efficient society is therefore not one in which people run around doing whatever they want. Sometimes the best way to ensure that individual choice leads to an efficient outcome is to impose some limits on that choice.

The outcome of a prisoner's dilemma is often so dumb that some people have a hard time believing that anyone could really get stuck in one. After all, the outcome is so *obviously* inefficient. It seems that we should be able to get out of these situations with just a bit of common sense and self-restraint.

The examples in this chapter are intended to show, contrary to these suspicions, that common sense is often not enough, and that people really do get stuck in prisoner's dilemmas—routinely. You can't drive around a city street for more than five minutes without getting into one.

But that's not the worst of it. A prisoner's dilemma is what we call a "one-shot" game. Sitting in the police station, you get one choice—deny or confess—then it's game over. However, when people are able to interact on multiple occasions over time, it becomes possible for them to get stuck in a sequence of repeated prisoner's dilemmas. Not only that, it is easy for them to wind up in a situation where each time the dilemma is repeated, the outcome gets worse and worse. This is called a race to the bottom.

If getting stuck in a prisoner's dilemma seems dumb, then getting stuck in a race to the bottom must be *really* dumb. Nevertheless, we do it all the time.

Anyone who has lived in an apartment building with thin walls is probably familiar with the following scenario: For some reason, there is something uniquely annoying about listening to your neighbour's music. Even if your neighbour has decent taste, it's still annoying. Music from next door can easily set off a race to the bottom. It all begins when your neighbour puts on some tunes a little bit too loud. You get annoyed, but instead of knocking on the wall, you decide to put on some of your own music in order to drown out the stuff coming from next door. Unfortunately, one of the more mysterious laws of the universe seems to be that in order to effectively drown out a neighbour's music, your own has to be a fair bit louder. So while putting on some music helps to make your own environment more enjoyable, it also has the effect of seeping into your neighbour's apartment, annoying her. The real trouble starts when she then turns up the volume on her own music in order to drown out the stuff that's coming from your apartment. You respond by turning up your own music, and the race to the bottom has begun.

Why is this a race to the bottom? Once the music reaches a certain volume, both you and your neighbour might be a lot happier listening to nothing at all. As the volume creeps up, the situation gets worse for both of you. The problem is that you can turn off your own stereo, but you can't turn off your neighbour's. Once the volume goes up above the comfort level, you would like to call the whole thing off. But you can't. Assuming that you don't want to actually talk to your neighbour, the only choice you have is between listening to your own music, too loud, or to your neighbour's. As long as your neighbour's music is more irritating than your own, you will keep cranking up the volume. Furthermore, as the volume increases, it will become harder and harder to call it all off, because your neighbour's music will have gotten that much louder. In other words, as the outcome worsens, the incentives that generate that outcome are reinforced. At each step of the way it is in your interest to intensify the competition, even though the competition as a whole is bad for both of you.

This is why the quest for security often generates inefficient outcomes. Security is often best achieved through deterrence. When trying to deter an assailant, the key is usually to be better armed than he is. It is not so much the absolute level of armament that matters, but the relative level. This can lead states to spend enormous amounts of money on armaments at the expense of other social priorities (hence the high concentration of very poor states in Africa that spend more than 5 per cent of their GDP on defence).

This kind of competition, incidentally, is not just male posturing, as some have been inclined to suppose. I have found, for instance, that a depressingly large number of women of my acquaintance, after having children, began suddenly to express the desire to own an SUV (sports utility vehicle). Typically, they claim to feel "safer" in a big huge four-wheel drive. This is, in a sense, true. Unfortunately, the reason that SUVs are safer has nothing to do with the design of the vehicle. Cars must meet much stricter safety standards than SUVs, so in single-vehicle accidents most cars are safer. One survey reported that "the death rate for every 10,000 registered small SUVs, such as the Ford Bronco II or the Suzuki Samurai, is more than 10 times the rate for the largest passenger cars. Overall, SUVs have rollover fatality rates per million registered vehicles between two and three times that of passenger cars. The incapacitating rollover injury rate per occupant is 27.6 percent higher for SUVs than for the average passenger vehicle on the highway."

Single-vehicle accidents are one thing, but running into somebody else is quite different. In a multiple-vehicle collision an SUV is safer, simply because it is bigger than most other vehicles on the road. It is a general principle that if you slam into something smaller than you, it is going to hurt a lot less than if you run into something bigger than you. This means that if you are in an SUV and you run into someone driving a car, you are less likely to get killed (in fact, the person you have run into is four times more likely to die that you are). So the increase in security that comes from driving an SUV is entirely a free-rider payoff. Being big increases *your* safety, but only by making you more dangerous to other drivers. Here are the collision scenarios, again in decreasing order of desirability:

1. You're driving an SUV; the other person is in a car.
2. You are both in cars.
3. You are both in SUVs.
4. You are in a car; the other person is in an SUV.

Thus purchasing an SUV for increased "security" is collectively self-defeating. As more SUVs come onto the road, it makes the roads more dangerous for everyone. However, it also sets off a race to the bottom. The trick is to have an SUV that is bigger than everyone else's. After all, the increase in safety (and status) comes from being not just large, but larger than the others. This a major component of the dynamic that has seen the average size of North American vehicles drifting upwards over the last decade (and has generated such crimes against good taste as the Ford Excursion—a.k.a. the *Fordosaurus*, a.k.a. the *Ford Valdez*—which won't even fit through a standard-sized garage door).

Again, it is worth noting that most of the people who contribute to this race to the bottom have no idea that they are doing it. Buying an SUV is, in some sense, a deeply antisocial action. You increase the security of yourself and your children only by endangering the lives of others. You could achieve the same effect by installing gigantic spikes on the bumpers of your car, thereby encouraging other drivers to give you some space. But then the antisocial character of your actions would be much easier for others to detect.

The inefficiencies that follow from unrestricted freedom of choice are easy to see just by looking at some of the social problems that arise south of the border. In the United States, there is a very strong tendency to assign individual liberty priority over efficiency. In many ways, American civilization is like a great social experiment, designed to see just how much inefficiency people will be prepared to tolerate in the name of liberty.

The most serious inefficiencies in American society come from people's unwillingness to pay taxes (on the grounds that taxes interfere with individual liberty). This is what produces the well-known "private opulence, public squalour" that characterizes American cities. The outcome is often equal parts comedy and tragedy.

In the late 1970s, for example, the city of St. Louis found that it was having difficulties maintaining city streets. Tax revenues were simply not high enough to pay for all the work that needed doing. The result was a predictable decline in the quality of the roads (not to mention the schools and other public services), and the beginnings of an exodus to the suburbs. Of course, this being America, raising taxes was out of the question. So in a desperate bid to solve the problem, the city started selling streets. People living in residential neighbourhoods were invited to get together and buy their street from the city. This turned out to be very popular—in some parts of town, almost all the streets quickly became private. (Of course, it cost a lot more to buy these streets than it would have cost just to pay the taxes, but that's not the point. The point is that people had a *choice* whether or not to buy them.)

Once these streets were privatized, people started to get picky about who was using them. Residents figured, somewhat reasonably, that if they were the ones paying for their streets, then they should be the only ones with access to them. And so, one after one, streets started getting closed off, with large gates and no trespassing signs springing up at every other corner. But this had another consequence. Throughout several parts of the city, it become impossible to travel in a direct line from point *a* to point *b*. This became especially problematic when Washington University found that many of its students could no longer walk to school because all the streets across the north side of the campus had been privatized. The university was forced to negotiate with the neighbourhood associations to create a special corridor that students could pass through.

When Canadians look at this sort of situation, they find it difficult to avoid the conclusion that some mild form of insanity prevails south of the border. But it is not insanity. It is of course inefficient to have a city in which people must take a wildly circuitous route in order to get anywhere. But the only way to achieve the efficient outcome in this case involves a restriction of individual liberty. Canadians are, in general, willing to accept such restrictions, while Americans are not. This is the major reason why our society is more efficient.

The Moral Economy

Anyone who has ever lived with roommates understands the Hobbesian state of nature implicitly. When I was a student, I shared a gigantic old apartment in the east end of Montreal with four other people. The place was beautiful: it had a fireplace, stained-glass windows, moulded plaster ceilings, and two balconies overlooking Boulevard de Maisonneuve. Unfortunately, after about a year, it became significantly less beautiful. Some might even have called it decrepit.

What we discovered—what everyone living with roommates seems to discover—is that buying groceries, doing the dishes, sweeping the floor, and a thousand other household tasks are all prisoner's dilemmas waiting to happen. Cleaning is a typical example. If everyone "pitched in" and cleaned up messes as they occurred, everyone would be happy. Unfortunately, there is a free-rider incentive—before cleaning, it's best to wait around a bit to see if someone else will do it. As a result, the dishes will stack up in the sink, the floor will get dusty, and so on. Things will get cleaned less frequently than anyone would like because everyone will be sitting around waiting for someone else to do it. This is an inefficient outcome.

(For what it's worth, I should point out that my roommates were hardly self-styled Hobbesian individualists. In fact, one was a communist, one a radical feminist, and the other two anarchists. They still didn't clean up after themselves. Nor did I.)

Food turned out to be an even bigger problem. Because this was a "left-wing" household, it was initially assumed that the food bill should be shared communally. What we discovered, to our dismay, was that this arrangement gives everyone an incentive to overspend. Because the majority of the cost of anything you buy is passed on to the others, everyone has an incentive to buy more expensive food than they otherwise would. Why buy frozen orange juice when you can get the fresh stuff? After all, it only costs you a couple more cents. As a result, everyone's share of the food bill turned out to be higher than it would have been if everyone did their own shopping. This caused so many fights that the sharing of food eventually had to be eliminated. (As a result, we were all treated to the delicious spectacle of our favourite communist yelling, "Hey, who's been eating *my* cheese?")

In any case, people who have lived with roommates also know that the "state of nature" is not so hard to get out of. People can counteract their tendency to fall into inefficient interaction patterns in a variety of ways. The most common is to *make rules*. What roommates usually do, as the house begins to decline, is call a meeting and draw up a chore list. If it is decided that the floor should be swept every week, then someone can be assigned to do that job. If dirty dishes should be washed every night, then people can take turns doing them in the evening. If there is a problem with food pilfering, then one can make it a rule that no one touches anyone else's food.

Of course, everyone also knows that just telling people to do things does not automatically translate into a willingness on their part to do them. There is still an incentive problem that needs to be resolved. People can be expected to "forget" that it is their turn to do the dishes, or to become mysteriously absent on the day that everyone is scheduled to pitch in and clean up the bathroom. In order to make the rules effective, people have to be given some kind of motivation to comply.

So why do people follow the rules? The first thing about rules that most people pick up on is the fact that we are generally punished for breaking them. In the case of roommates, "forgetting" to do your chores has consequences. You may be given a rude reminder, or you may be kicked out onto the street. Because these punishments are quite visible, and because we have no difficulty figuring out how they serve to motivate people, there has been an enormous tendency to focus only on enforcement of rules as the solution to the problem of compliance. In fact, Hobbes tried to develop an entirely general theory based on the idea that all social rules are followed simply because the person in question fears the punishment associated with failure to comply.

However, Hobbes's theory was so unpersuasive that many social theorists began to take its explanatory failure as good reason to suppose that more than just sanctions are at work in our everyday rule-following. The fact is, many people follow the rules, sometimes at great cost to themselves, even when they could easily get away with breaking them. There is clearly an internal motivational component to rule-following. We often feel shame, guilt, or remorse when we break the rules. And we often obey them out of a simple sense of obligation. This internal mechanism is much more difficult to understand than the operation of external forces. But without some analysis of these inner motives, our understanding of how social institutions function will be deeply distorted.

That having been said, it should still be noted that many theorists continue to deny that inner constraint plays any role in motivating individuals. They are prepared to explain away any example that appears to suggest inner constraint, claiming either that the agents, deep down, simply *want* to follow the rule, or that they fear some hidden form of punishment.

Personally, I have always found this sceptical attitude difficult to understand. I often find myself following the rules even though I would much rather break them. For instance, every morning I take my dog for a walk around the block. Every morning I stop to clean up his *ordure*. And every morning I ask myself, "Why am I doing this?" This question becomes extremely pressing when it is 7:00 a.m., absolutely no one is around, and there is a foot of snow on the ground. It would be just weird to say that I somehow want to do it. I find the task offensive, and I would really rather not do it. Furthermore, my chances of being caught breaking the rule, much less punished, are almost nil. There is no one around to see me. And it cannot be that I am concerned about keeping the park clean. My one dog's meager output makes very little difference to the overall cleanliness of the park, and in any case its effects won't start to show up until some time in April when the snow melts.

So I have no desire and no external incentive to clean up after my dog. At the same time, I can see that the choice is a classic prisoner's dilemma. What I do makes very little difference to the park. Combined with my distaste for the act, this is what gives me an incentive to break the rule. At the same time, I can recognize that if no one cleans up, the park will quickly become disgusting. Thus self-interested behaviour would generate an inefficient outcome. According to the Hobbesian view of things, it should then follow quite automatically that I break the rule. And yet I don't.

So every morning I find myself obeying a rule that I have no desire to obey, and every morning I am confronted with something of a philosophical puzzle (even before my first cup of coffee!). Why do I do what I do?

The best answer, in my view, is that my actions are governed by a straightforward sense of moral obligation. I do it as a matter of principle. The principle in question is closely related to the prisoner's dilemma structure of the choice. When tempted to ignore the rule, I ask myself, "What if everyone did that?" And recognizing that it would be very bad if everyone did what I was about to do, I refrain from doing it. Thus I "do my part" in helping to avoid a prisoner's dilemma among fellow users of the park even though, strictly speaking, I don't have to.

This kind of voluntary compliance is clearly a central component of every moral code and accounts for the popularity of "golden rule" laws in essentially every major world culture and religion. In the Western philosophical tradition, this idea was given its most forceful expression by Immanuel Kant, who argued that our central moral obligation is simply not to make an exception of ourselves. Since I want other people to clean up after their pets, then I am under an obligation to do so myself. Simple as that.

Morality, in this view, is a kind of internal control system that helps us avoid prisoner's dilemmas. Kant's supreme principle of morality— "Don't make an exception of yourself"—amounts to a moral prohibition against free-riding. If you can improve your own situation only by making others worse off, then this is not something that you could will to be a "universal law." You are clearly hoping to make an exception of yourself. And so morality prohibits that course of action.

Some people think that this sort of reasoning is pie-in-the-sky. When push comes to shove, they say, we will set aside these moral niceties and do what is in our interest to do. To think otherwise is nothing but naïveté.

The problem with this sort of hard-boiled realism is that it leaves us at a loss to explain all kinds of co-operation that we see around us every day. In general, people do not require a policeman at their elbow in order to be kept in line.

But then here is a problem. According to the claim I am advancing, we are sometimes able to avoid prisoner's dilemmas by respecting a moral principle that prohibits us from making an exception of ourselves. And yet the previous chapter was larded with examples of people getting themselves into all sorts of prisoner's dilemmas. So how do we reconcile the fact that sometimes we are able to avoid inefficient outcomes, while other times we seem incapable of escaping from them?

In all the examples of prisoner's dilemmas given in the previous chapter, the crucial ingredient missing in each case is trust. People are often willing to do their part in implementing some kind of solution to a collective action problem, but only if others are prepared to do their part as well. They are willing to forego the benefits of free-riding, but they are not willing to be suckered. As a result, in order for people to co-operate, they must all believe that a fair number of others will co-operate too. They must trust one another.

This is something that I think about whenever I ride the subway. A number of years ago I saw a very odd little poster in the Toronto subway encouraging people not to litter. The basic message of the poster was pretty unspectacular—something like "Please don't litter." What made it more interesting was the fine print. Beneath the basic slogan were a couple of sentences that purported to explain precisely why one should not litter. The argument was quite unusual. According to its authors, some study had shown that as soon as one person drops a piece of litter in a subway car, everyone else starts to do the same thing. So, we were invited to conclude, when you think about dropping that first piece of litter, keep in mind that through your actions you will cause everyone else to start leaving all their garbage behind as well.

This claim is interesting on a number of different levels. The philosopher in me was initially intrigued by the argument itself. It struck me as ingenious, definitely weird, and probably fallacious. The subway authorities were trying to use the results of the study to impose a sort of Kantian moral reasoning on potential litterers. Before acting, Kant invited us to ask ourselves, "What if everyone else did the same?" The problem for Kant was that whether or not others "do the same" is completely outside your control. You aren't deciding what everyone will do, only what you will do. So why not litter? The subway poster tries to suggest that you *are* in fact deciding what everyone else will do, because your littering will cause everyone else to start littering. So in this case, the world is organized in such a way that you must think like a good Kantian.

Sadly, the fascinating question of whether or not this argument is fal-lacious cannot be answered here. But even setting aside this issue, the poster raises a number of interesting questions. The empirical facts uncovered by the study are quite strange. A subway car can stay perfectly clean for hours on end, but then someone drops one piece of litter, and the car instantly becomes a trash can. The first piece of litter is the hole in the dike that subsequently unleashes a flood. But we are not talking about water here, we are talking about people. People decide whether to drop their garbage or carry it to a trash can. So what is going through their minds that could cause such a sudden change in mass behaviour?

Here is one suggestion: subway litter is a prisoner's dilemma. People like to ride in clean subway cars, but they are also lazy when it comes to disposing of garbage. (According to another study, the average Canadian will carry a piece of garbage only twelve steps before dropping it.) Leaving a piece of garbage behind when you get off the train is therefore a classic free-rider strategy. It benefits you, but you would rather that others not do the same.

As a result, as a society we have adopted a rule that prohibits dumping one's garbage in public places. This rule, however, is almost never enforced. The subway police don't give out a whole lot of fines for littering. So we depend almost entirely upon voluntary compliance. People are, by and large, willing to comply. But while they are willing to forego the benefits of free-riding, they are still not willing to be suckered. Their willingness to comply is accompanied by the proviso "as long as others do so as well." Thus the practice as a whole requires an element of trust. People will comply only if they believe that others will comply as well.

So what happens when a person finishes reading her morning newspaper while riding the subway? Suppose our imagined passenger knows it is wrong to litter, but also doesn't feel like hanging on to the paper until her stop is reached. She looks around. She may see no litter at all, only an immaculately clean car. This will make her feel quite conspicuous leaving the paper behind. The fact that everyone else has been respecting the rule makes her feel obliged to do so as well. But suppose instead that, in looking around, she spots a piece of litter. She then thinks to herself, "To hell with that. If other people aren't following the rule, why should I?" And so she drops the newspaper. Of course, this makes the next person on the train even more likely to drop his newspaper. And so on.

What makes the "moral" solution to the collective action problem unravel here is that it is very easy to see whether or not others are co-operating. People who defect from the co-operative arrangement leave behind a visible sign of their defection—their garbage. This visible sign has the effect of undermining trust—the belief that others are going to play by the rules. And without this belief, no one can be confident that doing the "right thing" will not leave them open to exploitation by others. Despite the Christian injunction to "turn the other cheek," it seems that, as a matter of sociological fact, most people are not willing to.

Amateur criminologists (aren't we all?) will recognize, incidentally, that the mechanism at work here is very similar to the one underpinning the so-called "broken windows" theory of crime popularized by New York Mayor Rudolph Giuliani. The theory gets its name from the observation that a car can supposedly sit unoccupied on the street for weeks without being molested, but that as soon as someone breaks one of its windows, it will quickly be stripped down to the frame. Thus the broken window seems to send some kind of a signal that attracts the criminal element.

It is possible that the broken window suggests that no one is watching the car or that no one cares about it, and so the potential criminal is less likely to get caught breaking into it. Another possibility, however, is that when people notice that a rule is being broken or that it has been broken, many feel that it relieves them of the responsibility to obey the rule. Hence the commonly observed—and widely televised—fact that during riots many perfectly law-abiding citizens suddenly start helping themselves to store merchandise. The important thing is that someone *else* breaks the shop window. Once the window is broken, it doesn't seem so bad to take home a few items.

In this way, the erosion of trust becomes an autocatalytic process.

An enormous number of the moral rules we follow in everyday life have the function of eliminating inefficiencies. We tend to think that not littering, not stealing your roommate's cheese, or not cutting off other drivers in traffic are just common courtesies that we show to one another. But they also have a deeper rationale. In each of these cases, the rule prevents us from falling into a type of prisoner's dilemma. This means that the rules are efficiency-promoting. They make everyone better off—in terms of their own goals and projects—without making anyone worse off.

Of course, it often doesn't *feel* that way. Often the rules feel like outrageous impositions, unjustifiable restrictions on our freedom. But this is usually just the old free-rider incentive rearing its head. You would be better off if you could break the rule—but only if you were the *only* person who could break it. If everyone broke it, then you would be worse off, along with everyone else. Thus the rules improve our well-being precisely because they do *not* let us do what we want to do.

Even the most trivial of social rules can have an important role in promoting a more efficient outcome. Minor points of etiquette, for instance—which spoon you use for the soup, how you introduce yourself, whether you offer the last meatball to others before taking it— while not intrinsically efficiency-promoting, have the important function of building trust. A person who makes polite conversation over dinner is less likely, we figure, to attack us with his steak knife than someone who has been flying into a rage all night. This makes it much easier for everyone to enjoy his or her food. In general, we assume that someone who respects the rules in minor affairs is also more likely to respect them in major affairs (which is why so-called "confidence artists" are able to take advantage of us so easily).

If any of this seems odd, it is because we are not used to thinking of either morality or etiquette as promoting efficiency. We are much more likely to think that efficiency is primarily a feature of the economy, and that the complex, baroque set of rules that prevail in more "social" settings—such as dinner conversations or supermarket checkouts—are the antithesis of efficiency.

In fact, many economists pick out the practice of standing in line as an example of an "irrational" or inefficient social convention.

What irritates them is that, in general, people standing in line do not allow others to buy their way in. In principle, there is no reason why this should be prohibited. Instead of waiting for fifteen minutes in line at the bank during your lunch hour, why not pay someone at the front of the line ten dollars for her place? If you're in a big hurry, this might seem like a good deal. The person who sells you her place has to wait a bit longer, but comes out ten dollars richer. As long as both people are happy with this arrangement, isn't it a win-win transformation? And if so, isn't any rule that prohibits such transactions inefficient?

There is of course something to be said for this argument. After all, what harm is done if someone buys his way into a line? As long as the person who sells his place leaves the line, then the transaction doesn't actually slow down any of the people behind (unlike the practice of "saving a place" for your friends, which does actually slow down the people behind). Of course, if it became common for people to buy their way into line, this might give rise to a new class of professional "liner-uppers"—people who line up for a living, hoping to sell their place to some rich person who comes along. And of course it would be a problem if people started to hold up the line by spending a long time haggling over prices. Nevertheless, the economists' essential point is sound.

What this argument overlooks is the more basic fact that the practice of lining up is itself an efficiency-promoting institution. The reason we line up for things is that any kind of rationed access to a good generates a prisoner's dilemma. Everyone has an incentive to push his or her way to the front, but when everyone does this, the mob scene that ensues results in everyone getting through more slowly. This is especially true in the case of emergency exits. When I was young, it always seemed strange to me that parents and teachers expected us to line up to escape from burning buildings. The reason, I later discovered, is that more people can escape in a given time if the exit is conducted in an orderly fashion. This is not much comfort to those at the back of the line, and so the rule requires fairly powerful moral incentives in order to have any force.

The general point is that just because we can sometimes think of ways to make social institutions more efficient, this does not mean that they are not already performing some kind of useful, efficiency-promoting function.

It will be helpful to keep this in mind when we start looking at the economy. It is certainly the case that our economy—a market economy—is very efficient. It is also notoriously true that it does not require especially moral behaviour from individuals. Under capitalism, people are generally free to pursue their own self-interest in managing their affairs. And they are certainly not wrong to do so. The last thing we want the manager of a store to think about just before declaring a giant year-end clearance sale is what this will do to the competition, and how he would feel if they did the same thing to him.

This can be misleading, however, because our economy is the product of a very long series of historical developments. You don't have to go too far back in human history to find a time when every economic transaction was founded on a type of moral relationship. In the beginning, every economy was a moral economy, governed by a set of explicit rules and regulations. It was only much later that we started "tweaking" this system to secure increases in efficiency above and beyond what the basic moral rules were able to secure (in the same way that we might consider "tweaking" the practice of lining up, in order to allow people to buy places in line).

One need only think about a group of roommates drawing up a list of chores to understand how primitive economies were organized. The situation of five people sharing an apartment is a microcosm that contains all the challenges that originally confronted all human societies. In fact, the discipline of economics begins, with Aristotle, as literally the science of household management. When roommates get together to organize their chores, they don't create little miniature markets or joint-stock companies. They come up with a set of rules that assign particular jobs to particular individuals. And for the most part, they trust each other to comply with these rules. Thus they create a miniature economy that is governed by a moral code that organizes all productive activities.

⚬⚬⚬

In a sense, every society that wants to last more than a few days has to have *some* commitment to efficiency. While this commitment need not be conscious or fully explicit, there is good reason to believe that it must still be there. Even the legendary Ik of northeastern Uganda, the most antisocial and misanthropic people in the history of anthropological research, adhered to a number of social norms that mandated sharing and co-operation. Despite an ongoing famine, for instance, they would still offer their food to anyone who came upon them while eating (which is apparently why they would go off and hide whenever they found something to eat).

People are sometimes able to get along without encountering too many collective action problems. But there are some areas in which these seem to be endemic. In particular, anything that involves effort or work tends to generate prisoner's dilemmas. This springs from the fundamental fact that people are lazy. When faced with some kind of task that involves exertion—say, washing the car—and given a choice between doing it myself and having someone else do it, most of the time I prefer that someone else do it. At the same time, that someone else will probably prefer that I do it. So neither of us will do it.

The simple fact that work is hard creates a free-rider incentive. If there is any chance that someone else will come along and do the job, people are often willing to hang around for a bit before throwing themselves into the task. Thus the reason that efficiency considerations are so often associated with the economy is not that the economy is so efficient, but that the economy is a sphere in which the most serious *inefficiency* problems often show up.

We even have a special word for free-riding at work—shirking. To shirk is simply to avoid doing the work that one is assigned, while still benefiting from the efforts of others. Our society has such a strong work ethic that it is easy for us to underestimate how serious a problem shirking can be. People have been known to literally starve themselves to death because they are caught in a collective action problem. The most famous North American example of this occurred in the Jamestown colony, established in Massachusetts in 1607. Like many early pilgrim colonies, Jamestown was initially organized on the model of a giant work crew. Every citizen was expected to pitch in and help build the palisade, sink the well, work the corn fields, etc. In return, everyone was entitled to an equal share of the colony's produce.

The latter turned out to be the weak point in the arrangement. The fact that everyone got a share of the produce, regardless of how much he or she contributed, generated a massive free-rider problem. Nobody had any incentive to actually do any work. Colonists found a million and one reasons why they just couldn't show up for work on any given day. Contemporary observers estimated that the colony's agricultural output was about one-tenth of its capacity. But in the midst of chronic scarcity and occasional starvation, visitors were amazed to see perfectly able colonists passing the time bowling in the streets, instead of working the fields.

Since human survival used to be a lot more precarious than it is now, societies that failed to correct these sorts of inefficiencies were subject to fairly drastic correction. During the winter of 1609, the period of most acute starvation, the population of Jamestown was reduced from five hundred to just sixty. This may seem unbelievable at first. We know that people can be lazy, but we also know that hunger begins to outweigh laziness at a certain point. So we tend to assume that people will never starve themselves to death through laziness alone. But this overlooks a crucial point. In order for hunger to translate into an incentive to work, a society must be organized in such a way as to make shirking a less attractive strategy than working.

Contrary to our usual intuitions, it is possible for people to starve to death simply because their society is badly organized. Chronic mistrust and shirking can be lethal. As a result, societies that are not at least minimally well-organized must either adapt or perish. The forms of social organization that we see in the world around us are at least minimally efficient—enough to reproduce what Marx called the "material basis" of society. And in most of these cases, morality is the primary mechanism used to achieve economic efficiency.

❧

There was a time when the European population derived almost all of its sustenance from bread. This is why riots used to break out whenever the price of bread went up—without it, most people would starve. Of course, the importance of bread has since dwindled to the point where it makes up an insignificant component of our diet. Yet when we go to a French or Italian restaurant, bread is still served symbolically at the beginning of the meal. A similar process is happening with rice in wealthier parts of Asia. Whereas rice used to be a staple of the diet, ordering a big bowl to go with your meal now generates a loss of face. After all, why would you want to eat like a peasant if you can afford better? In both cases, food that was once a core component of the diet has, with increased prosperity, become merely a symbolic supplement.

As it turns out, many of our little rituals—such as serving bread before meals—have their origins in far more serious concerns. Some practices that now have purely symbolic value were once a matter of life and death. For example, in our society, people usually give each other gifts only on special occasions—at weddings, birthday parties, or on certain holidays. But there was a time when gift-giving was one of the central institutions in our society, just as important to the smooth functioning of the economy as trade is for us now.

This may seem surprising, since gift-giving is a notoriously inefficient social institution. I have a basement full of things people have given to me that I don't really want but can't throw away or exchange. Furthermore, my friends probably have their fair share of things I've given them that they're not too fond of either. Clearly, if we could give all this stuff back, or get rid of it, or just buy presents for ourselves instead of for our friends, we would all be much better off. In fact, there are various ways in which people have tried to "tweak" the practice in order to make it more efficient. Bridal registries and gift certificates are two examples that spring to mind. But we can only go so far. Giving someone money may be the most efficient thing to do, but it is also regarded as unfeeling, insensitive, thoughtless. There appears to be a tension between the value of efficiency and the spirit of gift-giving.

This tension reflects the fact that gift-giving is no longer functional for our economy, but has a largely symbolic importance. This was not always the case. Gift-giving was once, and in many cultures remains, extremely important. The essence of gift-giving is a norm of reciprocity—whenever someone gives you a gift, you are obliged to repay him or her at a later date with a gift of comparable or greater value. As a result, gifts can serve as something like an insurance policy in economies that are subject to irregular returns.

For tens of thousands of years, humans survived as hunters and gatherers. The most basic problem with this form of subsistence is that it is subject to cycles of feast or famine. A hunter is likely to make a large kill very infrequently. When he does succeed, he then finds himself with a lot of surplus meat, most of which will spoil if it is not eaten right away. So based on his own individual efforts, he will tend to have either too much food or not enough.

One way to break out of this cycle is to pool some of the risk associated with the erratic returns of hunting. Although any one hunter is unlikely to make a large catch every day, in a large enough group *someone* is likely to make such a catch every day. If there is a practice of gift-giving, then the lucky hunter has an incentive to give away as much of the meat as he can to the others, knowing that they will be obliged to give some to him when they make their next kill. That way, on days that he is not so lucky, he will still have something to eat. Thus gift-giving can produce a distribution system that breaks the feast-or-famine cycle, guaranteeing everyone a steady supply of meat. Most importantly, the gift-giving norm allows people to avoid the collective action problems associated with hoarding. No meat will ever go uneaten, because the hunter would rather give it away—as insurance—than let it spoil.

Ethnographic reports suggest that gift-exchange systems of fabulous complexity, extending over vast territories, have been developed and sustained. The larger the group included in the gift-exchange system, the more significant its insurance functions. Farmers may give some of their surplus grain to fishers on the coast so that, if the weather turns bad, they can "call in the favour." It is a simple diversification strategy. The important thing is that it is organized and motivated entirely by a set of moral principles. Ultimately, nothing compels you to return a gift but your sense of honour and your obligation to the giver.

Trust has always been the glue that holds together human society. Trust is ultimately what prevents human interaction from degenerating into a Hobbesian state of nature. Nevertheless, trust is not the *only* thing that keeps society together. In fact, institutions based on trust alone are subject to very clear limitations. There are good reasons that explicitly moral practices such as gift-giving no longer play a central organizing role in our economy. It is simply impossible to organize a modern, industrial society on these foundations.

The key problem with trust as a basis for the organization of social relations is that it is extremely fragile. Building up trust can take a very long time. Undermining trust, on the other hand, takes no time at all. Furthermore, once trust has been undermined, it may become impossible to re-establish. It only takes a few rotten apples to eliminate a lot of the trust that may prevail in a community. Perhaps because of this, trust seems to depend quite heavily on personal contact. Many people find it difficult to trust anyone outside of their immediate circle of acquaintances, and especially difficult to trust someone they have never met.

As a result of these limitations, we very seldom see social relations that are grounded entirely in trust. Most often, trust relations are supplemented by a set of sanctions. When two people are stuck in a prisoner's dilemma, it is clearly in their interest to adopt some kind of co-operative solution. However, if they do not know each other well and so are unable to trust one another, they may not be able to implement such a solution. They can, of course, just take a leap of faith. But there are other, less risky solutions. One of them is to find a third person whom both of them trust to enforce the agreement. If this third person makes a credible commitment to punish anyone who fails to do his or her part in the co-operative solution, then it becomes possible for two people who do not trust one another directly to nevertheless establish co-operative relations. Of course, sanctions don't allow you to eliminate trust from the picture. If the person doing the punishing isn't trustworthy, it will be possible for either party to simply buy him off. This will undermine co-operation. Thus sanctions allow people to *expand* the circle of trust relations, not do without it.

The way that sanctions can expand trust can be seen clearly in the case of organized crime. As the original scenario of the prisoner's dilemma shows, it can be very easy for the police to persuade criminals to rat on each other. As long as there is no honour among thieves, they will tend to turn each other in. Thus criminal conspiracies are more successful when there is some kind of honour, or basis for trust, among those involved. This is why organized crime arises only in certain social contexts and tends to crystallize around institutions that promote strong, but particularistic, loyalties. The family provides the perfect foundation precisely because kinship ties generate a level of trust and loyalty that can outweigh any counterincentive that the police might provide. The family may adopt a code of silence. It's much easier to believe that your partner will respect the code and refuse to rat on you when that partner is your brother or sister.

This explains why organized crime tends to start out with a set of "crime families." The family is needed in order to contribute the *organized* component to the organized crime. However, once the criminal family expands beyond a certain size, it may start to run out of family members. As it gets larger, the basis for trust may also begin to erode. People may start to violate the code of silence (or just as bad, they may start to have doubts about whether *others* in the group will respect the code). As a result, the family may be able to grow only by supplementing the core trust relations with a set of sanctions. Thus the code of silence can be beefed up, as it generally is, with a credible commitment on the part of family members to kill anyone who testifies against another member. Whereas these sanctions would not be credible on their own, when combined with the background trust conditions, they generate a very powerful form of social control.

❧

One of the most commonly noted—and frequently lamented—features of human society is our tendency to establish hierarchical social relations. On *Star Trek*, the first thing the alien xenobiologists notice about human beings is invariably the hierarchical or "chain-of-command" organizational structure that prevails on the representative spacecraft. This sociological feature of the show, in fact, provides ample fodder for critics who lament the quasi-militaristic ethos that seems to pervade this supposedly utopian vision of the future. But such criticism in some ways begs the question. After all, who says that the military has to be organized hierarchically? In principle, it could be organized any way we like. If every military we know of is organized hierarchically, this may say something important about the virtues of organizational hierarchy. It may reflect, for instance, a principle of selection. Perhaps non-hierarchical militaries are too easily defeated.

One way of understanding the ubiquity of hierarchical organizational forms is in terms of their superior efficiency. Anyone who has spent time working in a '60s-style commune or co-operative knows how impossible it can be to get anything done when everyone must be consulted. A hierarchy still depends upon trust relations, but it supplements these with sanctions in a way that makes decision-making considerably more economical. In a standard chain of command, leaders have the power to punish subordinates who disobey orders. But orders are enforced only as a last resort, and in many circumstances leaders are not in a position to actually compel obedience. They depend upon moral incentives to motivate their subordinates. The most effective hierarchies are ones in which subordinates have enough loyalty to the organization and to its leadership that they obey without needing to be forced. Thus hierarchies provide a perfect example of the way sanctions can be used to *extend* trust relations to secure co-operation in larger groups.

Of course, there are various problems with this mode of organization. It is, for instance, subject to diminishing returns as its size increases. It is also very bad at handling certain types of distributed information. Its core virtue, however, is that it helps us to avoid collective action problems.

The basic trust relations that bind each individual to the group project, when amplified by a set of social sanctions that reward compliance and punish deviance, create an organization that is capable of very large-scale concerted, co-operative action. There are very few other ways known to us for organizing and mobilizing people on such a scale. This is why the institutions around us—not just the military, but also schools and universities, governments and corporations—are all hierarchies. The alternatives to hierarchy tend to be extremely inefficient.

Historically, hierarchies have played a very important role in the development of human societies around the world, precisely because they permit large-scale organization. For example, no agricultural society has ever succeeded in building an irrigation system without at the same time developing a centrally organized state. This is largely because the construction of irrigation systems is subject to serious free-rider problems. (Instead of digging a canal from your field all the way to the river, why not wait until your neighbour digs one, then just hook yours up to his?) A hierarchy institutionalizes the trust needed to eliminate these free-rider problems—you can go to work digging the canal knowing that your neighbours will be forced to help out as well—along with providing the straightforward co-ordination required to assemble and mobilize work crews, and so on.

Hierarchies did come under sustained criticism in the 1960s, when the hippie counterculture made a sustained effort to eliminate hierarchical forms of organization—substituting instead "horizontal" forms of direct decision-making. In the end, none of this had much effect, primarily because we lack effective substitutes for hierarchy. Thus the major impact of the '60s was to give us a society whose overall *style* is anti-hierarchical, but which resorts to hierarchical patterns of organization whenever it needs to get anything done.

Growing up in the '70s, kids of my generation were constantly subjected to hippie teachers trying to create a less hierarchical ethos in the classroom—the old "let's put our desks in a circle" routine. The problem is that there is no way to get around having a hierarchy in the classroom. Teachers know more than students, which is the whole reason for them to be there. This superior knowledge puts them in a better position to judge what should and should not be learned, and how it should be learned. As a result, the teacher-student relationship is either hierarchical or pointless. Making us put our desks in a circle did nothing to change that. If anything, its function was not to make us feel better, but rather to make them feel less uncomfortable with the authority they were wielding.

One of the virtues of hierarchy as an organizational form is that it is very easy to construct. A hierarchy is generated through recursive application of the basic authority relation. The leader appoints a sub-leader. The leader has the power to issue directives to the sub-leader, and also to sanction the sub-leader's performance. The sub-leader then appoints a sub-sub-leader, who receives directives and whose performance is subject to sanctions . . . An arbitrary number of layers can be constructed in this way. Goals are formulated at the top and then passed down the chain of command. At each node, the individual has a choice between completing the task or passing it down.

No discussion of this pattern would be complete without mentioning one fateful little tweak we have introduced into the set of rules that governs these types of organizations. This tweak is what makes the difference between a simple hierarchy and a bureaucracy. Whereas a traditional hierarchy appoints individuals from outside the organization to the various leadership roles, a classic bureaucracy relies upon internal promotion. It allows its members to move up through the ranks as a reward for successful completion of their assigned duties within the organization.

This small innovation, which is generally credited to the Chinese, can generate significant improvements in organizational efficiency. A traditional hierarchy relies quite heavily upon negative sanctions in order to keep members "in line" at every tier. These sanctions tend to accumulate in force as one moves downward through the hierarchy, so that those at the very bottom often get "dumped on." As a result, the overall quality of life of subordinates generally deteriorates as one moves down the organizational hierarchy. As they say in the corporate world, "Shit rolls downhill." Bureaucratic forms of organization, however, turn this into a virtue. The prospect of moving up is used as an incentive to improve performance at every level. There is something vaguely diabolical about the incentive structure that is offered to subordinates, of course, because it organizes things in such a way that the only chance to reduce the amount that you get "dumped on" in the long term is to let people dump on you for now. But there can be no doubt that this incentive structure works.

This in part explains the love-hate relationship we have with bureaucracies. On the one hand, bureaucrats can be difficult to deal with. They are inflexible, unfeeling, and generally impatient. And working in a bureaucracy, as we all know, is soul-destroying. On the other hand, as customers and clients, we often like to deal with people in a bureaucratic manner. We want fast, efficient service, and we usually don't want to have to cultivate a personal relationship with everyone that we do business with. So at the same time that we complain constantly about bureaucracy, we ourselves are generally the source of the demands that impose a bureaucratic organizational form on institutions. (For example, despite our constant complaints about government red tape, we are also the ones who demand such a high level of "accountability" from government officials. Generating these accounts is precisely what requires a lot of paperwork.) The world is full of fast-food restaurants precisely because we often want our food to be prepared *fast*. In the same way, the world is full of bureaucracies precisely because we demand organizational results that only bureaucracies can deliver.

Ultimately, hierarchies and bureaucracies are a permanent feature of our institutional landscape because they are efficient, and that makes them a necessary evil. Winston Churchill famously suggested that democracy is the worst system of government—except for all the others that have been tried. The same might be said of bureaucracy as an organizational form.

But this would be a bit too quick. There is one organizational form that has the power to outperform the moral economy—whether that economy be organized through trust obligations, authority relations, or bureaucratic planning. This is the market. Even a century ago, Marx could state without exaggeration that capitalism, "during its rule of scarce one hundred years, has created more massive and more colossal productive forces than have all preceding generations together." Marx was in fact one of the few people in his time to fully grasp just how powerful the productive forces unleashed by the market would be. "Subjection of nature's forces to man, machinery, application of chemistry to industry and agriculture, steam-navigation, railways, electric telegraphs, clearing of whole continents for cultivation, canalisation of rivers, whole populations conjured out of the ground—what earlier century had even a presentiment that such productive forces slumbered in the lap of social labour?"

What is phenomenal about these changes is that they were not brought about by a technological breakthrough or a scientific discovery. Capitalism has revolutionized our entire relationship to the world and to each other because it permits a more efficient organization of our productive activities.

Part II. Institutions

The great conflict between capitalism and communism is over. Communism has collapsed; capitalism has won. Or so we think. But if you take a closer look at the structure of these victorious capitalist nations, it is not clear just how "capitalist" they are. In Canada, government spending adds up to well over 40 per cent of GDP. Universal social programs protect the weak, the sick, and the disabled. Government pensions have generated huge reductions in poverty among the aged, and public education provides a wide range of opportunities for the economically disadvantaged. If the core principle of capitalism is survival of the fittest, we seem to have strayed a long way from the true path.

There is a temptation to view economic arrangements of the type that prevail in Canada as a sort of uncomfortable hybrid, an unstable compromise between socialism and capitalism. We like the wealth that a capitalist economy produces, but we are uncomfortable with some of the other consequences, such as social inequality. So we have grafted a welfare state onto the market economy in order to redistribute some of this wealth and make the consequences of the capitalist order less unpalatable for those on the bottom. We talk about a "third way" between capitalism and socialism. But it is unclear whether such a path actually exists, or whether we are simply trying to take two different routes simultaneously.

This is all a misperception. There is a third way. It's the path that we've been following for quite some time. The key concept is efficiency. The primary function of the Canadian welfare state is not to redistribute wealth—it does almost none of that. Government is involved in the economy because, in many cases, the state is able to deliver goods and services more efficiently than the market. From highways and pest control to health insurance and pensions, government is able to get the job done better. Thus the welfare state, far from being an unstable compromise between capitalism and socialism, is a perfectly logical arrangement—one that is designed to promote the overall efficiency of our economy.

How I Learned to Stop Worrying and Love the Market

5 *We live in a capitalist society.* This means that the major decisions about what we should produce, how much we should produce, where and when we should produce, are made not by a central authority, but by private individuals or associations. The conditions under which these decisions are taken are established by a set of markets. The task that these markets are assigned is to adjust these conditions—most importantly, the prices at which goods and services trade—in such a way that the decisions taken by these private agencies will be the *right* ones for society as a whole. When the right decisions are made, it means that we will spend our time producing things that we need in approximately the right quantities and at approximately the right time and place.

Markets work so well that it is easy to forget how tricky the task is that they perform. Think for a moment about all of the resources that are needed to run a complex operation such as an airport. In order to function properly, an airport requires pilots and flight crew, air traffic control, refuelling, fuel storage, aircraft maintenance, baggage handling, seat reservations and ticketing, food services in the terminal and on planes, timetables for aircraft and personnel, maintenance of buildings and runways, weather forecasting, emergency services, etc. This means that, as a society, if we want airports, we need to make a sufficient quantity of all these resources available. If any of these components are missing, then the whole thing grinds to a halt.

When you stop and think how difficult it can be to get a group of, say, six people to choose a restaurant, you start to realize what a minor miracle it is that any airplane ever makes it off the ground. And in fact, there are plenty of societies around the world that just can't get it together for long enough to produce an airport that works properly. It is a considerable organizational achievement.

Step back from the airport now and consider the case of the entire economy. An airport requires the co-ordination of maybe one hundred or so major resources. Around the time of its collapse, the Soviet economy produced approximately twelve million distinct types of products. The task confronting their planners was to decide exactly how much of each good to produce, when to produce it, and where to ship it. Such a problem is, in principle, solvable. But this is a mathematical curiosity more than anything else, since the calculations required to solve it are of such staggering complexity that even if we threw all the computing resources in the world at it, centuries would pass before we could come up with even a *vague* approximation of the correct answer. And by that time our needs would have changed.

The consequences of this computational problem, however, are more than just a curiosity. If we can't calculate exactly what we need to produce, then we are bound to produce a lot of the wrong stuff. Producing the wrong stuff means that people will waste their time consuming energy and raw materials, producing goods that no one wants. It means that society will be using its resources inefficiently.

In a moral economy, people have very little choice but to work out a planned solution to the question of what to produce, how much to produce, and where to produce it. The moral economy is just a somewhat expanded version of the type of economic institution that roommates or families create when they sit down to work out a chore list. Because the chores are assigned directly to individuals, the group has to first sit down and decide collectively what needs to be done. The difficulty in collecting and processing the information needed to make such a decision is what places the ultimate constraint on the growth of moral economies. The reason that large-scale industrial societies have not appeared until quite recently—the last two hundred years—is not that people lacked the resources needed to build them, but that they lacked the organizational machinery needed to achieve co-operation on such a large scale. The piece of organizational machinery that was missing was the market.

There is a tendency in our society to overestimate how easy it is to put together a market. We are sometimes told that markets will spring up naturally whenever people are left free to trade. Nothing could be further from the truth. Markets are extremely sophisticated legal constructions. Furthermore, getting them to work properly requires people to think about their society in a very counter-intuitive way. As a result, markets represent a very unobvious and improbable institutional development. (If they weren't so unobvious people would have thought of them ages ago.) The central virtue of markets is that they allow individuals to organize productive activities using far less information than any other type of economic institution. They allow us, in a sense, to solve the basic problems of our economy without actually working out a solution. Precisely *how* they do this is the question that has fascinated economists for the last two hundred years.

Unfortunately, economics is a discipline with a public-relations problem. And for good reason. My first economics class ranks up there as one of the biggest disappointments in my life. I took it as a summer class at McGill University. Initially, things looked good. The location of the class was close to idyllic. It was held in a charismatic old wood-panelled classroom in the Arts building. This building is in many ways everything that a university building should be—a beautiful old stone mansion, set just high enough on Mt. Royal to afford a stunning view of the downtown. It even has ivy growing on it. During the warmer months, the front steps were *the* place for students to hang out, talk, and smoke. I couldn't imagine a better way to spend my summer.

So what was the big problem? To put it briefly, the professor was a right-wing hack. There we were in 1988, still caught in the cold war, that epochal conflict between two rival economic systems. All of us were eager to get the straight dope, the inside story. We wanted to really understand what the economic issues at stake were. That was why we had signed up for an economics class. On the first day, however, our professor explained to us that we were going to be studying only capitalist economies, not communist ones. The primary difference between the two systems, he went on to say, is that capitalism motivates its workers by offering them rewards, while communism motivates its workers through threats of punishment. While we were still trying to figure out why unemployment, starvation, and freezing to death on the street did not count as forms of punishment, he then launched into a discussion of how markets miraculously balance supply and demand, without addressing any of the more fundamental questions, such as "What about the 'demands' of people with no money?" By the end of the hour, it was difficult to avoid the impression that "economics" was nothing more than crude right-wing ideology. It took me years to overcome this first impression.

What really set me on edge in the class, though, was not just the right-wing ideology. What bothered me even more was a sense that lying beneath the surface of these remarks was a form of moral bankruptcy much more profound than anything I had yet encountered. This early impression, initially quite inchoate, was gradually confirmed as I learned more about the discipline. In fact, a number of studies have since shown that studying economics can actually make you a bad person.

The most widely publicized study was conducted by a team at Cornell University who compared the behaviour of first-year graduate students in economics with students from other disciplines. Students were given a sum of money to invest in one of two accounts, one "private" and the other "public." The money in the private account went directly to the student at the end of the term; the money in the public account earned a much higher rate of return, but the proceeds were divided equally among all the students. A classic prisoner's dilemma.

Economics students contributed on average 20 per cent of their funds to the public fund, while students in other disciplines contributed 50 per cent. In a more general set of studies, economics students were found to adopt free-rider strategies in prisoner's dilemma games 60 per cent of the time versus 39 per cent for students in other disciplines.

The reasons for this are not hard to find. Economics departments are dominated by a peculiar strain of utopian thinking, according to which markets eliminate the need for morality. As a result, economists persistently equate rational action with the pursuit of self-interest, narrowly construed, and regard moral constraints as irrational or inessential. In fact, many professional economists take perverse pleasure in "exposing" supposedly moral actions as merely covert self-interest. Of course, anyone impressed by this sort of view will therefore be less likely to co-operate in a prisoner's dilemma. The consequences of this, however, are quite outrageous. Economics is, if anything, the science of efficiency. And yet the way economics is taught has a tendency to subvert precisely the sort of co-operative impulses that are needed to secure efficient outcomes in many circumstances. Economists are often their own worst enemies.

In point of fact, the central "discovery" that led to the development of the market economy is not that one can do without morality but that one can permit a selective *decline* in morality without having society fall apart. This is why markets are an unobvious institutional arrangement. Anyone who has the slightest bit of experience in human affairs knows that when individuals disregard the interests of others in order to further their own, they are unlikely to promote harmony or general happiness. Because economic activity throughout most of human history has been organized as a system of moral obligations and entitlements, people have had, and still have, an automatic tendency to assume that some sort of shared values are essential for the maintenance of social order. If there was one lesson to be learned from history, it seemed to be that duty, honour, loyalty, and obligation were the glue that held societies together. So when economists came along claiming that people much like themselves—rich, well-educated men—should be given free rein to pursue their own interests with the assurance that it would all work out well in the end, many people quite naturally assumed that it was some kind of trick.

All of this is quite tragic, not because what the economists are claiming is false, but because what they say is true. Markets really are efficient, vastly more efficient than any other form of economic organization. The pursuit of profit, under proper conditions, does generate collective benefits—win-win outcomes. Markets are quite amazing. But because this sounds so unlikely, the fans of global capitalism have had a marked tendency to overstate their case. After all, it is hard to imagine that haggling, price-gouging, profit-seeking, personal enrichment, usury, or any of the other rough-and-tumble practices of the marketplace have beneficial social consequences. Self-interest is usually bad. Why should this be any exception? As a result, proponents of the market have been very reticent to admit that the market pattern of organization has any flaws or limitations. When combined with the utopian streak of many right-wing economists, this has given the debate over markets unnecessarily ideological and often quasi-religious overtones.

Setting aside all this hyperbole, one important fact remains. What capitalist institutions manage to do when they function correctly is harness the free-rider incentive that in the state of nature serves to worsen the human condition, and use it to increase both the productive capacity and the distributive efficiency of the economy. The "race to the bottom" is thereby transformed into a "race to the top." The way the system accomplishes this is very clever, and understanding how it works is absolutely fundamental to understanding how the explosion of wealth and prosperity that created modern societies came about. Understanding how markets work is also essential for understanding how the personal freedoms we now take for granted came to be institutionalized. The fact that our society is able to get along with less morality means that we are able to live with significant disagreements over substantive questions of value. This is one of the reasons we are able to accommodate such unprecedented levels of cultural and religious pluralism. It is therefore impossible to have a serious discussion about how our society works or should work without first establishing a deep appreciation of the contribution that markets make to its organization.

There's a lot more to markets than just trading. Adam Smith's throwaway line about the "propensity to truck and barter" has misled an awful lot of people in this respect. People have been trading for ages without it having any revolutionary consequences for society as a whole. Trade alone doesn't bring capitalism. What makes a market economy a market economy is that trade is combined with competition. This is the explosive mixture. While trade generates efficiency gains, *competition* introduces the dynamic that forces the system to constantly increase the level of efficiency. Both these elements need to be in place before the whole thing can take off.

While the various components of the capitalist system are as old as the hills, the idea of combining them in the particular way we do is not. Canadians know this from their high-school history lessons. (Studying Canadian history, for those who haven't had the pleasure, involves spending an implausible amount of time hearing about the vicissitudes of the fur trade.) In the seventeenth century, as the story goes, the Europeans wanted to buy lots and lots of beaver pelts to make hats. (For a long time I was confused on this point, since I had trouble imagining what *sort* of hats they could be making, and I didn't remember seeing too many pictures of Europeans running around with big furry hats on. The secret, it turns out, is that beaver fur was used to make felt, and the felt was used to make hats.) In order to get all the pelts, they set up a vast system of trade routes and then licensed corporations to operate them. But it never occurred to them to allow more than one corporation into an area. That's why the Hudson's Bay Company is called the Hudson's Bay Company (also why the East India Company was called the East India Company, etc.) Each company was granted an exclusive right to operate in a particular region. So even though the British knew all about trade and were anxious to achieve any gains that they could from it, they did not take it as obvious that trade should be ruled by competition.

Part of what this illustrates is that you don't need to have full-blown capitalism in order to get some of the benefits of markets; you don't even need to have full-blown markets. It is possible to realize efficiency gains through trade alone or from competition alone. Similarly, there is no reason that the entire economy has to be organized through markets. They can be, and have been, introduced piecemeal. The average first-year economics textbook starts out with a highly idealized picture of a thoroughly capitalist economy, with perfectly competitive markets, perfectly rational individuals and firms. It then turns out—surprise, surprise—that such a system will also be perfectly efficient. It takes a very peculiar sort of mental deficit to think that this is a useful conclusion. It is more helpful to take a look at how each of the pieces of the market function, independent of one another, before taking a look at how they can be combined to generate increments in the efficiency of a society.

The past decade has seen a huge amount of excitement about globalization. While protestors battle it out with riot police in the streets, international think-tanks with vaguely conspiratorial names have lined up to offer their opinions about the perils and promises of the new global society. Promoting international competitiveness has become a key policy objective of many Western governments. According to one influential study, this competition is a "major source of wealth generation" and "one of the driving forces behind technological innovation and productivity growth." Competition is even credited with having "lifted human aspirations" around the world.

This is all nice, but in some respects quite unhelpful. Throughout all this discussion, there is a sort of persistent vagueness about where exactly the *benefits* of competition come from. All the talk about "promoting excellence" does not really explain why competition is needed to promote excellence. Can't you just go off by yourself and be excellent? Compounding the puzzle is the fact that while co-operation is designed to deliver win-win outcomes, competition is specifically designed to deliver win-lose outcomes. After all, it's not a very good competition if no one ever loses. But if efficiency gains are win-win transformations, then how can competitiveness possibly deliver increased efficiency?

The answer is actually a bit complicated. In itself, competition is generally a bad thing. This is why people hate it when their friends or co-workers start to "get competitive" with them. Competition is also associated with certain forms of characteristically obnoxious male behaviour. Conan the Barbarian summed up the competitive mindset quite nicely when he described the "good things" in life as being "to crush your enemies, to see them driven before you, and to hear the lamentation of the women"—a sentiment that probably, despite protestations to the contrary, still resonates with a lot of men. Anyhow, not many people want to work with a bunch of little Conans, and for good reason. What could the benefits be?

The primary advantage of competition, it turns out, has nothing to do with its intrinsic merits. Competition is good when it is able to generate beneficial *side-effects*. The most important characteristic of a competition is that in order to win, you have to be more than just *good*, you have to be *better* than everyone else. This forces all of the competitors into a constant escalation of individual effort. A good competition is one in which the net outcome of this combined effort has beneficial consequences that outweigh the suffering of the losers. This is how it is able to improve efficiency. In fact, the escalation of effort induced by competition can help us to escape from various collective action problems.

One of the areas in which our society actively cultivates competitive impulses is in the field of sport. Just as gifts are a symbolic remnant of a practice that once served an important social function, sports are also a symbolic re-enactment of what was once a very important practice. This can be seen most clearly in the case of the Olympic games. Consider the following completely fictionalized account of the origins of the Olympic games:

The first Olympic games were held in 776 B.C. in Greece. One of the most important developments in Greek culture at the time was the discovery of specialization. Previously, the most celebrated virtue in this civilization was versatility. The hero Odysseus, for example, is described throughout Homer's great epic as "the man who was never at a loss"—a jack of all trades, the MacGyver of the ancient world. Citizens of the various city states were expected to cultivate more or less the same qualities so that they could work the fields in the morning, go to war in the afternoon, and discuss theatre in the evening.

One of the most formative discoveries in ancient Greece, however, was that one or two full-time soldiers, properly trained, could easily take out a dozen irregular, militia-style troops. This lesson made specialization all the rage in ancient Greece (which had enormous consequences for Western politics right down to the present age. Plato's *Republic*, for instance, is governed throughout by the view that society needs to be stratified into different classes of specialists, each of which would make a unique contribution to the harmony and prosperity of the city.) More specifically, the discovery of specialization led to the development of standing armies throughout the Mediterranean world. Instead of expecting farmers to drop their ploughs and take up swords every now and again, cities began to employ full-time military professionals.

Standing armies, however, can be very tricky to maintain. It sounds strange, but one of the most serious problems with standing armies is that they may suffer a decline in the overall physical fitness of the soldiers. After all, it is a structural feature of standing armies that they spend a lot of time just standing around. Farmers have to spend their days in the fields working, but professional soldiers have nothing to do but loiter around the barracks, waiting to be called into action. As a result, they tend to get out of shape.

One might imagine that the prospect of being called into action would give each soldier an incentive to stay fit. After all, no one wants to wind up short of breath when hacking at the enemy or fleeing an assault. Unfortunately, soldiers are confronted with a massive collective action problem. Your own personal level of physical fitness is unlikely to have any significant impact on the overall performance of your army. And whether you live or die depends almost entirely on how well your army as a whole does. This creates a free-rider problem. If all the other soldiers are going off to practise their spear-throwing, you might want to use this opportunity to catch up on some lost sleep. After all, how well you throw your spear is not really going to affect your chances of emerging from a battle unscathed.

Of course, while no *particular* soldier's fitness level has much impact on the outcome of a battle, the average fitness level of the whole army has an enormous amount to do with how the battle turns out. This was especially true in ancient Greece, when warfare involved manually dismembering your opponents. So soldiers can get stuck in a huge multi-person prisoner's dilemma. They would all be better off if they stayed fit, but none of them have an incentive to actually do so.

The standard strategy for counteracting this tendency was to impose an extremely strict disciplinary regime on the military. This solution to the collective action problem relies upon a mixture of moral constraint— in the form of classic martial virtues—and liberal use of sanctions, the strict military code of discipline. The overall outcome is then more efficient from the standpoint of all members of the military. The soldiers should be happy doing their exercises, knowing that when everyone exercises, they are all more likely to survive their next military encounter.

But the Greeks were very clever people. Using strict discipline to maintain fitness is still an imperfect solution. In particular, it encourages the soldiers to do something that economists call "satisficing." It is in the interest of each soldier to do exactly what is required of him, but no more. Thus discipline alone can guarantee a certain level of fitness, but it doesn't maximize fitness. There will always be room for improvement. Unfortunately, it's hard to know just how much room for improvement there is, and it's even harder to motivate people to attain it.

One can imagine an ancient general mulling over this problem, looking for possible solutions. Suddenly, the answer hits him like a ton of bricks. Take the standard military exercises—running, wrestling, spear-throwing, etc.—and organize a contest to see who can do them the best. Offer something quite valuable to the winner, such as a gold coin (and maybe something a bit less valuable to the runner-up, such as a silver coin). Organize a giant festival and invite everyone to come view the events.

In this way, the Olympic games were born. Of course, we are all used to these games, so it is easy to overlook just what a fiendishly clever invention they are. As soon as the commander offers the gold medal to, say, the soldier who can run the fastest, the soldiers are confronted with a new type of collective action problem. In general, they would rather lounge around in the barracks than do sprints around the camp. Training for a race is hard work. But because each competitor also wants to win the gold and is willing to put in a bit of work to improve his chances of winning, training now acquires the structure of a prisoner's dilemma. Imagine that you are a soldier and that you are in a two-person race. Here are the likely scenarios:

1. You train; your opponent doesn't. Chance of winning: 75 per cent
2. Neither of you trains. Chance of winning: 50 per cent
3. Both of you train. Chance of winning: 50 per cent
4. Your opponent trains; you don't. Chance of winning: 25 per cent

Consider what happens if the two of you develop an informal agreement that you will *not* train: "We'll both keep lounging around," you say, "and then when the day of the competition comes, the medal will just go to whoever happens to be fastest." This agreement sounds fine, but it ignores the fact that both of you have a free-rider incentive. If one of you is going to lounge around the barracks, then the one who sneaks out and trains on the sly will be very likely to win. But if one of you is going to be training, then it is essential that the other train as well, just to have a fighting chance. So either way, both of you will be better off breaking the agreement and training. In terms of your preference for leisure over training, the outcome that results is worse for both of you. If you both sneak out and train for two hours, the effects of the training will cancel each other out, and neither of you will improve your chance of winning the race. However, instead of spending a pleasant afternoon playing cards in the barracks, you will both be out sweating on the track.

Not only does the competition generate a collective action problem, it even sets off a race to the bottom. If your opponent is going to train for two hours, then it is in your interest to put in a bit more time, say three hours. Training one hour more than everyone else will improve your chances. But because this is true of everyone, everyone can be expected to train three hours instead of two. But then to get the advantage, you need to train four hours instead of three. Eventually, everyone winds up spending all their time training (which is why in many sports people have to give up their entire lives to become Olympic-calibre athletes).

So this competition is clearly bad for the competitors from their own point of view. But the result for society at large is excellent—the city gets a slim and trim military whose legendary speed and prowess will deter any invasion. The competition thereby harnesses the incentive structure of the prisoner's dilemma and uses it to provide a social good. Better yet, it arranges things so that people try to outdo each other in providing this good. Thus "healthy" competition creates a collective action problem among the competitors, so they can't stop themselves from doing something that is uncomfortable for them but generates benefits for the rest of society. In the end, even the soldiers wind up happier. If they win the Olympic games, their neighbours may be scared off and simply not attack them. That way they don't have to risk their lives fighting at all.

These examples illustrate the point that there is nothing specifically "capitalist" about competition. Competition is a generic institutional mechanism that can be used to spur people on to greater effort. This can be quite useful in the economic sphere, regardless of how the economy at large is organized. For example, workers on a collective farm, instead of just heading out to harvest their crops, might organize a corn-picking competition with special prizes for the person who is able to bring in the most. This has the effect of restructuring everyone's incentives so that instead of wanting to hide out in the field and shirk their responsibilities, each will try to outdo the others in picking as much as possible.

It is a common feature of ancient economic systems that alongside the production of everyday goods there is also a "prestige economy" governed by competitive production. Certain goods are accorded higher status, and the person who produces the most or the best is rewarded with special honours, gifts, or privileges. As a result, the prestige economy has an internal structure that gives each producer an incentive to work harder, to produce more, and to improve quality. In this way, competition is used to overcome the classic problem of economic co-operation.

Competition is also used extensively within bureaucracies. The military is, after all, one giant bureaucracy. Competition for promotion creates extremely important incentives within most hierarchically structured organizations. This is why we find competition everywhere, not just in capitalist economies. It's an invaluable organizational tool. Even the Girl Guides have a contest to see who can sell the most cookies.

However, because competition figures so prominently in much of the popular plaudits for capitalism—as if capitalism alone were able to harness the raw energy of human competition—for a long time it was an object of deep suspicion on the political left. What this amounted to was a sort of moral utopianism, the view that moral incentives alone could be sufficient to overcome the collective action problems that typically afflict all economic activities. This was an important sentiment in the 1960s, particularly during the salad days of Che Guevara and the Cuban revolution, when a very ambitious attempt was made to restructure the Cuban economy to eliminate individual material incentives.

In fairness to idealists of the left, it is worth noting that in times of crisis people quite often demonstrate a phenomenal level of spontaneous social solidarity. During the ice storm of 1998, thousands of Quebecers voluntarily took complete strangers into their homes, sometimes accommodating them for several weeks. Similarly, during the 1997 Manitoba floods, people dropped everything in order to help lay sandbags, evacuate their neighbours, and so forth. All sorts of collective action problems disappeared because people simply chose to set aside their self-interest in favour of the common good.

This can be a bit misleading, though. Revolutions are essentially a type of crisis, and they often inspire exactly the same type of spontaneous solidarity that people show in the face of natural disasters. Unfortunately, many revolutionary socialists have been misled into thinking that this kind of spontaneous solidarity can be maintained in the long term, or worse, that it can be used as an organizing principle of the economy.

The problem is that people's willingness to disregard their own comfort and satisfaction seems to last about two days, after which time all the usual bitching and griping starts to set in again—about how So-and-so isn't doing his fair share of the work, or about how people need to worry about their own children's future, and so on. Everyone is quickly plunged back into the old collective action problems, unless something can be done to keep them sufficiently pumped up. (This goes a long way towards understanding the kind of mass psychoses that communist regimes often sponsored, such as the Cultural Revolution in China.)

There was some hope that people's tendency to revert to this set of fairly parochial concerns was itself a product of capitalism, and so could be solved by the revolution itself. Hence all the talk about the "new socialist man" who would be, in effect, invulnerable to collective action problems. Unfortunately, such a person has yet to appear, despite many good-faith efforts to summon him.

In the 1970s, in the face of growing inefficiencies in the Cuban economy, the government made a significant move towards the reintroduction of personal incentives for workplace performance. Fidel Castro described this as an attempt to "correct idealistic mistakes" that were made early on in the revolution. Competition would be introduced as well—although not the "bad" type of competition that characterized capitalist economies, but a new, more fraternal type of competition, officially referred to as "socialist emulation." Work crews and factories would compete with one another to see which could produce the most—prizes would go to the winners. All this was tacit acknowledgement that love of country or service to the revolution were not enough to sustain efficient levels of co-operation in the long term.

Che Guevara, characteristically, put the matter more bluntly. "Competition," he said, "is a weapon to increase production."

Of course, even though competition can persuade people to sacrifice their own comfort in an effort to resolve collective action problems, this isn't what actually motivates the competitors. Their goal is to win, not to generate beneficial byproducts for others. The trick to designing a successful competition is to arrange things so that this private interest coincides with the more general public interest. While competition has the capacity to generate efficiency gains, it certainly does not guarantee them. Competitions need to be designed just right. They can easily degenerate into unproductive personal vendettas. Many more are just pointless. Who has the nicest lawn? Whose car can go from zero to one hundred the fastest? Who can name the 1974 Grey Cup champion? Who cares? These sorts of competitions generate no external benefits.

The situation is quite different in the case of trade. Trade generates efficiency gains almost by definition. When two people voluntarily exchange goods, it means that one person wanted what the other had more than what she had, and the other wanted what she had more than what he had. After the exchange is concluded, both of them should be happier. And since no one else is affected by the trade, the transaction represents a Pareto-efficiency gain for society as a whole. If the parties involved have no regrets afterwards, then it is a win-win transformation.

There is a subtlety here that is often lost in popular discussions. Through trade it is possible to increase the efficiency of the economy without increasing its actual productivity. The amount of physical stuff that our economy generates can be quite irrelevant. What matters is that we produce the *right* stuff, and that it end up in the right hands. There is an enormous tendency to think of the efficiency of our economy in very material terms. A firm is efficient, it is sometimes thought, because it produces a lot of output, using the minimal amount of input. But efficiency is only concerned with the amount of *useful* output. If we can reorganize things so that the same amount of stuff becomes more *useful* to people, then that represents an increase in efficiency. Again, an economy that produces one million left shoes and no right shoes is grotesquely inefficient compared to one that produces even one hundred *pairs* of shoes.

Thus the efficiency gains that come from trade can be quite intangible. Increasing the efficiency of a society is not at all the same as increasing the wealth of a society, since it is possible to increase efficiency while keeping wealth constant (or even while *decreasing* it). Trade makes everyone better off simply by shuffling around the existing goods—not by actually producing anything more. As a result, trading can generate efficiency gains in any economy, regardless of how its production is organized.

Consider the case of a gift economy. One of the paramount rules of gift-giving is that you are not allowed to treat a gift like any old commodity. Not only is exchanging, or refunding, gifts frowned upon, but "re-gifting" is strictly prohibited. (This is a *Seinfeld* expression. It refers to the practice of passing along gifts that you don't like to others as gifts. Clearly, it does happen. I read somewhere that the average fruitcake is given away seven times before it is actually consumed.) The morality of gift-giving requires that the recipient keep the gift, even if it is not something that he particularly wants. This is why we all have closets and cupboards full of useless presents that we hold on to out of politeness.

This is, needless to say, inefficient. It is especially so when two people receive gifts and each one likes the other's more than his or her own. If they were to swap gifts, both of them would be happier.

Such exchanges are a sufficiently obvious source of improvement in the quality of life that even completely moral allocation systems, such as gift economies, will tend to generate "black markets," in which people surreptitiously exchange goods. But this does not show that there is some natural human "propensity to truck and barter." Even in our own society, the situations in which goods can be freely exchanged are quite sharply restricted by social norms. For instance, most people are highly reluctant to swap food from their plates in restaurants, or buy leftover wine from people at the table next to them. The result is that restaurants throw away an enormous amount of perfectly good food. Thinking about the amount of readjustment it would take to get restaurant patrons to freely resell food is helpful in trying to imagine the way our ancestors initially responded to the suggestion that other kinds of goods, such as land, should be bought and sold in markets.

The basic reason for the discomfort people feel about trade is that the practice contains a very strong element of self-interest. When you exchange a gift, you are, in effect, assigning greater significance to your own happiness than the feelings of the person who gave it to you. Similarly, when you make a trade you are not really responsible for the ultimate satisfaction of the person who buys from you. Your job is to look after your own interests; his job is to look after his. As a result, within "high trust" relationships and communities, trade has traditionally occupied a very marginal role. Merchants have, until recently, always been viewed as individuals of somewhat dubious character.

As a result, trade has developed primarily as a way of dealing with outsiders. Generally speaking, people are held to a much higher standard of conduct when dealing with friends and neighbours than when dealing with strangers. This means that a "low trust" relationship such as trade is much more appropriate as a way of establishing co-operative relations with people down the road than it is with people in one's own village.

Historically, the development of the market economy involved the importation of trade practices from external relations into internal affairs. The greatest obstacle to the generalizing of these practices was the sense that trade was morally suspect. In particular, it conflicted sharply with the old-fashioned honour ethic, which emphasized generosity and high-mindedness, not penny-pinching. Up until the late nineteenth century, the "spirit of commerce" was still seen as an object of contempt and derision. As Nietzsche observed, in the marketplace "[t]hey punish you for all your virtues. They forgive you entirely—your mistakes."

Faced with a choice between making an advantageous trade and suffering a serious loss of face, many people throughout history have chosen to save face. The gains from trade were simply not *sufficient* to motivate people to disregard other social virtues. Part of the reason is that while trade generates efficiency gains, trade alone has no tendency to maximize these gains. In other words, there is no guarantee that when you trade you will get an especially good deal. This can make the appeal of trade only lukewarm. When trade is governed by competition, on the other hand, the situation changes entirely. Competition has the capacity to maximize the efficiency gains realized through trade. This means that it is able to ensure that all parties to the exchange get the best deal possible.

When two people trade goods, it suggests that one person values these goods more than the other does. The other day I sold my old motorcycle helmet to an acquaintance for twenty dollars. Both of us were happy about the trade. This means that the friend who bought it from me wanted it more than I did. In a sense, the helmet was worth more than twenty dollars to him, and it was worth less than twenty dollars to me. This is why the trade made us both happy.

But how did this particular price come about? Ever since we got rid of the family motorcycle, the helmet has been completely useless to me. I would have been willing to give it away. Similarly, if I hadn't come along, my friend would have had to buy one from a store, which would have cost him at least fifty dollars. So at any price between zero dollars and fifty dollars, this would have been a mutually advantageous trade. I could have held out for fifty dollars, and he probably would have gone for it. Similarly, he could have offered me one dollar, and I probably would have settled. Of course, because we are acquaintances, both of us felt morally prohibited from making serious lowball offers. But between strangers, no such constraints apply.

This is why trading in a marketplace between individual buyers and sellers often involves an enormous amount of posturing. There are a huge number of prices at which individuals may be willing to exchange goods. But because neither party knows exactly how high or how low the other will go, the exchange becomes a game in which each one tries to convince the other that he will not accept anything lower (or higher, as the case may be). Since there is a clear conflict of interest between the two parties when it comes to fixing the price, both sides will try to hold out for the best deal possible.

This is why sellers often start out claiming that "all prices are firm." When they start to negotiate, they will then make a lot of "take it or leave it" offers. Eventually, they will start to complain about the rent, the number of children they have to feed, and so on. All this is designed to convince the buyer that the seller could not possibly, under any circumstances, accept a lower offer. And since the trade is mutually advantageous at pretty much any price near the zone of negotiation, once the buyer becomes convinced that the "final offer" is, in fact, the final offer, she will take it.

A seller who is extremely good at this game can get very high prices. These prices may be so high, in fact, that at the end of the day he will have unsold goods. This can be perfectly rational for the individual seller, because it is possible to make more money selling small quantities at high prices than large quantities at low prices. But it is not good for society as a whole, because it is a source of inefficiency. The unsold goods go to waste. This means that the economy would have been more efficient had these goods not been produced, or had they wound up in other hands.

This is where competition comes into the picture. As soon as there is more than one seller or one buyer, it becomes impossible for anyone to "hold out" for the best price. If one seller demands a price that is too high, the buyer can simply threaten to go to the shop next door. This completely undermines the seller's negotiating position. When the asking price is too high, not all the goods that are available to be sold will actually get sold. Someone is going to wind up with excess inventory at the end of the day. When there is more than one seller, the question becomes *who* will wind up holding the bag at the end of the day. If all of them charge the same amount, then they will all wind up with excess inventory. However, if one of them lowers his prices somewhat, then he should be able to clear out his entire stock, leaving his competitors with unsold goods. But here is the catch: it may be less profitable for all to sell at these lower prices, but the free-rider advantage of clearing out one's inventory may offset this reduced profitability, thereby making it in each seller's interest to lower prices.

This is what makes it a competition. The two sellers are caught in a prisoner's dilemma. They would like to charge high prices. It's in their collective interest to charge high prices. However, they each have an incentive to "free-ride" off the other's pricing strategy and clear out their own inventories.

Suppose that you and your competitor each are holding substantial quantities of some good. If you both charge six dollars per unit, buyers will purchase 100 units total, probably 50 from each of you. However, at a price of five dollars, buyers would be willing to purchase 120 units. Suppose that your cost is three dollars per unit. Here are the possible scenarios:

1. You lower prices; your competitor doesn't. Sold: 120 @ $5. Profit: $240.
2. Neither of you lowers prices. Sold: 50 @ $6. Profit: $150.
3. Both of you lower prices. Sold: 60 @ $5. Profit: $120.
4. Your competitor lowers prices; you don't. Sold: 0. Profit: $0.

Whether you are chasing after windfall profits or simply trying to avoid getting frozen out of the market, your best strategy is to lower prices. The same goes for your competitor. As a result, you will both lower prices, and so instead of making profits of $150 each, you will make only $120 each. It is clearly not in your interest to pursue this competition, but you don't have much choice.

This collective action problem is also quite likely to degenerate into a race to the bottom for the sellers. If you are both charging five dollars and everyone still has unsold goods, then everyone has an incentive to lower their prices further. This process stops only when the prices get low enough that all the inventories clear.

This is why they say every free market is but a failed cartel.

Of course, the opposite side of this equation is that if prices get too low, it means that there will not be enough of the good to go around. Not everyone who wants to buy it will be able to find it, and so the buyers will start to compete with one another and bid the prices up. In the very tight Toronto housing market, I've seen people offer landlords more than the asking rent in order get an apartment downtown, just as homebuyers will often bid up the price of a house to above what the seller is asking. It is not in the collective interest of buyers to do this either, since it means they all wind up paying more. But they'd rather pay a bit more than live on the streets—or worse, in the suburbs.

While these competitions are bad for both sellers and buyers, they have side-effects that are beneficial for society as a whole. The prices that eventually get fixed in a competitive market represent an equilibrium between the needs of buyers and sellers. What is unique about this equilibrium is that, under properly structured competitive conditions, it generates a *perfectly* efficient use of resources. Since there are no unsold goods at the end of the day, it means that from the perspective of society as a whole, nothing has been wasted. Exactly the right number of goods were produced.

This is why society tolerates unbridled self-interest and competitiveness in the marketplace. The people involved don't benefit from being permitted to pursue their self-interest. In competing with one another, sellers and buyers are actually harming themselves. What matters is that they are harming themselves for the benefit of society as a whole.

Of course, it is not entirely obvious that competition plays such an important role in our economy. Most of us work in very large organizations—bureaucracies—and so are not involved in selling things on a day-to-day basis. Our primary form of engagement in the marketplace is as consumers. Here we find very few circumstances in which we actually compete head-to-head with other consumers or negotiate prices with sellers. Auctions and big-ticket items, such as houses and cars, are the rare exception. No reasonable person goes into the Gap and tries to talk down the price of khakis with the clueless teenager behind the counter.

This has led some people to doubt that competition plays much of a role in our economy. Prices seem to be dictated to us by big corporations. But this is more the appearance than the reality. Hang out around the street vendors in some Third World country and you will see hard-core negotiation. In our society, the competition is still there, but it is a great deal more sublimated.

The fact that consumers are constantly in competition with one another is something that struck me quite forcefully when I moved from Montreal to Toronto. I lived in Montreal through ten years of fairly constant, self-induced economic stagnation. Shopping for clothing at the time was a very relaxed business. If you spotted something you liked, the best thing to do was hang loose for a few months, then go back and buy it at the store's liquidation sale. Stock just didn't move, and so everything eventually went on sale.

Moving to Toronto, where people have real money, was quite a shock. I started working my usual laid-back approach to shopping. I soon discovered that upon returning to stores after a suitable delay, everything I liked was long gone. The sale racks contained nothing but weird, ill-fitting, ugly, or otherwise offensive garments. All the good stuff had been snapped up long before it became a candidate for the sale racks.

Pretty soon I started to feel the pressure. See something you like? Better buy it right away, because it won't be there tomorrow.

The net effect is that in Toronto I wind up paying full price for things. If I don't, other consumers will snatch them up. Of course, by paying full price, I am just intensifying the competition. It is not in our interest as consumers to be doing this. If we all just held off, eventually retailers would have to put things on sale. Thus the primary form of competition among consumers in our society involves buying things *before* they go on sale.

Each consumer who holds off on a purchase in order to wait for a sale generates a slight benefit for all other consumers in the form of increased pressure on suppliers to lower the price. Similarly, each supplier who delays putting things on sale produces a benefit for other suppliers in the form of increased pressure on consumers to buy at that price. In both cases, this generates a free-rider incentive—consumers may break ranks and buy at full price, or suppliers may break ranks and have a sale. The consequence of these two collective action problems will be downward pressure on the price of plentiful goods and upward pressure on the price of scarce goods. The only equilibrium will be the point at which the amount of each good exchanged is just right. Inventories will clear, and the resulting allocation will be maximally efficient.

To see what an achievement this is, it is helpful to put it in more concrete terms. Part of the task assigned to clothing manufacturers in our society is not just to produce garments, but to produce the right number of garments in the right sizes. This is a very complicated problem, since people come in all shapes and sizes. The most direct approach to this problem would be to go around and measure everyone and figure out on average how many size twos there are, how many size threes, etc. This is more or less how the military does it. The problem is that, unlike the military, where each individual is simply issued a fixed number of garments, in society at large there is enormous variation in the number of outfits that people feel a need to own. Some people want ten pairs of shoes, while some would rather spend their money on something else. Once this demand-side variability is factored in, the problem of calculating how much of what to produce becomes extremely difficult.

The marketplace, however, quickly solves this problem. If there aren't enough size threes being produced, all the size threes will sell out right away—at full price. And if there are too many size sixes, these will need to be put on sale. As a result, stores will put in orders for more size threes and will be willing to *pay more for them*. And this makes it in the interest of manufacturers to supply more clothes in these sizes.

Thus the prices at which goods sell form something like an image of what the population needs. Instead of having to go out and actually measure the population, you can just let people measure themselves, then compete with each other for clothes that fit them. Once the dust settles, you can look at the sale racks and the inventory logs of clothing retailers to see what kinds of clothes people need.

This market mechanism is more than just a neat trick. Let me draw attention, once again, to the fact that we have produced more goods in the past one hundred years than the rest of humanity produced over the entire course of human history. Human beings are, to put it mildly, not organizational geniuses. If it is difficult to collect information about what people want, it is even harder to get people to do what they are supposed to do. Markets make it possible to collect information and co-ordinate interactions in a way that is truly effortless by comparison.

Thus the attraction of the market economy is not that it promises big gains in efficiency but that it promises *huge* gains in efficiency. It's the difference between living in the Middle Ages and living in the twenty-first century. Once the blueprint has been laid down, it's not hard to see why people around the world have wanted to restructure their societies in order to realize these gains.

Imagine the following scenario. You live in a small village community that grows all its food in a large, collective vegetable garden. All the pro-duce is harvested in the fall, and one person is assigned the task of dis-tributing it to the members of the community. This year it is you. Being scrupulously impartial, you decide to give everyone exactly the same amount. So you assemble a basket of vegetables for each person, putting exactly the same number of carrots, potatoes, corn, and so forth, in each. But then, just before handing out the baskets, you ask yourself, " Have I done a good job here? Is this the best way to distribute these vegetables?" You then realize, with a sinking feeling, that the allocation of vegetables you are about to implement is inefficient. It would be possible for you to change the allocation in order to make some people better off, without making anyone worse off. What made you think of this is your recollec-tion that Fred hates potatoes, and that Susan is allergic to carrots. You could give Susan's carrots to Fred, and Fred's potatoes to Susan, and they would both be better off.

Once you start thinking this way, you realize that everyone has slightly different vegetable preferences, and so, if you want to make everyone as happy as possible, you will have to give them each a basket that is specifically tailored to his or her particular needs. So you hand out a little questionnaire, asking people to rank all the vegetables in order of preference. However, when you get the questionnaires back, you realize that you now have a bewildering amount of data, and that figuring out how best to satisfy each person's preferences is going to involve solving a very complex set of linear equations. By the time you do the math, the vegetables will have gone bad.

But your trusted adviser, who has been dabbling in foreign trade, makes an attractive suggestion. Traditionally, people have felt obliged to eat whatever they are given in order not to seem ungrateful. Your adviser suggests that you give everyone an identical basket of goods, but then encourage them to trade with each other, exchanging anything they don't want for something they do. That way, Susan can just exchange her potatoes for Fred's carrots, and you don't have to worry about it. Instead of having to figure out who likes what, you can just let the people sort it out themselves. That way no one needs to collect information about who likes what. The people, without even knowing it, can do your job for you.

Suppose that you proceed with this suggestion. A market for vegetables soon appears. Once this market is in place, patterns begin to emerge in the prices at which vegetables trade. These patterns may turn out to reveal interesting things. For instance, suppose that even though the garden produces exactly the same amount of potatoes as carrots, a pound of potatoes sells for twice the price of a pound of carrots. This must reflect the fact that, on average, people like potatoes more than carrots. (A taste for potatoes makes them less willing to sell their share, thereby reducing the supply, but also more eager to buy them, thereby increasing the demand.) Thus using a market to allocate goods creates a set of prices that reflect the underlying system of needs. The key difference is that while needs are unobservable, prices are publicly available. Prices are therefore like a visible image of an invisible preference structure (just as an infrared photograph uses the visible spectrum to represent light waves that we cannot see).

Now that prices have made this information available, a new opportunity for improving the well-being of the village presents itself. You begin to think, "Perhaps we don't need to grow so many carrots. Maybe we should plant more potatoes next year." Exchange may improve allocative efficiency, but this does nothing to improve productive efficiency. Redeploying the resources used to grow carrots into potato production could make everyone better off. However, deciding exactly how much land should be switched over can be a tricky matter, involving a complex set of calculations.

Once you start thinking about it, you realize that not only the village land, but some of the other resources may be misallocated as well. For instance, everyone in the village takes turns working the whole field, but some people are better at some jobs than others. Despite the fact that Susan is a very good potato-digger while Fred has a way with carrots, both of them are taking turns doing both jobs. It would be better to have Susan focus on potatoes and leave the carrots to Fred. But deciding who is better at what, and dividing up the work to everyone's satisfaction, would also be a costly and time-consuming business.

Again, your economically sophisticated adviser intervenes. "Instead of managing the allocation of resources for the whole farm," she suggests, "then giving everyone an equal share of the vegetables, why not give everyone an equal-sized plot of land? Take the collective farm, divide it up into individual plots, and give it away. This will involve some paperwork, and you will have to set up a legal system to keep track of what people own and regulate disputes over what they have exchanged. But once this is done, you can let people grow whatever they want on their own plots and then exchange their produce as they see fit."

Under this new arrangement, when the price of some vegetables is high, this gives everyone an incentive to grow more of those vegetables (either to sell them or to avoid having to buy them). If some people are especially good at tending particular crops, they can specialize in that area, then exchange their produce with others. Everyone can do their own cost-benefit calculation to see how much of each type of vegetable they should grow. People may grow vegetables for their own consumption, or they may grow vegetables that they intend to exchange. As long as everyone is trying to get the most that they can out of their plot, i.e., to get the best possible bundle of vegetables for themselves that they can, then the *resulting level of consumption will be both allocatively and productively optimal*. All the resources will be put to their best use, and all the goods will be in the hands of those who want them most.

What the adviser has just suggested is the basic structure of a *laissez-faire* economic system—the state assigns property rights, then leaves everyone free to make their own decisions about what to do with their share. The "moral economy" is eliminated not just from distribution, but from production as well. Without even realizing it, you have now introduced full-blown capitalism into your village. And you did it not because you stood to gain from it personally or because you felt like promoting greed and avarice, but because you wanted to make sure that everyone was happy, that everyone got the bundle of vegetables best suited to their tastes.

Of course, despite these good intentions, you may someday come to have second thoughts about your decision.

When Markets Fail

6 *According to an old Kwakiutl story,* Fast-runner and Throw-away were two great chiefs who had long been friends. One evening at a ceremonial banquet, Throw-away made the mistake of serving Fast-runner food in vessels that had not been adequately cleaned. Fast-runner protested and accused his friend of being cheap. In order to demonstrate his own superiority, Fast-runner took one of his ceremonial "coppers" and threw it onto the fire—thus demonstrating, quite literally, that he had money to burn. Throw-away responded in kind, tossing his own copper onto the fire. Fast-runner then took another copper and destroyed it. Throw-away didn't have another one handy and was unable to borrow one from the assembled company, so he was forced to withdraw.

The following night, Fast-runner was scheduled to hold a feast for Throw-away. By that time, Throw-away had secured another copper. So when the banquet began, Throw-away destroyed the copper. Fast-runner responded by having four canoes demolished and burned. But feeling this response to be inadequate, he also had one of his slaves killed and dismembered. He then presented the scalp to Throw-away. Throw-away still refused to admit defeat, so Fast-runner had two slave girls thrown onto the fire. Being crafty, however, he managed to persuade

Throw-away that he had just burned his own daughters. Unable to match this feat, Throw-away finally withdrew in humiliation.

This is an example of a competition that got a bit out of hand.

Social status in traditional Kwakiutl society depended primarily on the ability to throw magnificent feasts—potlatches—with gifts for all of the assembled company. The more that was given out, the more status and prestige accrued to the chief. Everyone who received a gift was then obliged to return a gift of greater value when it came his turn to host a potlatch. All of this was just fine, and was a typical example of a prestige economy. But at some point, in order to show just how wealthy he was, some chief got the bright idea of burning the goods, rather than handing them out. This idea, like most bad ideas, quickly caught on. The potlatch system then began to generate a cycle of "conspicuous waste," with each chief trying to outdo the others in showing just how much of his property he was willing to destroy.

While the story of the rival chiefs may or may not be true, the historical record does contain many examples of potlatches turning into orgies of destruction. At one potlatch in the late nineteenth century, for instance, observers recorded the guests heaping seven canoes and four hundred Hudson's Bay blankets onto the fire. Not be outdone, the host had so much candlefish oil poured onto the blaze that the roof of his own lodge caught fire. The entire clan remained seated, trying to look unperturbed as it burned.

At one time, the potlatch was clearly an efficiency-promoting institution. The desire to amass large stores of surplus goods was a huge spur to production within clans and was largely credited for the affluence of Kwakiutl society. People work a lot harder when their family honour is at stake. But with the introduction of competitive destruction, the race to the top that characterized the old prestige economy turned into a race to the bottom.

This illustrates a very general principle. Competition may work well, but it always requires supervision. When left unattended, competitions have a tendency to get out of hand. And this is no less true for us than it was for the Kwakiutl.

The biggest mistake people make when evaluating the effects of competition is to confuse the virtues of the competition as a whole with the virtues of the individual competitors. Whenever the overall process generates beneficial consequences, it is very tempting to think that the specific individuals involved in the competition are somehow great people for having done so. Hence our tendency to glorify athletes and business leaders. But there is absolutely no reason to think that these people are any more virtuous than the average person. They may be highly skilled in an activity that generates enormous benefits for society as a whole, but this does not mean that they are engaging in that activity in order to provide these benefits. They may just be in it to win.

The fact that competitors often have much narrower interests at heart is clearly shown whenever the integrity of the competition is compromised. Take the case of athletics. Sport generates a wide range of social benefits. At its finest, sport provides an extraordinary level of aesthetic pleasure. Great athletes such as Wayne Gretzky or Michael Jordan inspire us, as any virtuoso would. Competition clearly has a lot to do with the production of these great performances. In order to win at sports, you have to be more than just *good*, you have to be *better* than everyone else. As a result, everyone must train just a little bit harder than everyone else and push themselves just a little bit further. But this only "raises the bar," so that whoever wants to win has to train harder still, push themselves further still. Thus sporting competition forces us to be the best that we can be.

But this doesn't mean that people go into sports in order to improve the human condition. More often they go into it for the fame, glory, and money. The key to the success of sports lies in the fact that people can only get the fame, glory, and money by turning out performances that are better than everyone else's. Thus a properly structured sporting competition is one in which the only way to win is through practice and performance. But as the Tonya Harding/Nancy Kerrigan scandal in figure skating reminded us, there are lots of ways around this. Instead of training, athletes could simply get thugs to injure their competitors. That certainly improves one's chances of winning, but from society's point of view, it undermines the whole *point* of the competition. The goal of figure skating is not to see who is left standing at the end of the day, but to see who can perform the fanciest on-ice manoeuvres.

Athletes do not share the same interests as spectators or society at large, but society often expects a lot more from them than from mere mortals. Michael Jordan was constantly criticized for frittering away his money on gambling and golf rather than helping the poor children in the ghetto that surrounds the stadium where the Chicago Bulls play. But what reason did anyone have to think that Michael Jordan should be less selfish than the average man? The fact that his ball-playing inspired these children and made them happy does not mean that his foremost desire was to make them happy. It was a positive side-effect of his true desire, which was to win basketball games and ultimately tournaments.

A competition is healthy when the positive side-effects it generates outweigh the negative effects of the competition proper. A competition becomes unhealthy when these positive side-effects are diminished to the point where they no longer outweigh the negative ones. A competition becomes simply vicious when all its side-effects are negative. Generally speaking, what keeps a competition healthy is not the good intentions of the competitors, but the set of rules that constrain the competition. In other words, it is the design of the competition that keeps it worthwhile.

In sports, this shows up most clearly in the problem of steroids and other performance-enhancing drugs. If one competitor starts taking steroids, then everyone else is pretty much forced to do the same just to stay even. But this changes the nature of athletic competition so that instead of demonstrating who has the most ability, the competition only determines who has the best doctor. This can generate results that are positively freakish. Still, the athletes won't stop unless someone forces them to.

Competitions can become unhealthy through either deviance or excess. Deviance occurs when people break the rules (e.g., by hiring thugs). The desire to control deviance is what underlies our emphasis on being a "good sport" or not engaging in "unsportsmanlike conduct." (In fact, one of the reasons that sports are thought to build character is that it is so difficult in the heat of competition to resist breaking the rules.) In cases of excess, nobody breaks any specific rules, but the competition just gets carried to a point where it loses any redeeming social value. Women's gymnastics, for instance, has largely become a parade of diminutive preadolescents and sadistic coaches. Many people are beginning to wonder what the point of it all is.

This makes it a bad idea to romanticize competition too much. Competition is, as we say in the business, *prima facie* bad (i.e., presumed bad until proven otherwise), because every competitive outcome is inefficient for the competitors. Under very specific institutional circumstances the positive side-effects will outweigh the harm that competitors generate for each other. However, competition will always have a tendency to break through these institutional boundaries and become a race to the bottom. So healthy competitions require constant care and nurture.

Whether or not athletes take steroids and beat each other up off-court is ultimately not a big deal. Nothing really important hangs on it. The case is quite different when it comes to the organization of the economy. Here the tendency to romanticize competition can have disastrous social consequences.

Ironically, it is often the most tough-minded, no-nonsense right-wingers who go all soft when it comes to economic competition. People who would never be so naïve as to suggest that athletes might "voluntarily" refrain from taking steroids will turn around and push for "industry self-regulation" over government intervention, as if corporations might just choose to stop polluting or refrain from producing false advertising. It's difficult to imagine a more total misunderstanding of the underlying dynamic of capitalism.

Part of the problem involves the familiar failure to distinguish between the virtues of the market and the virtues of particular firms *in* the market. When the competition is staged just right, corporations will deliver unparalleled levels of efficiency. But it is almost never in a particular firm's interest to produce at a level that will generate efficient outcomes for society as a whole. Companies are forced to operate efficiently by the rules of the competition. If they can find any way around these rules, they will naturally go for it.

So despite the fact that markets deliver very efficient performances, there is nothing intrinsically efficient about the private sector. It is not because firms are privately owned that they are efficient. It is because they are forced to *compete* with one another that they are efficient. This means that when markets are not organized just right—if firms can somehow avoid the rigours of competition—then the private sector will not have any tendency to deliver efficient outcomes.

This is most obvious in the case of monopolies. Sometimes a product is of a type that can be produced efficiently only in very large quantities. In this case, a market may not be able to sustain more than one firm. The recent antitrust case against Microsoft illustrates the problems that can arise in such cases. In the personal computer market, there are advantages to using the same operating system that everyone else is using. As a result, it is very difficult for new competitors to enter the market. Under these conditions, there is no reason to think that the private sector will deliver efficiency.

The process that led to the entrenchment of Microsoft Windows in the PC market is sometimes referred to as the QWERTY phenomenon—named after the standard typewriter keyboard. This layout of keys became popular at a time when typists used to routinely "overtype" their machines—typing so fast that the keys would jam. The QWERTY configuration was specifically designed to prevent this by placing commonly used vowels and consonants off the home row, in a number of odd locations. Of course, "overtyping" hasn't been a problem for decades, and yet the QWERTY configuration persists, despite the availability of more efficient alternatives. Why? Most people can only learn to type one way. So if you're going to pick a layout, the best thing to do is to pick the one that *most people* use. This is QWERTY. The advantage of being able to use pretty much any machine that you come across easily outweighs the disadvantages of typing more slowly.

This is exactly how Microsoft's Windows operating system came to dominate the market, despite the availability of superior alternatives. (Saying that you like Windows in the company of technically sophisticated people is like asking for "something cooked" at a sushi bar. It suggests that you are beyond redemption.) But even in the Microsoft antitrust case, there were plenty of critics who took the government to task for "interfering" in the natural processes of the market. In fact, there is an enormous tendency to think that markets are somehow "natural" and that government is "artificial." According to this view, all government has to do in order to get a market going is just leave people alone or withdraw from a particular sector. Once this is done, apparently, a market will just spontaneously spring up and supply an efficient supply of goods and services. The example of Windows or of the QWERTY keyboard clearly puts the lie to this claim. Goods may be provided, but there is no guarantee that they will be provided efficiently.

Ultimately, the whole business about markets being more natural than governments comes from John Locke. Unlike Hobbes, who realized that the natural condition of humanity would involve a total failure of co-operation, Locke argued that we are all born with a set of natural rights, which allows us to start accumulating property even before we enter political society. We also have a mysterious impulse to respect the property rights of others and so find ourselves naturally disinclined to steal. (When it comes to explaining why we have these particular rights and not some other set, Locke does a lot of handwaving. In the end, he claims that this is just how God intended things. Note: whenever a philosopher starts bringing in God, you know he's run out of steam.)

In any case, Locke argued that we all have a natural set of property rights and can happily go about our business trading with each other and creating all sorts of prosperity. Only much later do we get together and form governments in order to eliminate certain "inconveniences" associated with the state of nature. This sets up the basic contrasts: economy = natural; government = artificial.

The impact of this type of thinking can be truly disastrous. No one knows this better than economic planners in Eastern Europe, who were unlucky enough to ask a bunch of American economists for advice on how to make the transition from communism to capitalism. Naturally, the Americans had no experience in these matters, but they did have an overarching ideology that stipulated that markets are nothing more than the expression of our natural "propensity to truck and barter." So their advice to the East Europeans was quite simple— don't do anything. Just destroy all your existing public institutions and markets will magically pop up and take their place. Nothing could be easier.

Any country foolish enough to take this advice quickly found that when it scaled back the government's role, what it wound up with was rampant criminality, not orderly markets. In a sense, the experience just proved once again that Hobbes was right and Locke was wrong. "Force and fraud" is more fundamental than "truck and barter." Even today, observers claim that as much as two-thirds of Russia's economy is controlled by criminal gangs.

The so-called "Goulash capitalism" episode in Hungary clearly illustrated the problem. In 1994, shortly after the privatization of agriculture and food production, the country was swept by an epidemic of lead poisoning. After searching far and wide for the cause, doctors and scientists finally tracked down the source of the problem. Manufacturers of paprika—a staple of Hungarian cuisine—had been grinding up old paint, much of it lead-based, and adding it to the spice in order to improve its colour. The practice was so widespread that Hungarian officials were forced to order all the paprika in the country removed from store shelves and destroyed.

At the time, no laws were in place to prevent such a catastrophe, simply because it had not occurred to anyone that this kind of thing would happen. Under communism, in which firms had no competition, no one had any incentive to poison their customers, and so consumer protection laws were unnecessary. In making the transition to the market, policy-makers assumed that producers would compete with one another to produce the best-quality paprika. They didn't realize that producers would compete only to produce the best-looking paprika.

Of course, poisoning your customers is not really in the long-term interests of any firm. But anyone can see how naïve it is to think that athletes will voluntarily refrain from taking steroids because, in the long run, they're bad for one's health or for the sport. It is just as naïve to think that companies will voluntarily refrain from poisoning their customers just because, in the long run, it's bad for the firm or for society. To imagine otherwise is to fundamentally misunderstand either the structure of competition or the nature of humanity.

The truth is that our market economy is a finely tuned legal and moral system that has evolved over hundreds of years. It is not a natural condition, but an extremely sophisticated institutional construction, one that requires constant monitoring and enforcement. The system of property rights alone requires a massive legal-bureaucratic apparatus just to keep track of who owns what and who owes what to whom. Consumer protection laws, which establish the basic rules designed to ensure that competition remains "healthy," are also an enormous legal apparatus. (It was estimated, for instance, that after the "velvet revolution," the Czech Republic needed to pass eighty thousand pages of law in order to get its product standards up to minimum European Union levels.) Furthermore, the number of regulations must increase every time someone finds a more ingenious way of circumventing the old ones (in the same way that the number of rules governing sport increases every time someone finds a new way of cheating).

It is important, therefore, to always maintain a balanced view of markets. There is something extremely elegant about the way they allocate goods and resources, and the way the price system automatically adjusts the system of production in response to changes in demand. There is a clear sense in which markets achieve a level of co-ordination and efficiency that no other form of social organization is able to provide. However, markets are not magical, and they will not solve all our problems. They work properly only under very specific institutional conditions.

As long as I'm on the subject of maintaining a "balanced" view of markets, I may as well say a few words about some of the more seriously unbalanced views in circulation. The success of capitalism has created its own strains of utopianism conviction. Just as "left-wing" utopians are inclined to think that moral incentives alone can provide an adequate foundation for the economy, "right-wing" utopians maintain that morality has become completely obsolete and that unbridled self-interest is all that we need to keep things purring along.

The idea at the heart of this utopian vision was captured quite nicely by the philosopher David Gauthier, who suggested that markets provide us with "freedom from morality." There is something quite enticing about this idea. After all, everyone can agree that morality is a drag. Having to care about other people, worry constantly about their feelings, having to keep promises and tell the truth—it gets to be a pain. Life would be a lot more fun if we could do whatever we wanted. But this is just what we can do, according to right-wing utopians. Thanks to capitalism, you can act like a complete jerk, and yet everything will work out fine in the end. This is because the market miraculously transforms self-interest into public benefits.

This idea has been around for a long time. It was popularized by Bernard Mandeville, whose "Fable of the Bees" suggests that private vices are actually "publick virtues." Modern audiences are more familiar with the argument from Gordon Gekko's classic "greed is good" speech in the movie *Wall Street* (where Gekko manages to convince a group of perhaps somewhat gullible shareholders that his getting rich was ultimately in *their* interest). Many stockbrokers can recite his triumphant conclusion from memory: "The point is, ladies and gentlemen, that greed, for lack of a better word, is good. Greed is right. Greed works."

One especially extreme version of this utopia can be found in the writings of Ayn Rand, whose novels *Atlas Shrugged* and *The Fountainhead* continue to be a staple of the literary diet of teenaged girls. (Strangely enough, this popularity has survived even though in both these books the primary female protagonist gets raped and enjoys it. This is very much on purpose. Rand believed that women have a "natural" desire to subordinate themselves to men. It is a testimony to the seductiveness of the literary form that many people don't even *notice* these rapes, much less find them offensive. This despite the fact that, in one case, Roark—the high-minded architect—actually sneaks in through the woman's bedroom window at night.)

According to Rand, the triumph of capitalism shows us not only that morality is unnecessary, but that it is actually a *bad thing*. The primary virtue, according to Rand, is selfishness. The idea that we should care about other people is actually a pernicious fraud perpetrated by those who are too weak or lazy to advance their own interests. They are free-riders, parasites, trying to drag everyone else down to their level.

Rand's basic idea—that morality is a conspiracy perpetrated by the weak against the strong—actually comes from Nietzsche. Of course Nietzsche came right out and blamed the Jews and their "slave morality" for all this. Since then, the right has been forced to adopt a more subtle vocabulary for use in mixed company. In any case, Nietzsche's famous injunction to move "beyond good and evil" is just the insistence that we put an end to this fraud, that we call it for what it is.

There is clearly something seductive about this view, especially since almost all readers of Nietzsche seem to imagine themselves to be among the strong, not the weak. (In the same way, more than 80 per cent of people believe that their driving skills are above average, or that they are more productive than the average employee.) This seduction, however, has something profoundly adolescent about it. Nietzsche tends to be a "phase" that people go through. Part of becoming an adult is finding a way to reconcile yourself with adult responsibilities, and these include moral obligations.

In any case, Rand's tendency to dilute this Nietzschian animus towards morality with a fawning respect for capitalism ultimately produces a more plausible doctrine. When push comes to shove, there is in fact something to be said for her view (although much less than many people imagine). One of the perverse features of living in a capitalist society is that not only does acting in your self-interest often lead to beneficial consequences for society as a whole, but the flip side is also true—often not acting in your own self-interest generates harmful effects.

When consumers want some kind of scarce good, the appropriate thing for them to do in a market economy is to start competing for it. Their actions will bid the price up, thereby sending a signal to producers that they should provide more of it. But suppose that, instead of competing with one another, they decide to be nice and share it. This may seem like the "moral" thing to do, but ultimately the consequences are bad. Without competition, the price will stay right where it is and producers will have no incentive to increase production. The result will be an ongoing scarcity of this good and overproduction of goods that people don't want so much.

Thus it is one of the more peculiar features of capitalism that we often have reason to refrain from acting upon our "moral" impulses. An excellent example of this occurred recently during the ice storm in Quebec. When millions of people suddenly found themselves caught in the dead of winter with no electricity, the demand for generators quickly shot up. The people who sell generators naturally responded by increasing their prices. Of course, this seemed at the time like an extremely opportunistic thing to do—taking advantage of people in their moment of need. In response to complaints, the government stepped in and prohibited vendors from price-gouging.

This struck many people as a good idea. But consider the broader consequences. Thousands of people in Ontario have old generators sitting around at the cottage, unused throughout the winter. Many of them could have driven up to their cottages, picked up their generators, and sold them to some desperate people in Quebec. But with used generators selling for, say, $500, this would hardly be worth the trip. On the other hand, if people are willing to pay $2,000, it just might become worthwhile. Similarly, some hardware store in Florida might have had a pile of generators sitting in the back room. At the right price, it might have been worth shipping them up to Quebec. The fact that Quebecers were willing to *pay* more for generators reflected the fact that at the time, they *needed* the generators more than most people. Government interference in the price system, in this case, eliminated the incentive that many people might have had to help satisfy this need. So while Quebecers continued to get their generators at reasonable prices, the population as a whole almost certainly did not get as *many* of them as they wanted.

Naturally, this cuts both ways. If we don't want consumers sharing things with each other, we also don't want suppliers getting too chummy either. It is important that businesses compete. Any moral restraint—such as not putting your competitor out of business when you have the chance—is ultimately bad for the consumer. It allows an inefficient firm to remain in business, continuing to consume resources that could be put to better use elsewhere. This is why governments need to constantly monitor markets to ensure that businesses aren't colluding, price-fixing, or what have you.

The point is that markets do not just permit competitive behaviour, they *require* this behaviour in order to function correctly. Morality is a mechanism primarily used to resolve collective action problems. It helps us to get out of prisoner's dilemmas. In a market, however, we *want* both buyers and sellers to remain stuck in their respective prisoner's dilemmas, which often means that they must resist their moral impulses. This obvious perversity is responsible for a lot of the moral qualms that many people have about capitalism.

Be that as it may, none of this suggests that we can do entirely without morality. When we're trying to win a competition, in one sense we are just following our self-interest. But the competition will remain healthy only so long as we abide by a set of rules, and it is generally not in our self-interest to obey these rules. In the same way that "good sportsmanship" is essential to any game, "good citizenship" is still essential to the operations of capitalism. Just as it is in the "interest" of figure skaters to cripple their competitors, so it is in the "interest" of corporations to blow up each others' factories or to assassinate each other's CEOs—something the Russians have discovered first-hand. The first line of defence against this is simply moral restraint. The law then steps in when morality fails.

In order for capitalism to function smoothly, we need to refrain from stealing, from using violence to achieve our ends, from making fraudulent misrepresentations, etc. The list goes on and on. These are all legal and *moral* obligations. If people did not respect these basic rules, the entire system would fall apart. The race to the top would become a race to the bottom. The irony of Ayn Rand's position is that if too many people took it seriously, it would quickly undermine the foundations of capitalism. Altruism may be unnecessary within markets. But the market system as a whole is sustained only by moral behaviour.

Thus the capitalist system still requires a lot of morality. It just requires a bit less morality than some other forms of economic organization.

As we have seen, the virtues of competition come from the set of rules that govern the contest, not from the intentions of the competitors. So whether or not a market economy is healthy or unhealthy will depend upon the design of the rules. Unfortunately, it is often not so easy to design a set of rules that works right. Markets tend to work very well when it comes to exchanging medium-sized dry goods. Other types of exchanges can be much more difficult—sometimes impossible—to organize.

When markets don't work right, they generate inefficient outcomes. This is referred to as *market failure*. Market failure is the key to understanding the entire macrostructure of welfare state capitalism.

The most common strain of market failure stems from the impossibility of enforcing certain types of property rights. The function of prices in a market economy is essentially to ration scarce goods. For example, it would be nice if we could all use as much gasoline as we wanted. Unfortunately, there is only so much gas to go around, and it takes a lot of effort to get it out of the ground and refine it into something usable. This means that whenever we use up some gas, we impose a cost upon other people. Each litre that I burn is a litre that someone else doesn't get to burn and that other people spent a lot of time and energy to produce. This is why I have to give something of my own up in exchange for it. I have to *pay* for it.

In order to ensure that the economy produces just the "right" amount of gasoline from an efficiency standpoint, it is important that the price reflects quite precisely the cost that consuming gas imposes upon others. This is what stops us all from using too much of things we don't really need or want. The system of property rights forces us to cover these costs. So when we fill up at the pumps, it is the gas station owner's property rights that entitle him to demand payment from us.

Unfortunately, some of the costs that burning gas imposes are never recovered and are therefore not reflected in the price. Most obviously, whenever we burn it we create atmospheric pollution. This is clearly a bad thing, which imposes a cost on other people. However, those affected are not able to charge us for the right to pollute the air that they breathe, because it's too hard to enforce this type of property right. Economists refer to this as a negative externality. It is a cost that is not factored into the price.

Externalities are the most common source of market failure, the effects of which can be far-ranging. Several years back, my aunt became extremely distraught when her neighbour in rural Saskatchewan decided to start up a pig farm. Pig farms can be a source of enormous tension, because they stink to high heaven. This would not be such a problem if it were possible to extract compensation from the pig farmer. Unfortunately, there is no market mechanism available to organize this transaction.

If the pig farmer had wanted to dump manure on my aunt's land, the system of property rights would have protected her. Because she owns the land, she could have prevented him from doing it, or at least charged him for the privilege. But the air around her farm does not belong to anyone, and so there is no way to prevent her neighbour from "dumping" noxious fumes into it.

Now consider the long-range consequences of this defect in the system of property rights. The pig farmer is trying to run a profitable operation.

The number of pigs he raises will be determined by the cost of raising them and the price at which they sell. This is how society ensures that the "right" number of pigs get raised—balancing the cost of producing them against the need for pork chops. However, not all the true costs are reflected in his production costs. He has to pay for disposal of manure, but he doesn't have to pay for disposal of stink. As a result, the balance between those who receive the benefits (the pork-chop eaters) and those who suffer the costs (those whose time and energy is spent sustaining the pigs) will be out of whack. The farmer will produce far more pigs than are actually warranted. Because of the negative externality, society will wind up with an excess of both pigs and stink. This means that efficiency gains could still be achieved by shifting resources out of pig farming and into something else. But the market cannot be counted upon to do this shifting; in fact, it will actively work against any such shift.

This is hugely significant. Whenever there are negative externalities, it means that markets will stubbornly overproduce the goods that create these externalities as by-products. Even worse, producers have a constant incentive to find new and better ways to externalize their costs. Pig farmers have to pay for disposal of their manure only because property rights protect land from dumping. But if they burn the manure, then they can get rid of it for free because markets don't regulate the use of air. So even if burning it is much more harmful to society than burying, imperfections in the market may give farmers an incentive to dispose of it that way. This is grotesquely inefficient.

What we call "environmental problems" are for the most part market failures of this type. If firms do not have to pay for waste disposal, they will generate too much waste. This sort of pollution is clearly a bad thing. However, when a firm is polluting, it also suggests that *too much* of a certain good is being produced. The fact that the firm is polluting shows that its cost structure is out of sync with the social cost. Thus society takes a double hit from an efficiency standpoint—first through the pollution itself, and then through overproduction of unwanted goods. Russell Hardin cleverly refers to this as the "backside of the invisible hand."

The goal of an efficient society, and of our economy generally, is to satisfy people's needs, or to satisfy as many needs as possible given the available resources. The advantage of the price system is that it produces an observable "image" of these needs. Again, recall the example of the infrared camera, which detects frequencies that are normally invisible to the eye and converts them to the visible spectrum. The system of needs, like infrared radiation, is invisible. The market takes these needs and converts them into something that is observable—prices. But whenever there are externalities, the image gets a bit skewed. Some of the needs get missed. As a result, the picture that emerges will be distorted; it may even be missing entire sections. Since this picture is what we use to determine what to produce, flaws in the image will lead us into systematic inefficiencies. We will waste resources producing stuff that we don't really want, instead of other stuff that we do want.

The price system is extremely good at detecting our need for medium-sized dry goods. If this is the sort of thing that makes you happy—if your car, your stereo, or your house is the centre of your existence—then the market economy will serve you well. But if you happen to be the unlucky type of person whose needs are focused on more intangible goods—such as going for a nature hike on a clear summer day—then the market will not serve you as well. In fact, it will serve you quite poorly, since it will have a tendency to shift resources away from the production of the type of goods that you enjoy.

Not all the by-products of economic activity are noxious. Just as we sometimes generate costs for other people, we are also able to create benefits. If you go out and plant a bunch of carrots in a field, you have just created a generalized social good by increasing the overall stock of food available for human consumption. Anyone can come along in a couple of months, pick one of these carrots, and enjoy a tasty snack.

Unfortunately, people don't usually run around showering benefits upon one another. They usually save that side of their personality for special occasions. Of course, we all perform the occasional altruistic act—some of us more than others. But most of our day is spent doing things that are in our own interest to do.

When people stick to their own interest, it generates collective action problems. Because of this, there are many cases in which we *want* people to produce goods for others. We want people to plant carrots. We want them to refrain from walking around with handguns. The function of property rights is not only that they allow people to charge others for costs that are imposed upon them, but that they allow people to charge for benefits that they create. Property rights, in effect, allow you to "capture" some of the benefit that your actions have for others. Thus owning the carrots entitles you to sell them and therefore partake of the benefits that your carrots create for those who ultimately eat them. This is what gives you an incentive to plant the carrots in the first place, and it is how property rights help us to escape from a wide range of collective action problems that can arise when people lack the incentive to help others.

A positive externality occurs whenever people are unable to capture some significant fraction of the benefits that their activities create for society at large. Again, positive externalities occur where the system of property rights is incomplete. One example of this, dear to my own heart, is mosquito control. I belong to the school of thought that says the only good mosquito is a dead mosquito. This makes killing mosquitoes, in my books, an unqualified good. (Anyone who doesn't feel as strongly about mosquitoes should feel free to vary the example somewhat, e.g., by substituting "rats" for "mosquitoes" throughout.) However, each mosquito I kill benefits not only me, but also every other person that the mosquito in question might have bitten. My bug-zapper therefore confers a slight benefit on all my neighbours. Unfortunately, the benefit that my neighbours receive from my pest-control efforts is so difficult to keep track of that I can't really charge them for it. It is a positive externality.

Whenever there is a positive externality, markets will tend to underproduce the good in question. As a result, the system of property rights as a whole will fail to solve a certain class of collective action problems.

Imagine a group of people who all live a stone's throw away from a brackish pool—the perfect breeding ground for mosquitoes. They could all save themselves a lot of aggravation by laying down some bug spray on this pond. Unfortunately, private markets don't provide anyone with an incentive to do this. Buying the poison and spraying involves significant cost and effort—not to mention personal exposure to some dubious chemical substances. Imagine that one person goes out, buys the stuff, and does the job. The next day, she goes around and tries to collect some money from her neighbours in order to defray these costs. Of course, their reactions will be pretty predictable. A couple of nice people will pay up, and the rest will just tell her to get lost. (The clever ones will refuse to pay on the grounds that they have "environmental" objections to bug spray. That way they can free-ride while still clinging to the moral high ground.) She can try to persuade them, but ultimately she can't force them to pay, because the system of property rights doesn't cover "reducing the risk of being bitten by a mosquito."

Since this outcome is entirely predictable, in most cases no one will even bother to do the spraying. They will just let the mosquitoes breed. This is why public spaces or goods to which no individual has clear title tend to get degraded when left to the market—a phenomenon often referred to as the tragedy of the commons. The important thing to note is that the tragedy of the commons is just a prisoner's dilemma. It is a collective action problem that markets fail to resolve.

What are some other goods with significant positive externalities? One extremely important example is education. Being able to read obviously generates significant benefits for the person doing the reading. But it also generates huge benefits for others. Being literate means that people don't have to tell you in person what to do, they can just put up a sign. The fact that we live in a society with a high general education level generates huge benefits for us all. However, because we are unable to charge people for all the benefits that our education confers upon *them*, individuals do not always have an incentive to choose an education level that is socially optimal. Even with massively subsidized education, plenty of people still drop out of high school. This may be individually rational, but it imposes significant costs upon society—decreased productivity being the most obvious. That's why we have to use all kinds of non-market mechanisms to keep them in school.

In general, most "symbolic" goods have significant positive externalities. This is because it is so difficult to control their reproduction. A piece of information, a good idea, a catchy tune—all of these get reproduced the instant that anyone comes into contact with them. If you compose a song and perform it, anyone who hears it may turn around and reproduce it. And anyone who hears that reproduction may reproduce it again. It is very difficult to "recapture" more than a fraction of these benefits because the property right is so difficult to exercise. Trying to own these goods is like trying to own a fire. You can charge people for a light, but what happens to "your" fire afterwards is completely beyond your control.

The concept of market failure is extremely useful, but it can also be very misleading. The typical introductory economics textbook starts out by presenting an idealized model of the perfect market economy. Such an economy will also be perfectly efficient. Market failure is then introduced as a sideline, something of a concession to the "real world." This creates the impression that efficiency is the norm and that failure is sporadic. Furthermore, market failure is often described as a consequence of "missing markets" or of an "incomplete" system of property rights—as if a "complete" system of property rights was even conceivable, much less feasible.

This is quite wrongheaded. Market failure is the baseline. It is the fundamental human condition. The Hobbesian state of nature is really just a state of total market failure. Out of this state of nature, we have been able to build up a set of institutions that promote co-operation and therefore improve efficiency. Markets are one institution of this type. But they are extremely limited in their range, since property rights apply only to a tiny fraction of the ingredients we require for successful living.

The best way to picture things is not to imagine a system of complete markets, with a few little failures here and there. It is better to start by imagining a state of nature in which there is total market failure. Imagine about ten billion prisoner's dilemmas. Each one that we resolve makes society just a little bit more efficient. The introduction of markets resolves perhaps one hundred million of them. The rest are not even touched.

To take an example of a collective action problem that markets cannot resolve, consider vaccination. In Canada, as in many other counties, it is illegal not to have your children vaccinated. At first glance this seems odd. After all, who wouldn't want to have their kid vaccinated against deadly diseases? It's like having a law against suicide. Self-interest alone would seem to take care of things.

The reason we have a law is that vaccination generates a free-rider problem. When a person gets vaccinated, it gives her certain benefits— she is less likely to get sick. But it also creates a positive externality. A person who is vaccinated is not only less likely to get the disease, she is also less likely to transmit it to other people. This means that if the majority of the people in your community *have* been vaccinated, you are much less likely to get sick, regardless of whether you yourself have been vaccinated.

Here's the problem: when you get vaccinated against many diseases, you run a slight risk of getting sick from the vaccine itself. Once enough people are vaccinated, the risk of getting sick from the vaccine may become higher than the risk of being infected from the population at large. In this case, it becomes possible to reduce your risk of disease by skipping the vaccine and free-riding off all the other people who have been vaccinated. This is of course anti-social behaviour, since your actions not only make you ultimately more likely to get sick, they make you more likely to infect others. But that doesn't mean people won't do it.

When left to their own devices, human populations will tend to choose inefficient levels of vaccination. At first, when a disease is rampant, everyone will run out and get vaccinated. The disease will then start to recede. Once this happens, people will start to free-ride, and many will choose to forego vaccination. After about a decade or so, a sufficient number of people will be unprotected that the disease will make a comeback. An epidemic will break out, and once again everyone will rush out to be vaccinated. This just sets the same cycle in motion again. So even though everyone would be better off if everyone got vaccinated, self-interest alone is not enough to ensure such an outcome.

This can be seen as a type of market failure. If the system of property rights were "complete," people could charge each other for the benefits that immunization confers. That way, a person who decided not to get vaccinated would have to compensate those who have been for the dangers that this decision imposes upon them. This would eliminate the free-rider incentive. But such a system would be crazy and impossible to organize. Why? Because immunity to disease is not a medium-sized dry good. In this particular case, it is much more efficient just to pass a law requiring people to do what under a system of complete markets they would choose to do. So while it is permissible to think of this as a market failure, doing so suggests some very unrealistic expectations about what markets are able to achieve.

Incidentally, the vaccination example shows once again just how deeply perverse our tendency to get into collective action problems can be. I actually know a fair number of people who have resisted having their children vaccinated. The vast majority of them are salt-of-the-earth hippie types, responding to some vague fear-mongering about the medical establishment or the evils of modern technology. The important point is that they are not callous egoists; they are sensitive, community-oriented people. Still, this doesn't seem to stop them from free-riding off others. Why run the risk of having your own children immunized when you can displace the risks onto your neighbours' kids? Of course, this is not how they think about it, but it is the underlying logic of their choice.

As Hobbes saw clearly, people don't have to be evil to get into collective action problems. They just have to be human.

Several years ago, I was tooling around Scotland and decided to visit the Glenlivet Scotch distillery. I went hoping to pick up a few free samples, or at least discounted wares, but found myself somewhat inadvertently getting caught up in a guided tour. This made me a bit self-conscious, especially when I discovered that everyone else on the tour was, believe it or not, a university professor. (This actually reveals a lot about the social construction of taste.) After a while I started to entertain myself by going up to complete strangers and saying, "So, where do you teach?"

The tour guide was a very pleasant young fellow. Naturally he was a graduate student in philosophy. He probably took the job so that he could develop contacts. He gave us a lot of interesting information about the plant. Like most continuous-flow manufacturing processes, the plant operated on three eight-hour shifts. On each shift there were four workers, for a grand total of twelve employees. That's right. All the Glenlivet in the world is manufactured by just twelve people.

You might think, then, that the Glenlivet plant made only a somewhat marginal contribution to the local economy. But you'd be wrong. Why? Because the plant also employed a small army of tour guides and gift shop employees, far more than were involved in the manufacture of the actual product.

This illustrates the most dramatic shift that our economy has undergone in the last forty years. Making actual, physical *stuff* has become easy. Manufacturing has become so highly automated that human labour is almost superfluous. This is the foundation of our society, the basis of our quality of life. And it is why junior faculty members—even graduate students—can now afford single-malt Scotch.

It also means that as our labour is shifted out of manufacturing, it becomes increasingly focused on the production of more intangible goods. The two most important examples are services and information. This is a very familiar fact, one that has been analyzed and dissected ad nauseum under the banner of "the information age," "post-industrial society," "the knowledge industry," and so on. What is seldom mentioned in the discussion is just how finicky many of these more intangible commodities can be. As we get away from the manufacture of physical stuff, the system of property rights becomes increasingly difficult to enforce. Information, in particular, is an incredibly difficult commodity to bring to market. The "knowledge sector" is therefore one of the areas most clearly prone to market failure.

The reason that information is hard to buy and sell is straightforward. In order for markets to be perfectly efficient, all parties to an exchange must have perfect information about the quality of the goods being exchanged and the prices at which all other goods in the economy are trading. If they don't have this information, there may be some other, more advantageous trade that they are overlooking.

Thus properly functioning markets require that information be not only complete, but symmetrical. It must not be the case that one person knows more than her trade partners. But then how can anyone buy and sell information? If you're in a position to sell someone information, then by definition you must have *more* information than they have.

When you buy a pair of shoes or a television, you like to inspect the quality first. This is the only way to ensure that the goods are actually worth what you are paying for them. Since the transaction is efficiency-promoting only if both parties are happy afterwards, efficiency requires that the buyer have pretty good information about quality before making a purchase.

Sometimes it is very difficult for a non-specialist to determine the quality of goods. In this case, we have to hire an expert. It is why we have to pay a mechanic to look at a used car before we buy it, or have an inspector look at a house before we finalize the deal. These information costs significantly limit the level of efficiency that can be achieved in such markets. For example, the average homebuyer looks at only six or seven houses before making a purchase, whereas you can easily look at twenty or thirty coffee makers before picking one out. This makes it almost certain that efficiency gains could be made if people could swap houses more easily.

Part of what limits these transactions is the fact that bringing in an expert to assess the quality of the goods is quite expensive. A home inspection can cost upwards of $500. Of course, if the house costs hundreds of thousands of dollars, this may be worthwhile. Sometimes, however, the cost of getting something checked out is just as high as the value of the goods being exchanged. A lawyer, for example, sells you legal advice. How do you know whether it is good advice? The only way to find out is to get another lawyer to check it. But this will probably cost you just as much as the first lawyer, so you're better off just taking the advice that you get. In cases like this, competition between sellers becomes almost non-existent, and so the prices determined by the free market are very unlikely to be the "right" prices from an efficiency standpoint.

The problem with buying and selling actual information is even worse. In order to assess the quality of the information you are about to buy, you need to take a look at it. But once you've had a look at it, you will know what it is, and so you will no longer have any incentive to pay for it. So no seller in her right mind will ever let you look at it. You'll just have to guess how much it's worth. As a result, the transaction is no more likely to promote efficiency than any other random process.

This is why markets for information do not function like markets for material goods. Most of the time they do not function at all. Several innovations, such as copyrights and patents, attempt to extend the property rights system to cover information, but they offer only partial coverage at best. The vast majority of markets for information simply fail. Of course, there are lots of nifty ways to get around this problem. Nevertheless, the term "information economy," when taken at face value, is an oxymoron. The institutional mechanisms that we use to organize the production and distribution of information are almost never markets.

This is one of the most persistent self-misunderstandings of our age. As information becomes a more significant component of our economy, markets become increasingly problematic as a form of economic organization.

Last but not least, in order to have a perfectly efficient market system, we must have a complete set of futures markets. Most goods are bought and sold in the present. You buy a television; you take it home. A futures market is one in which goods are bought and sold in the future. In order for capitalism to function at peak efficiency, there would have to be a complete market for each different type of good at each possible point in the future. Not only that, but the price at which each good will sell at each future point in time would have to be known by everyone today.

As far as economic idealizations go, this one is a real whopper. It amounts to the requirement that nothing unexpected ever occur. If anything unexpected did occur, then the future prices might change, and this would induce inefficiency. For example, because of some unexpected event, someone may find that he has chosen a rate of savings that is too low to meet his future consumption needs. Someone else may have chosen a rate that is too high. Shuffling the resources around could therefore create an efficiency gain.

Naturally, unexpected things do occur, and so it is inconceivable that we could ever have a complete set of futures markets. But all is not lost. One way to get around the problem of "missing" futures markets is to have complementary insurance markets. Whether or not a tornado will strike one particular farmer's field is quite uncertain. But the number of tornadoes that will touch down in some large region is more easily calculable. This is the law of large numbers. Insurance allows a group of people facing some uncertainty to take advantage of this law by pooling their risks. It allows them to set aside just the "right" amount of money to deal with tornado damage, and therefore prevents the misallocation of resources that might otherwise have occurred in this sector.

Unfortunately, insurance is also a very troublesome commodity. In order to secure efficiency, we should be able to buy insurance against any uncertain event. In reality, we are able to buy insurance against only a tiny number of risks. This is because insurance sales are especially prone to market failure.

The basic problem is one of information. If the people buying insurance have more information than the people selling it, then selling insurance is an easy way to lose money. Take the following example: People who use computers a lot know that data loss can be a huge problem. For a company that depends upon electronic databases or files, a hard-disk crash can be a catastrophe. But while it's easy to buy insurance against your building burning down, it's difficult to find insurance against data loss. In the United States it is very expensive, and in many other countries it is not available at all. Why is that?

Suppose that you decide to sell data-loss insurance. The first thing you need to do is figure out how much to charge people for it. One way to do this is to take a representative sample of your prospective customers, figure out the monetary value of the damage that they suffered from data loss last year, and divide that by the number of people in the sample. You can then take this figure, top it up a bit to handle your own administrative costs, plus the profit you would like to make, and set that as a premium level.

What will happen if you start selling insurance at this price? You will lose money—guaranteed. Why? Because the people who find it attractive to purchase insurance at that price are the people who expect their losses to be greater than the premium. Some people are extremely careful with their computers, and they always back up their files. For them, your insurance will not be worth the price. Other people are extremely careless. Not only do they never back up their files, they spill coffee on the keyboard, blow smoke at the CPU, and so on. For these people, your insurance will be good deal. Unfortunately, they know who they are, and you don't. As a result, when you start selling the insurance, you will automatically attract precisely the type of customer you don't want to have. This is called adverse selection.

So the first problem with insurance is that it tends to attract nightmare customers. But even more problems occur after the point of sale. One of the reasons that people who are careful with their data are so careful is that they want to avoid the damages associated with data loss. But once they are fully insured against these damages, they lose some of the incentive that they had to be careful. So even customers who were quite scrupulous before they bought the insurance may start to get reckless after they have bought it. This is called moral hazard.

Anyone who doubts that people behave recklessly when they are insured is invited to conduct the following experiment: Go out and rent a car, and decline the damage insurance. Now you know that every little nick and scrape on the car is going to come straight out of your pocketbook. Observe how much more carefully you drive. What does this prove? It shows that the way you normally drive is actually quite reckless, and that the reason you drive recklessly is that you are insured.

Moral hazard generates prisoner's dilemmas. When people buy insurance, they behave more recklessly. This increases the number of accidents, which in turn increases the premium levels. So we may wind up with more accidents than are necessary, and we may wind up paying more for insurance than we would like to pay. This is a type of market failure.

In some cases, it is possible to offset these problems. Adverse selection can be avoided by prescreening potential customers, having them fill out complicated questionnaires, or sending an inspector out to check up on them. Premium levels can then be adjusted to reflect the risk that a particular customer poses. Moral hazard can be mitigated through deductibles and periodic inspections. Sometimes this works, sometimes it doesn't. When it doesn't, the market for that type of insurance will fail completely. This is why we are unable to buy insurance to protect us against so many of life's little surprises. But when these insurance markets fail, it sends out ripples throughout the entire economy. It prevents us from adopting fully efficient investment and consumption decisions.

All these examples show that market failure is not the exception, but the norm. This means that markets are, at best, only a partial solution to the collective action problems we face. This doesn't mean that they don't work at all. When they do work, they work brilliantly. But it is important to keep track of their limitations.

The greatest weakness of the market system stems from the very limited range of goods that the system of property rights applies to. If you feel that you live in a crassly materialistic society, that's because you do. Markets work best when used to co-ordinate the production and distribution of discrete, material goods. As a result, markets produce more of these goods than we actually want.

This is the key to understanding some of the more perverse features of life under capitalism. For example, despite being the most outrageously wealthy society in the history of the world, the more populated regions of the United States are also relentlessly, preposterously, brutally *ugly*. American cities often seem to consist of nothing more than mile after mile after mile of aesthetically punishing tract housing, strip malls, and freeway overpasses. It's hard to think of any great civilization in the history of the world that has so systematically failed to invest its wealth in the creation of beauty. This is not just an outsider's prejudice either. Americans complain about it just as much. So why do they do it?

The explanation is simple. The material prosperity of Americans is due to the relatively unrestricted operations of the market economy in their society. It can cost a lot of money to make buildings beautiful. Once they are built, their beauty can be enjoyed for free by anyone who happens to pass by. Thus the enjoyment we all get from beautiful surroundings is largely a positive externality. As we have seen, market economies systematically underproduce goods with positive externalities. And so beauty suffers.

Of course, that's not a good reason to overthrow capitalism. There is a lot to be said for crass materialism. In any case, we are fortunate that this isn't the end of the story. Just because markets don't do some things right doesn't make us helpless. We have other institutional remedies available.

Big Business

7 One of the small peculiarities of Canadian civic life is that while the rest of the country enjoy a long weekend in August, people in Quebec remain hard at work. The big summer holiday in Quebec is the *fête nationale* (formerly known as St. Jean Baptiste Day), which lands on June 24, just shortly before Canada Day (also known in Montreal as "moving day"). So Quebecers usually take the whole week off. This is one reason why the distinct society in Quebec is more fun than the other, purportedly distinct societies scattered throughout the rest of Canada.

The highlight of this entire period is the St. Jean Baptiste parade, which shuts down all of downtown Montreal. The event has fairly strong nationalist overtones, which usually scares away the anglos. There's something about a huge crowd shouting "*le Québec aux Québécois*" that can be unnerving. But apart from this residual ethnonationalism, there is something else about the parade that speaks volumes about the distinct character of Quebec society. The year I attended, one of the major components of the parade was a series of floats celebrating the "giants of industry." All the big corporations in Quebec—Bombardier, Hydro-Quebec, Quebecor—were represented.

The suggestion that people should take pride in the fact that their economy is dominated by large corporations is one that would be quite foreign to most Canadians outside Quebec. It's hard to imagine people in Toronto cheering for Inco, or Vancouverites rallying around the MacMillan-Bloedel banner. In fact, lots of people in B.C. took perverse pleasure from seeing "MacBlo" get gobbled up by Weyerhaeuser.

In part, this is because people outside Quebec take the existence of giant corporations for granted. In Quebec, however, where society has only recently emerged from a period of relative economic backwardness, these corporations are the symbol of a modern economy. The only way to be a real player on the world stage is to have some big companies that can compete in the major leagues. Thus there is a natural harmony of interest between Quebec nationalists and the various and sundry home-grown tycoons.

Corporations are the public face of a successful capitalist economy. When we think about the world of business, we don't usually think about markets and trading. What comes to mind first are corporations. The most powerful symbols of American capitalism are Coca-Cola and McDonald's, not the stock market or the Federal Reserve Bank. The appearance of the first McDonald's in Moscow and later Beijing said more about the weakness of the communist system than all the economic analysis in the world. Similarly, opponents of the capitalist system almost always focus their energies on fighting big companies.

The irony is that in a perfect market economy there would be no need for corporations. The typical corporation is nothing but a giant bureaucracy. Markets, however, are supposed to be more efficient than bureaucracies. So why are there such huge bureaucracies in the private sector? Why don't the big corporations get outperformed by groups of small players organizing their transactions through markets?

The answer is that the transactions that typically take place within a corporation are especially prone to market failure. As a result, it is much more efficient to organize these exchanges using a good old-fashioned bureaucracy than through the market.

In other words, corporations, despite being the foremost symbol of triumphant capitalism, are actually a symptom of market failure.

The largest corporation in the world today is General Motors. The company has annual sales worth over $170 billion, more than the GDP of many small European nations such as Portugal, Belgium, or the Czech Republic. It has manufacturing operations in fifty different countries, employs more than six hundred thousand people, purchases goods from approximately twenty thousand different suppliers, and manufactures products ranging from cars and trucks to communications satellites and industrial robots.

General Motors is also a bureaucracy. While all its relationships to suppliers are organized through the market, everything that happens within the company follows a completely different logic. Managers do not buy and sell partially assembled cars from and to one another. Each division, subdivision, branch, plant, and workgroup is assigned its own particular tasks. The structure of the production process resembles a chore list much more than it does a market.

In its heyday, General Motors was a classic organizational hierarchy, with six major divisions and fourteen layers of management. Each worker and manager reported to his or her immediate superior, and instructions flowed down the chain of command. Control was exercised from the centre, with ultimate decision-making power vested in the CEO. This hierarchical structure was reinforced by control over information. Important information about the operations of the firm was available only to the CEO, and was disseminated to division heads on a "need to know" basis.

Getting six hundred thousand people to work together is an incredibly challenging task. General Motors is not an especially efficient firm, but the fact that it is able to secure co-operation among so many people at all is a phenomenal achievement. The credit for this success, however, should not go to the market, which has little impact on the internal operations of the firm. The credit should go to the modern science of management. It is managers, not entrepreneurs, who perform the day-to-day tasks needed to organize and maintain these giant bureaucratic structures.

There tends to be a lot of confusion on this point. Not even Adam Smith was immune to it. *The Wealth of Nations* starts off with a discussion of the fabulous efficiency gains achieved in an English pin factory, thanks to the division of labour. The production of a pin requires about eighteen different operations: pulling the wire, straightening it, cutting it, grinding the end, etc. Smith estimated that if one worker performed all of these tasks, he could make at most 20 pins a day. But when the tasks were divided up among different workers, factories were able to produce upwards of 4,800 pins per worker per day.

This is all well and good. But Smith goes on to say that the division of labour "is not originally the effect of any human wisdom," but an indirect effect of the market. This is a very odd conclusion indeed. It seems obvious that "human wisdom" had a lot to do with the organization of the pin factory. In fact, somebody probably sat down one day, thought about how pins were made, and decided to start dividing up the tasks. The market had nothing to do with it. The workers didn't start buying pin-parts from each other and selling partially assembled pins back and forth. They just did what they were told to do by a supervisor. If anything, the pin factory is an example of the efficiency gains that can be achieved through bureaucratic administration. It is only tangentially related to the operations of the market.

But why do things bureaucratically? Here the traditional explanation is unsatisfactory. The growth of large corporations is usually explained as an attempt to achieve economies of scale. Because of the way that cars are manufactured, the more cars you make, the cheaper it is to make each one. Thus the larger firm will always enjoy a competitive advantage over the smaller firm. As a result, firms will grow larger and larger, buying up or squeezing out competitors, until the market is dominated by just a handful of major players.

This analysis is fine, as far as things go. But it does not really explain the growth of corporations. It explains why we have only five or ten car manufacturing plants, not one hundred or two hundred, but it does not explain why these plants are operated by a single company and managed through an organizational hierarchy. One could, in principle, still use the market. One can imagine an automobile factory that would be organized entirely through private exchanges. Each worker on the assembly line would be an independent contractor, renting a position on the line. He would purchase a partially assembled vehicle from the worker immediately upstream from him, buy some parts from various inventory suppliers, install these parts on the vehicle, then resell it to the next worker downstream on the line.

Such an arrangement would seem to guarantee maximum efficiency. Because production is centralized, all the efficiencies of scale would still be realized. Each worker would have an incentive to purchase inputs at the best price, to install the parts as quickly and as efficiently as possible, to develop innovative production methods, and so on. There would be no need for supervision or quality control, as each supplier would compete with the others in order to deliver the highest quality goods at the lowest price.

So what possible benefit could there be in hiring workers on an hourly wage, then simply assigning them a job on the line? This kind of employment relation eliminates all the positive incentives that the market system provides and can require costly investments in supervision to eliminate shirking. Nevertheless, this is the primary form of workplace organization in most sectors of every capitalist economy—so much so that an assembly line run by independent contractors seems more like a bizarre thought experiment than a possible mode of production.

So why is this? If markets are so efficient, how are organizational hierarchies able to survive?

Ideal markets—the kind that economists sketch out on paper—are perfectly efficient. Real markets—the kind that exist in the world around us—are never perfect. One of the most basic reasons for this is that real markets exist in space and time. Material goods are not abstract quantities; they are physical objects that exist at particular locations. In order to be made useful, they often have to be moved around, and moving them around consumes resources and costs money. Thus instead of being perfectly competitive—i.e., with multiple suppliers providing goods at the same price—real markets tend to be a collection of partially overlapping regional monopolies.

An assembly line provides the perfect example. Workers on the line could purchase partially assembled cars from the person upstream from them. But once the purchase is made, they have no real choice but to resell the car to the person immediately downstream. Taking the car off the line and selling it to someone in some other plant would be prohibitively expensive. This makes it all but impossible to organize a competitive market for partially assembled cars.

Whenever it is impossible to organize a competition, the major advantages of the market pattern of organization are lost. There is no longer any guarantee that the prices charged will produce efficient outcomes. Every worker on the assembly line would be held hostage by the person downstream from them, who would be free to dictate pretty much any price to them.

This example is not entirely fictitious. One of the reasons General Motors became so large was through the purchase, in the 1920s, of Fisher Body. Originally, GM purchased the bodies of its cars from Fisher, which was a separate company. In order to improve efficiency, GM began pressuring Fisher to locate its assembly plants right next to GM factories. They also began asking Fisher to produce more specialized products, ones that would be tailored specifically to GM designs.

The problem with this, from Fisher's point of view, was that it made the company vulnerable to opportunistic action by GM. Once you build a manufacturing facility right next to a GM plant and install expensive equipment that allows you to make products that only fit GM vehicles, then you really have no choice but to sell to GM. This gives GM the power to dictate prices. Once you have built the factory, what is to stop GM from turning around and cutting the price they are willing to pay?

This was exactly what worried Fisher executives. Once Fisher built a plant next to GM, it would create an opportunity for GM to "lowball" them on price. GM could free-ride off Fisher's investment. And so they resisted GM's pressure, which in turn made the production process less efficient. This interaction is a classic prisoner's dilemma.

Because of this problem, firms that sell their products on the market will be unwilling to make "asset-specific" investments to meet the needs of a single customer. This may include not only refusing to locate facilities near the major customers and refusing to install specialized equipment, but also refusing to invest in the type of knowledge and training that would be required to meet one customer's highly specialized needs. Whatever efficiency gains are realized through use of the market mechanism can easily be wiped out by the inefficient production processes that the refusal to make asset-specific investments creates.

The solution to this problem, in the case of GM, was simply to buy Fisher. This is a classic case of "vertical integration." Instead of organizing their transactions through the "horizontal" medium of market exchange, GM absorbed Fisher into its own vertical organizational hierarchy, thereby giving GM the power to directly order Fisher managers to construct manufacturing facilities right next to GM assembly plants. The prisoner's dilemma is thus solved by suspending the operations of the market and substituting direct bureaucratic control.

Of course, the boundaries of the firm are not fixed once and for all. Changes in technology may make it easier for suppliers to change their production methods to meet the needs of different customers. This may make them willing to consider investments that they were once unwilling to undertake. Large firms may then find that they can do better by spinning off one of their units and outsourcing the production of certain parts. Because the market is constantly changing, firms must also constantly change their boundaries in order to adapt to new conditions.

The problem of asset-specific investments is a particular case of a general phenomenon. The state of nature contains billions of prisoner's dilemmas. The market does not make any of these go away. It simply creates a layer of incentives that keep them under control. But beneath this layer, there is still a simmering cauldron of anti-social behaviour just waiting for the opportunity to break through.

The law-abiding citizens of a market society tend to respect each other's property rights. But this does not mean that they would not like to skip out on a payment, or pocket some spare change, or otherwise engage in opportunistic behaviour. They still have an incentive to cheat; it's just that the law and the threat of legal punishment are sufficient to dissuade them.

This dissuasion doesn't come free. The system of property rights helps us to avoid a wide variety of collective action problems. But because the incentive to lie, cheat, and steal is still there, we have to spend a lot of time and energy making sure that people don't take advantage of such opportunities. We have to keep track of all the property and who it belongs to. Then when people enter into transactions, we have to keep track of exactly what their agreement consisted of, what they agreed to exchange, when they agreed to deliver it, and so on. Finally, we need to have all sorts of people around willing to interpret these agreements, resolve disputes, and possibly punish those who break their agreements.

The payoff we get from all this is a system of markets that enables people to engage in economic co-operation, even when the level of trust between them is very low. But there are also costs, even when it is possible to organize a properly competitive market. Using the property system to organize economic transactions requires a lot of paperwork, a lot of contracts, and ultimately, a lot of lawyers. In some cases, the benefits of using the market outweigh these transaction costs. But in many more cases, they do not. This means that people who already have high-trust relationships can avoid a lot of expense.

Consider the difference between going into business with a total stranger and going into business with your sister. If you come from a normal sort of family, chances are that you will trust your sister more than you trust a perfect stranger. So before going into business with a stranger, you will want to develop fairly extensive contracts, specifying in great detail what each person's responsibilities and entitlements are.

You will also want to keep an eye on your partner to make sure he isn't embezzling, or wasting company funds, or shirking, or any other of the millions of ways he could be exploiting you. Of course, the stranger will feel the same way about you. As a result, you will each waste a lot of time and energy monitoring each other. This is inefficient. If you go into business with someone you trust, such as your sister, you can dedicate a lot more time to the actual task of running the business.

The lesson here is that sometimes the moral economy is still superior to the market economy. Imagine how much negotiation would be involved in running a factory in which each worker was an independent contractor and each piece of equipment or inventory that changed hands was a separate market transaction. It would be a nightmare.

Most large companies have a division, often called "supplies," whose job it is to provide the company's employees with supplies. Suppose that, in an effort to take advantage of market incentives, a company decided to "outsource" its supply services and then have individual workers deal directly with this firm. Each employee would be asked to negotiate with the supply company directly and pay for each staple used, each paper clip, each photocopy, etc. In the abstract, this might seem like a good idea. After all, people are unlikely to waste so many paper clips if they know that it's coming out of their pocket. The problem with this arrangement is that the amount of time needed to keep track of all this junk—all these paper clips and staples—is prohibitive. It's much more efficient for the firm to just give away free office supplies.

So this is what companies normally do. All the little resources that are needed to conduct business are made freely available to employees. Of course, when the market mechanism is suspended and supplies are given away for free, it gives each employee an incentive to overuse. One can therefore expect that a certain number of paper clips and staples will be wasted, and that some unnecessary photocopying will occur. In order to keep this in check, the company relies upon the old-fashioned components of the moral economy—trust and sanctions. Employees are punished if they overuse supplies or get caught stealing toilet paper from the company washroom. But by and large, the company just trusts its employees to exercise some restraint. It does this because relying on trust, even if this trust is sometimes violated, is still cheaper in the long run than using the market mechanism.

As we have seen, markets work reliably only when they are backed up by the force of law. This comes at a price, and trust is often cheaper. Whenever this is the case, organizations based on trust will be able to outperform individuals who coordinate their action through markets. Naturally, trust works best in smaller, more intimate groups. So while it is impossible to organize the whole economy through trust relations, pockets of trust can survive and prosper. Corporations provide the principal environment in which this trust can be fostered.

The idea that corporations rely upon trust may strike many people as unrealistic. After all, competition among employees in a firm can be just as cutthroat as competition among firms. While a family firm may rely heavily upon the dedication of its members, this isn't the way we usually think about gigantic impersonal corporations.

But closer observation of the inner operations of the corporation tells a different story. Naturally, large firms are hierarchies. People do their jobs not only out of loyalty to the firm, but also because they want to get promoted or don't want to get fired. And people compete with one another, quite intensively, for job perks and promotions. But when push comes to shove, employees are still expected to be team players. They are not allowed to put their own interests above those of the company.

This is reflected in the way that compensation is organized. Even annual performance bonuses, which seem like highly individualized incentives, are seldom based on the contribution that any one individual has made to the firm's output. Within a typical organization, this contribution is seldom even quantifiable. Employees are usually rewarded for more intangible contributions, such as the level of commitment they exhibit or the contribution they have made to the organizational cohesiveness of the firm. Stock options, for instance, a very popular form of performance incentive, depend entirely upon collective achievement for their value. An employee can make money off stock options only if the value of the company's stock rises. Thus they have value only if the company as a whole performs well.

The company's demand for commitment, honesty, and loyalty from its employees is even legally enforceable. Any employee can be dismissed for failure to disclose information that is prejudicial to the employer's interest. Managers, directors, and officers are subject to even stricter control. Employees in such positions are generally considered to be "fiduciaries" of the firm, which means that they can not only be fired for breaches of trust, but also sued for damages.

The most efficient firms are the ones that are able to inspire high levels of loyalty and commitment in their employees. Current trends in management are all directed towards the promotion of "corporate culture" and the creation of a set of shared values within the firm. The goal is to increase the sense of belonging among employees.

One of the first to discover the connection between employee loyalty and increased productivity was the inventor of the assembly line, Henry Ford. Like Frederick Taylor and the efficiency movement, Ford is often denounced for having dehumanized the workplace. Ford saw, however, that improving employee morale might be a source of improved productivity. He responded by voluntarily paying wages that were much higher than the going rate. He introduced the now-famous five-dollar day at a time when standard wages for industrial labour were closer to two dollars. With this wage rate, Ford was, in effect, doing his workers a favour. He was paying them more than he had to. This naturally gave them a greater desire to keep their jobs. But it also tapped into the old norm of reciprocity: when someone does you a favour, you owe them something in return. As an employee, one of the ways you can return the favour is by working hard and making sure you do a good job.

Ford speculated that the extra money spent on wages would be repaid in the form of harder work, better quality, decreased absenteeism, and higher morale. He was right. It is highly significant that to this day, Ford's strategy—paying wages that are higher than the market rate—is referred to as an "efficiency wage."

The importance of dedication and loyalty within the firm was driven home in the early '80s, when people began to pay serious attention to Japanese management techniques. Part of the superior efficiency of Japanese firms flowed directly from higher levels of trust in the work-place. The most celebrated example involved pull-cords, through which any worker could bring the entire assembly line to a halt in order to cor-rect some manufacturing error or defect. Such a system has obvious advantages in terms of quality control—American workers were used to watching helplessly as defective goods moved past them on the line. But it also requires a very high level of trust between management and workers. After all, the system gives workers an obvious free-rider incen-tive to pull the cord whenever they feel tired or want a coffee-break.

Sometimes the desire to create a unified corporate culture can go too far. In 1998, Steelcase, the world's largest manufacturer of office furni-ture, set up a six-by-four-foot glass display case in the lobby of its New York City headquarters. Inside the display was a fully functional ant colony (pop. 1,500).

The ants were supposed to serve as an inspiration to workers, and as a model of how a good company should function. According to Steel-case manager Dave Lathrop, "Ants live to work, and work to live." This ethic is one that ants "silently represent," "simply by doing what they do." Unfortunately, the display set off a bit of a backlash. Since the ants only live for three or four months, the *Wall Street Journal* suggested that the company might adopt a new slogan: "You work and then you die."

In any case, the Steelcase display helps to drive home the point that corporations are not markets. Ants don't compete with one another, they co-operate. They are team players. They sacrifice themselves for the good of the colony. They are a symbol of the moral economy.

On August 24, 2000, more than fifty million people in North Amer-ica watched Richard Hatch win a million dollars. Hatch was one of the sixteen contestants on the TV show *Survivor*, which became a runaway ratings hit during the summer season. The game was fairly simple. Sixteen people from all walks of life were "marooned" together on an island in the South China Sea. Every three days, they got together to vote one person off the island. The last person left standing won a million dollars.

Most people agreed that Hatch—or "Rich," as he came to be known—deserved to win. While not the most likeable person on the island, he clearly played the game better than any other contestant. From the very beginning, he had a clear strategic perspective. He made selective use of his skills as a spear-fisher in order to survive the first few rounds. He then formed an alliance—which block-voted against the most threatening contestants—in order to carry himself into the final rounds.

In real life, Rich is a corporate trainer. Many people found this unsurprising. The skills that he displayed in the game—in particular, his calculated manipulation of the other contestants—seemed to be precisely the same skills that one needs to get ahead in business. The million dollars that he made on the island pale in comparison to the millions that he could certainly make on the lecture circuit, teaching junior executives to be just like him.

But many of his fellow corporate trainers were not amused. They felt that Rich's behaviour had blackened the entire profession. Corporate training, they insisted, is not about Machiavellian scheming and dog-eat-dog competition. According to one upset member of the profession, it is all about "togetherness, teamwork, and tolerance." Rich's ruthlessness violated the fundamental credo of the training profession.

This may sound pretty unbelievable. Touchy-feely talk may be nice, but it's hard to imagine that corporate trainers get paid to organize group hugs. But contrary to what one might think, many of them do. Touchy-feely talk is rampant in the corporate world. Many contemporary business books are almost indistinguishable from '60s countercultural manifestos. Pick up a copy of Stephen R. Covey's wildly successful *The 7 Habits of Highly Effective People*, and you'll see that almost none of it is about business or even time management. It's a weird blend of new-age spiritualism, abstract reflections about morality and character, and tips on building "synergistic" interpersonal relations. It even ends with a bizarre set of reflections on the nature of God and the role of higher spiritual forces in our lives.

What is the point of all this? According to Thomas Frank, who was the first to point out these remarkable similarities, "What's happened is not co-optation or appropriation, but a simple and direct confluence of interest." In order to be effective, corporations need to secure co-operation from their employees. The most effective way to do this is to secure their loyalty and commitment—in short, to construct a moral economy. Corporations use moral suasion in order to persuade their employees to eliminate collective action problems. Whatever spiritual values happen to be in circulation can easily be picked up and pressed into service.

Thus the corporate trainers who complained about Rich were not just making lame excuses for their profession. Corporate training really is about teamwork and co-operation. The problem with their complaints had more to do with a misunderstanding of how Rich won the game. He behaved in exactly the manner that a good corporate trainer should. He didn't set out to win on his own, he went out and formed a coalition. This *coalition* was successful because Rich was able to secure the trust and co-operation of other competitors.

At the beginning, it looked as though *Survivor* would be just a repeat of high school. The frat boys and pretty girls got together and started throwing out everyone who seemed a bit different: first the old people, then the black woman, and so on. Rich also looked like an easy target, both because he was gay and because he was irritating. Had it been a high-school popularity contest, he would have been gone in no time. But about halfway through, the show started to get much more interesting. Rich began turning the tables. Together with a few other underdogs, he formed a voting block and began throwing out the frat boys and pretty girls. By the time the other (somewhat dense) contestants caught on to what they were doing and got organized to resist them, it was too late.

From the beginning, Rich approached the game looking to build a team. His opponents tended to think in far more individualistic terms.

In particular, most of the college students thought that everyone should just "vote their conscience" and evaluate each person on his or her own merits. This type of individualistic thinking was their downfall. They were eliminated, not because they were victims of some dog-eat-dog free-for-all but because they failed to establish trust relationships, and because they failed to take advantage of the powers of *organization*.

Rich's behaviour, far from producing a stain on the reputation of corporate trainers, managed to show precisely why corporations are able to survive and prosper in a capitalist economy. Teams can be more powerful than individuals, and co-operation is often the most effective competitive strategy.

If corporations exist in order to correct market failure, then the organizational benefits of incorporation should be greatest wherever the potential for market failure is the greatest. This is clearly apparent in the case of knowledge. Of all the elements that make up the value of a commodity, knowledge is perhaps the most difficult to buy and sell. Whether it be something as mundane as familiarity with the company's filing system or something as sophisticated as the "in-house" libraries of code maintained by software and e-commerce companies, knowledge is an essential ingredient in any productive activity. But much of this knowledge cannot be traded on open markets.

The problem is illustrated quite well by a little joke that was popular among engineers a couple of years ago:

> There was once an engineer—let's call him Bill—who had worked at a certain manufacturing plant for as long as anyone could remember. When the time came for him to retire, he protested. But the company had a strict policy, and so Bill had no choice but to pack up his things and head for the golf course.
>
> Shortly afterwards, a piece of equipment at the plant broke down. The entire assembly line ground to a halt. The

junior engineers fiddled around but were unable to locate the source of the problem. "I wish Bill was around," they said. "He's the one who used to look after this stuff."

So the plant manager called Bill and said, "We really need your help. We're losing thousands of dollars every minute the line is shut down."

"Does this mean you want to hire me back?" Bill asked.

"No," said the manager, "just do this one job for us, and bill us for your services."

Bill came in, looked around, tapped the machine in a few places, and listened carefully. He then took out a piece of chalk and marked a large X on one component of the machine. "This is the broken piece," he said. "Replace it and you're back in business." The junior engineers did what Bill said, and soon the line was up and running again.

The next day the manager received an invoice from Bill for the sum of $50,000. This was a bit higher than he had expected, so he gave Bill a call. "That's a lot of money," he said. "I'll need to know how you came up with that figure. Send me an itemized bill."

The next day he received the following:

Item	Cost
One chalk mark	$1
Knowing where to put it	$49,999
Total	$50,000

The point of the joke is that Bill is pretty much free to charge anything he likes, and so an itemized bill is a pure formality. All the trappings of a market transaction are there, but the logic of the interaction completely undermines the organizational pattern of the market.

This is why firms seldom choose to purchase the services of specialized knowledge workers like Bill. Instead, they put people like him on salary, making them in-house experts. The salary is designed to secure their co-operation, not pay for the specific knowledge that they dispense. Thus forcing Bill to retire was a mistake. The horizontal market transaction is not an effective substitute for the employee-employer relationship.

In 1982, economists at the Brookings Institute estimated that about 62 per cent of the value of a typical American firm stemmed from its physical assets—everything from tables and chairs to factories and inventories. Everything else consisted of more intangible "knowledge assets." By 1992, the balance had completely reversed. They calculated that only 38 per cent of the average firm's value came from its physical assets.

With the shift towards more knowledge-intensive production processes, it is natural that firms should start to worry much more about employee loyalty. It is relatively easy to stop employees from making off with company property—just post guards at the gate. But when employees leave, they generally take with them all the knowledge and experience they have acquired, and there is no way to stop them. So the best way for a firm to retain control of its assets is to build a strong organizational culture, one that will inspire loyalty and allegiance from its employees.

From this perspective, it is entirely predictable that the firms that depend most heavily on the knowledge of their workers will also be the firms that put the most effort into employee retention. Software companies in particular are famous for their efforts to create a corporate culture that will secure employee allegiance.

Faced with the task of building a strong, cohesive corporate culture, many software companies have borrowed heavily from other organizations. Trilogy Software made headlines by sending its new recruits to a training "boot camp" for three months—with classes running from 8:00 a.m. to midnight, seven days a week, for the first month. Other companies, such as Scient, subject their new recruits to intense pep rallies, with constant repetition of the company slogan—

"I'm on *fire!*" The popularity of these tactics has even led to some hand-wringing about the cult-like character of many business initiation rituals.

One writer for *Shift* magazine captured the dilemma quite well in a brilliant article entitled "Why Your Fabulous Job Sucks." "Work is a blast. Your colleagues are cool and they dig having your dog around. But something evil lures you to the company beer fridge. Ever wonder why you're never home?"

The observation here is quite astute. Creating a cool work environment, holding fabulous office parties with great bands, letting people wear whatever they want, setting up the LAN for multiplayer gaming—this may all seem like corporate generosity. But it also has a sound economic rationale. All these devices help to build among young employees allegiance, loyalty, and a willingness to work. The easiest way to persuade people to pull an all-nighter is to make being at the office more *fun* than being at home.

For a long time, it was assumed that the reason corporations got larger and larger was that they wanted to acquire a monopoly position in the market. By eliminating their competitors, they would effectively escape from the prisoner's dilemma that suppliers are caught in. This would leave them free to set prices as high as they liked. Naturally, a high price level is unlikely to generate an efficient level of consumption, and so society has an interest in preventing such monopolies from being formed. This is the point of anti-trust legislation.

But while not denying that firms sometimes consolidate in order to acquire a monopoly position, it is important to realize that there are a lot of other reasons—good reasons—that corporations might grow larger. Whenever there is a market failure, it means that certain goods and services will either not be produced at efficient levels or not be produced at all. By substituting direct bureaucratic administration for the market mechanism, corporations are able to ensure that these goods do actually get produced in the right quantities.

Vertical integration can be a useful strategy when competition fails and when transaction costs are high. But corporations also correct market failures that are more difficult to detect. In many cases, markets not only fail to supply goods at efficient price levels, they fail to provide the goods *at all*. When this happens, corporations are sometimes able to provide benefits to their workers that would otherwise be impossible to purchase. This is especially true in the case of insurance.

Because they are so vulnerable to manipulation, the vast majority of insurance products are subject to total market failure. In other words, it is simply impossible to buy insurance against the vast majority of risks. But insurance is nothing more than a name we give to risk-pooling arrangements that are organized through private markets. When these markets fail, it is possible to pool risks in other ways. The corporation provides a perfect example of how people can arrange to share risks without the mediation of explicit market mechanisms.

For example, there are many types of production processes that call for very specialized skills. The division of labour is itself an enormous source of efficiency gains. Unfortunately, acquiring highly specialized skills can be extremely risky for an individual, because the future is uncertain. While I may know that there is adequate demand for my skills now, I have no idea what things will be like five years down the road. As a result, no one may be willing to invest the time and energy needed to acquire specialized skills, because it is too risky.

This efficiency loss could be avoided if it were possible to buy some kind of insurance that would compensate people when there was some fluctuation in the demand for their skills. Unfortunately, no one would ever want to sell this type of insurance because of obvious moral-hazard problems—people would lose all incentive to market or upgrade their skills. So private markets will simply fail to provide this type of insurance.

Corporations, however, are able to provide such insurance to workers through bureaucratic means. Companies can hire a variety of different workers with different skill sets to produce a range of different products. With this diversification, companies are able to ride out fluctuations in the demand for particular products or skills by levelling the peaks—using the returns from products that are currently in high demand to subsidize production of those that are not.

Thus corporate diversification strategies have the effect of protecting workers against certain risks. If you run your own business out of the basement, the chances that your company will go bankrupt are very high. If you do exactly the same job, but do it working for IBM, the chances that your company will go bankrupt are negligible. The chances that you will be laid off are still there, but are much more tolerable. Thus companies such as IBM provide a form of insurance to their workers, insurance that clearly has considerable value to them. They wouldn't have to go to IBM for this if they could buy the same sort of insurance in private markets. But they can't. This risk-sharing is part of the reason that large firms like IBM are so successful.

Every year, Americans buy more health care than they actually want to buy. Canada, along with most other industrialized nations, spends less than 10 per cent of its GDP on health care. The United States spends almost 15 per cent of its GDP on health care. In practice, this means that across a whole lifetime the average Canadian will spend about 10 per cent of her income on medical supplies and services. The average American will spend 15 per cent. What could explain this difference? Do Americans just have more of a taste for health care—in the same way that they have more of a taste for Velveeta or Pepsi-Cola? Or is someone forcing them to buy more health care than they need?

The answer is neither. Americans buy this much health care because they are stuck in a collective action problem. This collective action problem is a consequence of the way private health insurance works.

I didn't really understand this until the day I got free plastic surgery in Chicago. I went to graduate school at Northwestern University, which is in Evanston, just north of Chicago. Like most graduate students, I had a tuition waiver, so I got to avoid the US$15,000 annual fees. One of the things that came along with tuition was free access to the student health centre. Hospitalization insurance, on the other hand, we had to pay for. The university plan cost just over US$500 per year, which seemed pretty steep to me. But it was mandatory, so I had no choice but to pay up.

One of the things that I inherited from the German side of my family was a set of three colourless facial moles. (I apologize for the unpleasant details, but they're important to the story.) They weren't big ugly moles, but they weren't all that pretty either. One day, I noticed that one of them had changed colour and was looking a bit angry. I had heard some vague talk about moles and skin cancer, so I went down to the student health centre to have it checked out. The doctor poked it a bit, said it looked fine, but then suggested that I have it checked out by a dermatologist. "Fine," I said, thinking that I probably wouldn't bother.

The doctor wandered out of the room, then reappeared a few minutes later with another guy, a dermatologist. The dermatologist poked the mole a couple more times, said it looked fine, but added that "it probably bothers you while you're shaving. Maybe you should have a surgeon take a look at it." "Fine," I said, thinking again that I probably wouldn't bother.

But then the dermatologist disappeared and came back a few moments later with yet another guy. This time it was a surgeon, who just happened to be in the clinic at the time. The surgeon poked the mole a bit more, and said, "You might want to get that removed. Why don't you call my secretary and set up an appointment at the hospital?"

So within a space of about five minutes, my little mole had been examined by a general physician and two specialists. What service! Of course, none of this was free. These specialists charge for every consultation. They charge a *lot*. But I didn't care. The university was paying.

An appointment at the hospital, on the other hand, wasn't covered as part of the tuition package. And I wasn't sure that my hospitalization insurance would pay for such a minor procedure. So I asked the surgeon whether the operation would be considered medically necessary. He looked at me a bit oddly, then said, "Well, it probably bothers you when you're shaving." This wasn't what I wanted to know, so I just asked him straight out, "Will my insurance pay for this?" He gave me a blank look and said, "I have no idea. You'll have to talk to your insurance company."

The next day I called the university's insurance office and asked them whether mole removal was covered under the plan. I was told that whenever someone was referred to the hospital from the student health centre, the procedure would be automatically covered by the insurance plan. "But the surgeon is referring me to himself," I protested. "Doesn't matter," she said. "You will be reimbursed 100 per cent."

Great. So I hemmed and hawed for a couple of months, then finally booked myself an appointment at the hospital. When I showed up, the surgeon clearly had no recollection of me or my mole. "So," he said to me, "what would you like to have done today?" I showed him the mole again, and he quickly agreed to excise it. "What about those others?" he said, pointing to the two colourless ones. "Would you like me to take those off while we're at it?"

"What the hell," I said. So I had all my moles removed. And it was billed to the student health insurance plan, even though at least two-thirds of the procedure was totally cosmetic. In retrospect, I should have asked for a nose job while I was at it.

Again, none of this was cheap. I know this for certain in the case of the hospital procedures, because they sent me copies of all the bills. The surgeon charged US$300, $100 per mole. The hospital expenses came to about US$200, which included an itemized account of all the sutures, bandages, and Tylenol that I consumed. Finally, the surgeon sent tissue samples from all three moles to the pathology lab, which charged US$100 per sample for the analysis. Grand total: US$800.

But what did I care? After all, the insurance company was paying. And it felt good to get my money's worth out of the US$500 insurance premium that I had paid.

I wasn't laughing quite so hard the following year when I got the next bill for my health insurance. The premiums had gone up across the board by 15 per cent. Everyone's insurance now cost $575. The next year it went up again, to $650. The year after that it was $750.

What was happening? Clearly, the insurance company was not exercising adequate supervision. As a result, doctors were able to bill pretty much anything they wanted to the insurance company, and they were able to charge pretty much anything they wanted. As a result, students were "overconsuming" health care. I would never have paid US$800 for mole removal. I would have bought a computer instead. But because of the insurance plan, I was able to have the procedure, then externalize the cost, displacing it onto the other policy holders.

The premiums were going up because a lot of other people were doing the same thing. And since every procedure that is billed to an insurance plan is ultimately paid for through the premiums of policy holders, the inevitable consequence is that the insurance gets more and more expensive.

So we, the students, were collectively purchasing more health care than we were actually willing to pay for. But we had no way to stop, because the insurance plan locked us into a giant prisoner's dilemma.

This is moral hazard. Big-time moral hazard. People buy car insurance to protect themselves from financial catastrophe in the event that they have an accident. However, once they have bought the insurance, it decreases the incentive to drive carefully. As a result, the number of accidents will increase, and the amount paid out in damage claims will be higher. Health insurance works the same way. Big medical bills can be a financial catastrophe. But when people are fully insured, they have less incentive to avoid big medical bills. And so premiums go up and up.

In the case of car insurance, it is possible for the insurance company to conduct reasonable supervision of the claims that come in. This is because cars are fairly simple machines. It's relatively easy for the company to tell whether or not certain repairs are actually necessary. If you have to get the air conditioning fixed in your car, and you send the bill to your insurance company, they will probably tell you to take a hike. In the case of medicine, however, the information asymmetries are often too high. The insurance company usually has no way of knowing whether a particular diagnostic test or surgical procedure is needed. And so often they will just pay out any claim that comes in. This leads to market failure.

One way in which the failure of private health insurance markets shows up is in escalating health care costs. The function of the price system is to ration scarce goods. But when doctors can charge almost anything they want, the rationing system starts to fail. To take one example, in 1990 there were more than 10,000 mammography machines in the United States. But only 5,132 machines were needed to give every woman in America all the recommended screenings. So the country as a whole had about twice as many of these machines as it could possibly use.

How can this happen? In a properly structured market, the price of mammography should be determined on the demand side by how much people are willing to pay for a screening, and on the supply side by the cost of the machine. If the machine costs $10,000 a year to own and operate, and people will pay up to one hundred dollars per screening, then a hospital or clinic would need to attract one hundred paying customers per year in order to break even. If there are too many machines in circulation, they will start to lose money on their investment and so will impose a moratorium on the purchase of any new mammography machines.

What happens in real life in the United States is that because people are not actually paying for these screenings out of their own pockets, they don't really care how much they cost. And so hospitals can just jack the price of a mammogram up to $200, enabling them to break even with only fifty clients. The insurance company simply does not have the energy or resources to exercise adequate supervision and so often just accepts the bill. (Furthermore, the insurance companies themselves are caught in a collective action problem when it comes to inspection. Why have your own adjusters go in and check out what doctors are charging when, if you're lucky, a rival firm will do the same? Then you can just refuse to pay any more than they pay.)

The problem, from a societal point of view, is that all the time, energy, and resources that go into producing mammography machines would have been better spent somewhere else. It could have been spent on refrigerators, computers, cameras, or anything else that people happen to want more. But these decisions are ones that are supposed to be made by the market. When the market fails to perform this task, it means that people get stuck producing and consuming stuff that they don't really want.

This market failure is what accounts for the spectacular growth of HMOs (health management organizations) in the United States. The major problem in the health care sector is a breakdown in the horizontal relationship between two corporations—the health care provider and the insurance company. One easy way to solve this is simply to suspend the market mechanism for this particular exchange and absorb the two companies into a single, vertically integrated firm. This is precisely what a classic HMO does.

HMOs come in all different shapes and sizes, but the basic idea is pretty straightforward. An HMO is a big company that usually owns a number of hospitals and employs a small army of doctors. Individuals sign up with the company and pay an annual flat fee. The HMO then agrees to provide whatever health care services those individuals require during the year. When doctors provide service, the costs are no longer externalized to an insurance company; they are absorbed by the doctor's own employer. There's no longer a strong incentive to inflate prices, because the price system as a whole has been suspended. Delivery of health care is now under direct bureaucratic administration.

HMOs have been so successful that they now occupy a dominant position in the market for health care in the United States. Approximately forty-five million Americans are uninsured. Of the remainder, about half are enrolled in some type of HMO. Most others receive some sort of managed care plan. Less than 10 per cent of Americans still have classic fee-for-service private health insurance (down from more than 70 per cent in the late '80s).

So even though many people equate HMOs with private health care, these sorts of corporations exist only because of the failure of private markets to supply appropriate health care. HMOs succeed precisely because they are more efficient than insurance markets. There should be no illusions about the character of these organizations—they are giant bureaucracies. The largest of them, Kaiser Permanente, employs over eleven thousand physicians and has more than six million subscribers in the state of California alone. This makes Kaiser larger than most of the government-run health care systems in Canada. And while the Canadian system is extremely decentralized, Kaiser Permanente is a single, vertically integrated corporation.

Of course, the HMO system in the United States is still rife with problems and remains deeply unpopular with consumers (most Americans get shoehorned into HMOs by their employers). But the growth of HMOs shows how corporations are able to achieve efficiency gains by suspending the price mechanism and substituting direct bureaucratic administration. But as the comparison with the Canadian health care system makes clear, governments also have the same powers. There is no *a priori* reason to think that private-sector bureaucracies will be more efficient than public-sector bureaucracies. And in the absence of effective competition, they are likely to be very much less so. Thus the same forces that make it advantageous to form giant corporations also make it advantageous for the state to take on a strategic role in the economy. From an economic point of view, big business and big government are like fraternal twins.

Big Brother

8 *The quality of the air in most* North American cities is significantly better now than it was thirty years ago. No one ever believes me when I tell them this, but it's true. Ambient concentrations of sulphur dioxide, carbon monoxide, ozone, lead, and nitrogen dioxide are all lower than they were in the 1960s.

The reason that air quality has been so much improved is simple—environmental regulation. Until the late '60s there were almost no restrictions on what people could dump into the air, water, or ground. When I was a kid in Saskatoon, going to the local dump used to be a lot of fun. In order to decrease the volume of garbage, they used to set it all on fire. So there would always be more or less out-of-control wildfires burning in the garbage mounds. We used to have lots of fun throwing aerosol cans, tires, and anything else exciting onto the blaze.

In a modest concession to environmental consciousness, one day they set up a separate pit for "hazardous liquid waste." People were invited to separate their paint, industrial solvents, and used motor oil from the rest of their trash and dump it in this special area. Of course, the special area was just a big hole in the ground. What made it so special was that, unlike the rest of the dump, this area was not set on fire.

Such an arrangement seems inconceivable in this day and age. At the time, it didn't seem so odd. Standing in the middle of the prairies on a clear summer day, it's hard to get too excited about air quality. If there's one thing that Saskatchewan has lots of, it's air.

But that was the '70s, a different era. Back then, we thought nothing of taking our trash and throwing it out the car window. Finished with that drink? Out it goes. Need to empty the ashtray? Again, out the window. When Banff National Park started imposing—gasp!—one-hundred-dollar fines on people for dropping litter on the roadside, we felt this to be a significant infringement on our freedom.

So what changed all this? As far as air quality is concerned, the major improvements came from government either banning certain substances outright or else imposing significant constraints on the freedom to dump them into the environment. This regulatory intervention was, in general, quite successful. Unfortunately, it is a success story that is seldom celebrated. The left does not want to encourage complacency on environment issues—since there is still much work to be done—and so tends to avoid self-congratulation. The right simply doesn't want to admit that government regulation is responsible for such massive improvements in our quality of life. As a result, no one wants to pat government on the back.

The consequence, unfortunately, is that we wind up seriously underestimating the contribution that government is making to the efficiency of our economy.

If you want your car to run smoothly, one of the best things you can do for it is toss a bit of lead into your gasoline. The lead acts as both a valve lubricant and an engine coolant. In effect, it's a cheap way to increase the octane level of your gas. This is why a lot of racing cars still run on leaded fuel.

The problem with putting lead into gasoline is that it gets burned. Once burned, it becomes a toxic air contaminant, one to which there is no safe threshold of exposure. It has been associated with heart disease, kidney problems, and high blood pressure in adults, but even more significantly with learning disabilities, behaviour problems, and lower IQs in children.

You would think that with such serious health consequences, no one in his or her right mind would choose to use leaded gasoline. But you'd be wrong. Producing unleaded gasoline requires more sophisticated refinement techniques in order to maintain an adequate octane level. As a result, unleaded gas costs around three cents per litre more than leaded gas. And everybody knows how touchy people can be about the price of gas.

The result is a classic prisoner's dilemma. People have to pay for their own gas, but they don't have to breathe their own exhaust. The contribution that any one automobile makes to the overall concentrations of airborne lead is minuscule. While switching to unleaded gasoline costs you money, it does almost nothing to improve the quality of the air that you or your children breathe. So when given the choice between leaded and unleaded gasoline, people consistently choose leaded, despite its environmental consequences. It's a classic free-rider strategy.

Of course, if there were a "complete" set of markets, people could charge you for the pollutants that you dump into their airspace or for the damage it does to their children. Then you wouldn't be able to free-ride. But this is impractical. Markets will therefore systematically fail to generate a socially optimal level of lead consumption. The more efficient route is simply for government to intervene and ban leaded fuel. This is precisely what most advanced industrial nations did in the 1970s and most developing nations have been slowly doing since.

The net effect of government regulation in this case is a clear-cut efficiency gain. If you ask people how much they would be willing to pay in order to protect their children from airborne lead emissions, the answer would probably be "a lot." In a hypothetical market in which people could exercise property rights over the air they breathe, people who wanted to burn leaded fuel would have to compensate all those affected (thus "internalizing" the negative externality). This would drive up the price of leaded gasoline quite significantly.

Let us say, for the sake of argument, that internalizing the relevant externality would drive the price of leaded gasoline up by ten cents per litre. This reflects the additional cost imposed on society of burning that type of fuel (and is not an unreasonable assumption, given how protective people can be about their children). Similarly, the extra three cents per litre for unleaded fuel reflects the cost to society of having to use more intensive refinement techniques. We can now calculate the efficiency gain realized from switching to unleaded—seven cents for every litre of gas consumed. Since Canadians buy about thirty-five billion litres of gasoline every year, this gives us annual savings in the range of $2.45 billion.

Unfortunately, we don't *actually* save $2.45 billion. When we eliminate atmospheric lead, it gives us a benefit that is worth $3.5 billion to us. But we don't get this in the form of money, we get it in the form of clean air. And so all the calculations are hypothetical. Because the "market" for air doesn't exist, we can only guess how much it is worth. Unfortunately, there is a market for gasoline, and so the $1.05 billion cost of additional refinement is quantifiable. This means that the regulation may *appear* to be costing us money, imposing a drag on the economy even when it isn't. It just happens to be imposing a drag on that *portion* of the economy that is organized through private markets.

We could remedy this by trying to create an "air" market. Then we would know exactly how much we gain by eliminating leaded gasoline. But what would be the point? The outcome that we want is simply cleaner air. The same gain is realized, regardless of whether this outcome is achieved through the market or through government regulation. If government regulation is cheaper and more effective, then there are strong reasons for favouring a regulatory solution.

And there is good evidence to suggest that government regulation of lead emissions is an almost unparalleled success. In the United States, lead emissions dropped from 147 million tonnes in 1975 to 8.6 million in 1986. Concentrations of lead in the atmosphere dropped by 85 per cent during the same period. In Canada, ambient lead concentrations dropped by an even more impressive 97 per cent. The result has been a huge improvement in the welfare of Canadians at negligible social cost.

You don't hear many people singing the praises of government regulation these days, and I am certainly not claiming that it is always beneficial. The claim is simply that in many instances government is able to deliver goods and services more efficiently than the private sector. Clean air is just an example.

Inefficiencies are the result of collective action problems. Collective action problems result whenever people have an incentive to free-ride. Markets eliminate certain free-rider problems by allowing individuals to charge each other for goods and services that they provide. Sometimes markets are too cumbersome, and so people find it in their interest to create corporations, which then provide certain goods "for free" to their members. But corporations have very limited powers. Ultimately, a corporation is a voluntary organization. When push comes to shove, people can just quit their jobs or declare bankruptcy. So corporations are still vulnerable to free-riders.

In order to eliminate the really persistent free-rider problems, what we need is an organization with powers of compulsion over all members of society and whose membership is not voluntary. This is the state. (In fact, many social scientists simply define the state as the agency that exercises a monopoly on the use of force in a particular territory.) Thus the state is an important economic actor, because it is the only social institution whose decisions carry the weight of law.

Consider how we resolve the most basic of free-rider strategies—theft. The incentives to steal are clear. Why grow your own tomatoes when you can sneak into your neighbour's yard at night and steal hers? But then why should your neighbour plant tomatoes if she knows that they will all be stolen? Economic activity can't even begin until people find a way to eliminate this sort of free-rider strategy.

The most straightforward solution is to have everyone defend his own property. You could sit on your back porch all night with a shotgun, looking out for tomato rustlers. Most people, however, prefer to avoid violent confrontations. Not only that, but it's impossible to keep an eye on all your goods, all of the time. Eventually you have to sleep.

One way to solve this problem is to pay someone to keep an eye on your goods. But most of the time, this just isn't worthwhile. Some very rich people have enough property to warrant hiring private security guards, but most of us do not.

So it often makes sense to band together and purchase security services as a group. Instead of having a full-time security guard watching over your tomato patch, you could get together with your neighbours and pay a security guard to walk up and down the back lane, keeping an eye on everyone's yards.

The problem with this arrangement is that it creates a new free-rider incentive. The sight of a security guard usually scares away potential thieves, so your neighbours will benefit from having the guard on patrol, regardless of whether they have contributed anything to paying his salary. And because you can't exercise property rights over the benefits that your guard contributes to the neighbourhood, you can't force your neighbours to pay. So unless you live in a very high-trust community, the plan won't work. Private markets alone will fail to provide adequate levels of security.

One way to respond to this market failure is to form a corporation. Instead of having individuals own their own houses, you can create a large corporation that owns them all. The corporation can then hire a security guard, and anyone who wants to live on company property can be forced to contribute to paying the guard's salary. Of course, this is not a hypothetical example. It is more or less how a condominium association works. If you want to live in a condominium project, you have to pay "condo fees," which are then used to provide a range of shared goods, such as a security guard at the front desk, maintenance and repairs to the elevator, trash removal, and so on.

The reason that the condo corporation is able to eliminate the free-riders while a neighbourhood association is not is that the corporation has the power to force people to pay for benefits they receive. The condo solution has a number of disadvantages, however. It only works for certain types of property configurations, such as high-rise buildings or gated communities, in which entry and exit points are easily controlled. It also means that neighbours have a lot more power to meddle in your affairs. Condo corporations, for example, often bar people from keeping dogs. Some even enforce a ban on children. So this is obviously not the solution for everyone.

If a corporation is not feasible, the obvious alternative is government. In the same way that the corporation can say, "If you want to live here, you must pay condo fees," the state can say, "If you want to live here, you must pay taxes." It can then turn around and use these taxes to provide goods and services that private markets fail to provide.

This is just what happens. The government collects money in the form of taxes, then uses it to hire security guards. These guards are assigned the task of protecting our property, among other things. They're known as the police. And when they defend our borders, they're known as the military.

The important point is that when the state taxes us, then uses the money to hire police, it is achieving an efficiency gain. We want to have our property protected, and we're willing to pay for this protection. Unfortunately, because it's so easy to free-ride off protection services, we often try to get away with not paying. The state stops us from doing this, forcing us to pay for something that we are, in fact, willing to pay for. At the end of the day, everyone is happier.

Of course, the fact that we are forced to pay taxes rubs some people the wrong way. But this is inevitable whenever it is necessary to do something as a group. In the case of the condominium association, people have no choice but to pay for the security guard at the front desk. In the case of the state, people have no choice but to pay for the RCMP. In both cases, the freedom that is being restricted is nothing other than the freedom to free-ride. And that's a freedom we're all better off not having.

Economists sometimes distinguish between three types of goods: private goods, which can be purchased by *individuals* through the market; club goods, which can only be purchased by a *group* through some organization like a corporation; and public goods, which can only be purchased by whole *communities* through the state. This is a very helpful terminological distinction, but it should not be allowed to obscure one very important point. As the example of security guards shows, in many cases the good that is purchased is *identical*; it's just that the way it is purchased differs. Rich people pay their security guards personally. Condo owners pay fees to a condo association, which then pays security guards. Citizens pay taxes to the state, which then pays the police. Exactly the same economic transaction is taking place, but it is organized in a different way.

So if you ask whether security should be a private good, a club good, or a public good, the answer will be—it depends. Sometimes it is more efficient to deliver security services through the market; sometimes it will be more efficient to deliver them through the state. From the standpoint of society, the goal should be to choose the delivery system that works best in each case.

If you believe what I just told you, then you now believe that taxation and government spending can improve the efficiency of the economy. You'll also think it is pretty obvious that taxation can promote efficiency. So why does it sound so strange to say it? And why do so many people treat taxation as though it were a drag on the economy?

The answer has to do with the way we measure economic output. When we talk about the amount of wealth in our society, we refer to the GDP. But the GDP is not a measure of all the goods and services that we consume, the things that go to make up our quality of life. It is essentially a measure of the *private goods* that are produced and consumed. It does not measure the full value of club goods or public goods.

In order to calculate the GDP, statisticians start by counting up all the goods and services that are produced in the economy in a given year—the number of hamburgers served, new homes built, running shoes manufactured, and so on. With just these data, however, it's impossible to form a picture of what's going on in the economy. If the number of hamburgers served went down, but the number of running shoes produced went up, it's hard to know whether this is an improvement. In order to figure this out, we need some way to compare the two. The obvious way to do this is through the price. Find out how much a hamburger is worth relative to a running shoe, and then see whether the aggregate value of goods produced has declined or increased.

This works out swimmingly when prices are readily available. But as we have seen, prices are available only for private goods, not club goods or public goods. If I put my child in private daycare, the full value of these daycare services is added to the GDP. If the government provides free daycare services to its citizens, these services are not counted at full value. And if I stay home and raise my own children, the value of these services is not counted at all.

The problem arises because only private transactions generate prices, and without prices it's very hard to determine the value of goods and services. Of course, it would be ridiculous to completely ignore services provided by government. As a result, statisticians use the cost of government services in order to "guestimate" their contribution to the GDP. But this has a number of perverse consequences.

The first problem is that genuine costs to society often get measured as benefits. For example, governments in Canada employ approximately 63,500 police officers. The reason we hire them is that we want security. But we have no idea what the security these officers provide is worth, so we simply add the cost of providing it to the GDP. This can be very misleading. The United States employs well over a million police officers, more than twice as many per capita as in Canada. But the amount of "security" they produce is much lower—43 per cent of Americans say they feel unsafe walking alone, compared to only 27 per cent of Canadians. Thus Canadian police, with only half the number of their American counterparts, provide a much higher level of customer satisfaction. As Canadians, we spend less and yet get more for our money. But you would never know it from looking at the GDP, since the cost of all the surplus officers in the United States shows up as part of that nation's wealth.

It gets worse. Using cost to measure government output has the effect of making efficiency gains in the public sector show up as declining productivity. For instance, most municipalities in Canada supply water to the homes of all their citizens. No one really knows how much this water is worth, because there is no market price. As a result, the contribution is calculated by taking the amount of money that municipalities *spend* on water services and adding that to the GDP. If municipalities install new machinery in their water-processing facilities, which increases the productivity of their workers, they may not need as many employees as before. But if they reduce their staff, this will have a negative impact on the GDP and will therefore show up as a *decrease* in productivity. The reason is that in the public sector GDP does not measure the value of the water produced; it measures the cost of producing it. Thus a more efficient delivery of public services may look like a decline in productivity, but this is entirely an artifact of the way that economic growth is measured.

Because GDP measures the full value of private goods, the growth that it measures can often be illusory. Suppose that as a result of government cutbacks, the integrity of the public water supply is compromised. Citizens may become scared to drink the tap water and, as a result, begin to buy bottled water. This is, of course, a massively inefficient way to deliver water and for a society as a whole a total waste of time and energy. Think of all the resources used—the plastic bottles, the truck that delivers them, the guy who carries them to the door—and compare that to the ease and simplicity of plumbing. But rather than showing up as a decrease in efficiency, a shift towards bottled water will actually tend to boost the GDP. All this wasteful activity will be tallied up and counted as though it were wealth.

Economists are usually quite clear about this. The GDP does not measure the size of the economy; it measures only the value of goods that are exchanged *through the market*. (This is why, for example, developing nations sometimes post astronomical rates of growth. It is not that they are becoming that much wealthier, it is that people are starting to use the market to coordinate transactions. If instead of getting your brother-in-law to fix your fence in return for babysitting his kids one day, you go out and hire someone to fix it, then you are now contributing to the GDP. The fence gets fixed either way, but the value of the repairs gets added to the GDP only when the transaction is organized through the market.)

This is incredibly important. The GDP does not measure actual wealth. It measures the extent to which we use markets to organize the production and distribution of wealth. As a result, it is positively biased against other forms of economic organization. If we take exactly the same economic activities and organize them using some non-market mechanism, then this may appear as a decline in wealth, even if overall output levels are unchanged—or even if they increase.

Economists understand that the GDP provides at best a rough guide to what is going on, and freely acknowledge that it is biased against the public sector. In popular discussion, unfortunately, all these distinctions are lost. To take just one example, the fact that per capita GDP in the United States is higher than it is in Canada does not mean that people in the United States are necessarily richer. It may simply reflect the American preference for using markets instead of government to organize their economic activities.

In the 1980s, neoconservative governments were elected in both Canada and the United States, with a commitment to reducing the size of government. The overall ideology was summarized quite neatly by Ronald Reagan when he announced that "government is the problem, not the solution." But by the end of the decade, this neoconservative revolution was widely acknowledged to have been a failure, even on its own terms. Not only did these administrations fail to halt the growth of the state, but they actually presided over significant increases in the overall size of government.

One way of ascertaining the relative size of the state is to express government expenditure as a percentage of GDP. During the 1980s, Canadian government spending increased from 38.8 to 46 per cent of

GDP. During the same period, American government expenditures increased somewhat more modestly, but still increased—from 31.4 to 32.8 per cent.

Why is this? Why did government spending mushroom during the Mulroney years? And why does the right in Canada continue to pledge support for big-ticket items such as the public health care system? Why is the American right committed to keeping "hands off" Social Security? It is certainly not because their hearts bleed for the plight of the poor, the elderly, and the disadvantaged.

The simple reason is that government is quite efficient when it comes to delivering these services. Efficiency gains are win-win transformations, and as a result, they tend to be extremely popular. After all, when everyone benefits, what's not to like? This is ultimately the reason that neoconservatives didn't touch any of the major government social programs. People like these programs, and they tend to vote against politicians who tamper with them.

Many of these government programs are obviously just delivery mechanisms for public goods. Government provides basic infrastructure, such as highways, parks, and sewers, because any attempt to deliver these goods through private markets will be subject to insuperable free-rider problems. The same can be said for services like pest control and vaccination. Similarly, because markets for information are so prone to failure, government spends considerable resources collecting and disseminating information. Agencies such as Statistics Canada do so directly, while granting agencies such as the National Sciences and Engineering Research Council do so by funding research.

In many more cases, the "public goods" character of government services can be difficult to discern. Providing welfare payments to the poor, for example, is often regarded as a straightforward redistribution of wealth. But from another perspective, it is a way of delivering a range of public goods.

Most people are sensitive to the suffering of others. Most of us would rather not live in a society that allows the disadvantaged or unfortunate to starve or freeze to death. As a matter of pure individual preference, most people would rather not have to pass through a gauntlet of beggars and lunatics on the way to work. We would rather that someone take care of them. Furthermore, when people are homeless and starving, they have absolutely no stake in the existing social order. This gives them very little incentive to respect either the property rights or the personal integrity of others. Thus a small investment in welfare to eliminate the most abject states of poverty generates benefits for everyone in the society.

A former teacher of mine from Chicago once told me that he found it quite refreshing to visit Toronto. One of the major attractions of the city, he said, was that he could walk around without being "assaulted by the spectacle of human degradation." Anyone who has lived in an American city knows what he's talking about. Relief for the poor does a lot to improve the quality of the urban environment. When I was living in Chicago, I once passed a homeless man on my way to school. It was the middle of winter, and he had no shoes. It made me feel ill.

In some people, this feeling is strong enough that they are willing to donate some of their own money to charity in order to help relieve such suffering. Unfortunately, the fact that this preference is felt so strongly in some quarters gives others an opportunity to free-ride. People who don't care much about other people can get away with not donating anything to charity. They still get all the benefits that poor relief generates—in terms of improved environment and security—yet pay none of the costs. Thus charity leads to the exploitation of the moral by the immoral.

Because charitable donation is subject to this free-rider problem, a voluntary payment scheme will tend to generate inefficient levels of poor relief. (This is why even charitable donation is tax-subsidized.) A situation can arise in which everyone would prefer that the poor be better taken care of, yet no one actually does it. A simple solution is for government to make some minimal contribution mandatory—through taxation and welfare payments. Individuals are then free to make additional contributions above the minimum, if they feel so inclined. The general principle is that since everyone benefits from poor relief, everyone should pay.

Thus welfare, despite being redistributive on the surface, is simply one of the public goods provided by government. This is why conservatives in Canada, who are generally opposed to the principle of redistribution, have restricted themselves to just cutting welfare payments. They have not eliminated the programs entirely, because they aren't prepared to sacrifice the efficiency gains that these programs generate.

The "public goods" character of many other government programs is even more difficult to detect. We think of the social safety net as a set of government programs designed to protect the most vulnerable members of society—the sick and injured, the elderly, the unemployed. It is sometimes thought that government provision of these benefits is motivated by a desire to care for the less fortunate.

But it is not just the social safety net that protects the less fortunate. Every insurance scheme exists to protect the unfortunate. Car insurance protects those who are unlucky enough to get into car accidents the same way that government health insurance protects those who are unlucky enough to get sick. In both cases, all the participants in the plan are enjoying the benefits that come from risk-sharing. The only difference is that in the first case the risk-sharing is organized through the market, while in the second case it is organized by government.

Thus the social safety net is not fundamentally different from any other type of insurance. What makes it special is not the type of service that is provided, but the way that the provision of the service is organized. The social safety net is a set of insurance products that are provided by government. The reason that they are delivered through the public sector is exactly the same as the reason that highways and sewers are delivered through the public sector—because of an underlying market failure.

Take the Canada Pension Plan. Many people don't realize it, but a defined benefit pension plan is essentially an insurance product. Contributing to a pension plan is a way of purchasing insurance against not dying. (Thus it is the exact opposite of life insurance.) Saving for retirement is risky. If you knew exactly when you would die, then you would know exactly how much money to save. But since people generally don't know this, they may run out of retirement funds before they die.

But while individuals are uncertain when they will die, we are able to predict with great certainty what *portion* of a large group will die at what age. This makes it easy to predict how much retirement savings a group of individuals will need. So people can benefit from pooling their savings together and creating a retirement fund. Such a fund will then offer them a guaranteed payout during each year of retirement, no matter how long they live. The "losers" under any such arrangement will be those who pay premiums but die young, while the "winners" will be those who live for a long time—they will take out more than they put in.

The problem with private pension funds is that they are subject to adverse selection. Suppose (to simplify enormously) a pension fund starts up that offers to pay out $20,000 a year after the age of sixty-five. Since the average life expectancy in Canada is seventy-six for men and eighty-one for women, this plan will have an expected payout of $220,000 for men, and $320,000 for women. Assuming that the premium level is chosen so that the plan will exactly break even, this means that every man who joins the pool gets an expected loss of $50,000, while every woman can expect to gain $50,000. As a result, if a private company offered a pension scheme of this type to individuals, only women would sign up for it (and the fund would go bankrupt).

In this example, the adverse selection problem can be handled by underwriting. It's easy to tell whether someone is male or female, so the insurance company can respond by simply charging women higher premiums than men. (In the same way that men have to pay more for car insurance than women, because they are more likely to crash their cars, women would have to pay more for pensions than men, because they are more likely to live longer.) But while this may solve the particular problem, in many more cases clients will have information about their life expectancy that they are able to conceal from the insurance company (for example, whether or not the family has a history of cancer). As a result, companies may not be able to control adverse selection through underwriting alone and so may refuse to sell certain types of insurance products, even though in principle there is a market for them.

The adverse selection problem arises because in a private insurance market customers self-select into groups, choosing insurance products in a way that is highly disadvantageous to the insurance companies. Thus private markets will fail to provide certain types of insurance products, even though people want them and are willing to pay for them. Companies will refuse to sell to them until such time as they find some way to weed out the bad risks.

Government can easily solve this problem by simply eliminating consumer choice. Since self-selection is what creates the problem, if everyone is forced to deal with one insurer, then the problem disappears. Government can collect premiums from everyone (in the form of taxes or CPP contributions) and then provide more or less the same insurance product to all citizens (or create a Crown corporation to do the same). This is just how government pension plans work.

Despite this fact, pension plans are often classified as redistribution schemes rather than public goods. This is a misperception. Naturally, pension plans do result in a transfer of wealth. (Although it is often said that pensions redistribute wealth from the young to the old, this is not true. They redistribute from those who die young to those who die old.) In any case, this is no different from car insurance, which redistributes money from those who don't have car accidents to those who do.

Of course, there are limitations to the efficiency gains that can be achieved through government plans of this type. When government creates a universal insurance scheme, it gives some agency a monopoly over the provision of a particular service. This erodes the power of consumers, who can no longer threaten to take their business elsewhere. As a result, the incentive to maintain a reasonable level of customer service is significantly eroded. Creating an efficient organization in the public sector is a more sophisticated managerial task than it is in the private sector. But even if government services are poorly delivered, when the service that they provide is needed, and when this service is one that private markets would not otherwise have provided, the government will still generate an efficiency gain. It is just that this gain will not be as large as it might have been under better management.

Naturally, the efficiency gains associated with the public pension system are not the only reason that programs of this sort are implemented. In the case of pensions, one of the major motivations was to address the problem of poverty among the elderly. The efficiency gains are, however, the reason that the public pension system survives, even thrives, under conservative administrations, which are not particularly concerned about these other goals.

The single most important insurance service offered by the Canadian government is health insurance. Unlike many European states, where the government actually delivers health care directly to its citizens, in Canada the government's role is focused on delivery of insurance. The Canadian system is not true socialized medicine, since most of the actual health services are provided through the private sector. What distinguishes the Canadian system is that the government exercises a monopoly in the insurance market.

When you walk into the doctor's office for a checkup, chances are you're walking into a private business, just as when you take your car to the body shop. The difference is that when you have a car accident and the body shop bills your insurance for the repairs, they send the bill to a private insurance company. In the case of the doctor, the bill goes to the provincial government, which is your insurance company. This is referred to among health care cognoscenti as a single-payer system.

One of the major motivations for implementing a single-payer system is—no surprise here—adverse selection in the health insurance sector. Suppose you're a young woman planning to have a baby. In a completely private health care system, you could just walk in to the hospital with your Visa card (although it had better be a *platinum* Visa card) on the day of the delivery. But that would be very expensive. It makes much more sense to go out and buy health insurance before you get pregnant.

Of course, this makes you a very bad risk. The only reason you are signing up for the insurance is that you think your medical bills are going to be higher than your premiums. This makes you precisely the sort of customer that the insurance company does *not* want to have. So before accepting you as a client, they will want to have you checked out. You will undergo a physical exam, and they will ask you a few questions about your life. But are you going to volunteer the information that you plan to get pregnant? Of course not. And unless you do volunteer it, the company has no way of knowing. This makes you the perfect nightmare customer. You are going to cost them money—maybe a lot of money—and they have no way of knowing it.

This example is not farfetched. When I was studying in the United States, students in my class made a lot of strategic decisions regarding their health care. Since the market for philosophers is not exactly booming, people had fairly well-grounded concerns about unemployment after graduation. In the United States this is more of a big deal, because no job equals no health insurance. So anyone needing a major medical procedure was well advised to have it done before getting tossed out into the job market.

This is not a joke. Medical procedures can be very expensive. A friend of mine had a baby in her final year of graduate school. The child was born with a heart defect, which required immediate surgery. When all the dust settled, she was presented with a bill for more than US$200,000. No problem, she thought, and called up the same insurance company that had earlier been so gracious as to pay for my cosmetic surgery. The insurance company, however, drew her attention to some fine print, which specified that hospital procedures were covered up to a maximum of US$150,000. That's a pretty generous figure, but it still left my friend about US$50,000 short. Since both she and her husband were still graduate students, earning graduate student salaries, they managed to convince the state of Illinois that they were destitute. And so the government chipped in an extra US$40,000. This left them only US$10,000 short.

Of course, starting out one's career an additional $10,000 in the hole is not auspicious, especially when you have a degree in philosophy. But look at it from the perspective of the insurance company. Here it's an even bigger disaster. The limited payment of $150,000 is equivalent to the premiums paid by more than two hundred students. You can't afford to have too many bills of this size come in before the company starts losing serious money.

So if you're an insurance company, what do you do? If you want to stay in business, you have to start weeding out the bad risks. You might want to stop selling insurance to young women who are likely to get pregnant. ("Recently married? Just bought your first home? Okay, lady, you're outta here. . . .") One group that you will definitely want to exclude is old people. More than two-thirds of the health care resources that a person uses over his or her lifetime are consumed in the last five years of life. Anyone over the age of sixty-five is, to put it mildly, much more likely to be in the last five years of life than a person in his twenties. So old people are definitely a bad risk. You will also want to start excluding coverage for pre-existing conditions, so that people don't just sign up *after* they get diagnosed with diabetes.

The point is that in order to weed out the bad risks, you will have to stop selling insurance to entire categories of people—such as young women of childbearing age. This is because you have no way of telling whether they intend to have children or not. But as a result, a lot of women who *don't* plan to have kids will be unable to buy health insurance, even though many insurance companies should, in principle, be willing to sell it to them. This is the efficiency loss created by adverse selection.

Thus in a free market, perfectly healthy people may find themselves unable to buy health insurance, even if they have the resources to pay for it. This is one reason why no health care market is perfectly free. Even in the United States, where less than 40 per cent of the population has private medical insurance, much of it is purchased in the form of group plans. People with private health insurance usually receive it as an employment benefit. This is because corporations are more successful at purchasing insurance than individuals, because buying as a group minimizes adverse selection, therefore making insurance companies more willing to sell. (Although there are still cases of insurers dropping whole companies when one worker is diagnosed with an especially expensive ailment.)

Of course, an even easier way to eliminate adverse selection is to eliminate selection. By creating one insurance company and forcing everyone to deal with that insurer, the whole problem is instantly resolved. Hence the rationale for a "single-payer" health insurance system. "Universal" health care is attractive on a number of different levels, but one of the primary attractions is that universality eliminates consumer choice.

The single-payer system has a number of other fringe benefits. It massively reduces bureaucratic overhead. An American hospital has to keep track of every little detail of every patient's care so that the appropriate insurance company can be billed. In the end, each patient receives an itemized bill that includes such items as bandages, meals, and even orderly services, such as being pushed down the hall in a wheelchair.

After my surgery in Chicago, I noticed on my bill that I had been charged something like eight dollars for a Tylenol. Since the retail price of a single Tylenol pill is less than ten cents, administrative overhead presumably made up the balance of the expense. In Canada, the same agency pays for everyone's care, so there is no need to keep track of exactly who gets what. Hospitals can just buy Tylenol by the truckload and hand it out to whoever needs it. There's no need to *pay* someone to keep track of where all these pills go.

The extra bureaucracy can be very expensive. In 1987, the United States spent ninety-five dollars per capita on insurance overhead alone, whereas Canada spent only eighteen dollars. The amount of money being wasted here is significant. To dramatize this, consider the fact that the United States spent a whopping thirty-six dollars per capita on health research, versus only thirteen dollars per capita in Canada. Nevertheless, Americans managed to spend more than twice as much maintaining *superfluous* private-sector health bureaucracy as they did on research.

Another benefit of the single-payer system is that it reduces moral hazard—the temptation to rack up enormous charges because the insurance company is paying. These moral hazard problems are the primary motivation for the formation of HMOs, which are so unpopular with the American public. In Canada, much of the pressure towards HMO arrangements is mitigated because government is more effective than the market in controlling moral hazard. While Canadian doctors are still paid on a "fee-for-service" basis and so have a financial incentive to charge too much, the government is able to exercise far more effective supervision than private insurers.

Every year, each provincial government sits down with doctors and negotiates a schedule of fees. If doctors want to charge more for a procedure, they need to justify this demand. They can't just hand over a bill and expect payment. As a result, doctors in Canada can't get away with charging outrageous fees. The difference this creates can be dramatic. Physicians' fees in the United States are approximately 2.5 times higher than in Canada. To take one example, a doctor in Canada receives approximately $150 for performing a colonoscopy. The American government pays $475 for the same procedure. Private insurance plans in the United States pay, on average, $885.

As someone who is married to a surgeon, let me assure you that doctors in Canada have no trouble making ends meet. It takes a skilled practitioner about twenty minutes to do a colonoscopy. On a good day, my wife says she can easily do eight of them (gross revenue of $1,200), and still have time for other work. In the United States, she would bill more than $7,000 for the same procedures. Does this reflect a greater demand for colonoscopies in the United States? No. Doctors simply charge more. They do it because they can.

To see how perverse this is, recall that the whole function of markets is to ration scarce goods. The reason that we have to *pay* for things is precisely to stop us from using too much of them. But this arrangement only generates efficient levels of consumption if the prices are set at the right level. The only thing that keeps prices at the right level is competition. This means that in an improperly structured market, like the market for health care, prices will be all out of whack. As a result, soci-ety will wind up spending the "wrong" amount of money on health care—neglecting other priorities.

The United States spends close to 15 per cent of its GDP on health care. No other country in the world, Canada included, spends more than 10 per cent. But Canadians enjoy better overall health—longer life expectancy, lower infant mortality, and so on. It is tempting to think that Americans *must* be getting better care because they are spending so much more on it. The hard truth is that they are not. They are just wasting money: paying for unnecessary bureaucracy, paying doc-tors too much, paying for equipment that sits around unused, and pay-ing for treatments that they don't really need. This is all a consequence of market failure.

When markets fail so dramatically, government can often step in and do the job more efficiently.

Ever since the budget deficit was eliminated, the right in Canada has been harping about taxes. The big issue lately has been brain drain. The concern is that the best and brightest are all packing up and moving to the United States in order to take advantage of lower taxes. Despite Statistics Canada data showing that the drain is more like a trickle, the Business Council on National Issues issued an alarmist report calling for a steep reduction in Canadian taxation levels (mentioning, in particu-lar, the deleterious impact these taxes have on "senior executives and other high income earners").

Meanwhile, on the other side of the globe, business leaders in Hong Kong are also worried about brain drain. Companies there suf-fer from high turnover and complain about the difficulty in retaining their best employees. But the problem is quite different. In order to staunch the flow of talent, business leaders in Hong Kong want the government to take a more active role in the economy. In particular, the Hong Kong General Chamber of Commerce has issued an appeal for new anti-pollution initiatives.

Why? Because in Hong Kong, the most important problems involve the low level of public services. The air is polluted, the harbour is a mess, the city is dirty, and the roads are congested. People make lots of money, but they hate the city. They leave because the quality of the urban environment is appalling. In other words, they leave because the government does not supply an adequate level of public goods. The best way to redress this is to increase taxes and improve the level of public service.

There is a temptation to talk about taxation as if it were just a necessary evil, one to be minimized whenever possible. This is wrong. There is no absolute standard that dictates how high or low taxes should be. Taxation is just a mechanism through which we, as a community, purchase goods. Thus the level of taxation will reflect our preferences. The trick in setting taxation levels is simply to balance the supply of public and private goods in a way that most adequately satisfies these preferences.

As a result, it makes very little sense to compare taxation levels in different countries without taking into account the fact that preferences may vary. If people in one country happen to want more goods of the type that governments can best supply, then they will choose to pay higher taxes. If they happen to want more goods of the type that private markets supply, then their taxes will be lower.

Thus comparisons between taxation levels in Canada and the United States are almost meaningless. Taxation rates are just an index of how much people spend on public goods versus how much they spend on private goods. Complaining about the fact that Americans have lower taxes is like looking at your neighbour's house and complaining that their mortgage payments are lower. If their house is a dump and yours is beautifully renovated, then it's no surprise that you pay more for the privilege of living there.

If anything, the difference in taxation rates between Canada and the United States has the effect of sorting the population. Americans who have a strong preference for public goods—such as security, poor relief, or health insurance—will move to Canada. Canadians with a stronger preference for private goods—such as cars, VCRs, or suburban houses—will move to the United States. There's nothing wrong with this; it's just a matter of individual taste.

Of course, it is a problem when Canadians move to the United States while they are young but then come back once they have kids or get sick. The issue is not Canadians who leave the country, but rather Canadians who come back once they start needing more public goods. These are the real free-riders. Instead of trying to lure them back, we should consider making it more *difficult* for them to return. If we wanted to reduce brain drain, one fast way to do it would be to force people who temporarily leave the country to pay back taxes on their foreign income in order to regain access to the health care system or to get their children enrolled in free public education. This would prevent people from using temporary relocation to the United States or any other low-tax state as a way to avoid paying for Canadian public services.

Here's an odd fact about taxes. When you ask people if they want to pay lower taxes, a majority will invariably say yes. But when you ask them about specific government programs, their attitudes are quite different. Ask people whether they would be willing to pay higher taxes in return for an increase in education spending, and a majority will say yes. Ask them if they would be willing to pay higher taxes in return for an increase in health care spending, and a majority will also say yes.

This schizoid attitude towards taxes prevails in Canada and the United States. But how can people both support and oppose tax increases? One explanation is that they are "cynical about government" and so don't actually expect the money to go to these programs. They expect that it will be wasted. There may be some truth to this. A more plausible explanation is simply that a lot of them are expecting to free-ride. If you ask people, in the abstract, whether they want their taxes cut, they will say yes. This is because they don't imagine the cuts in government service that will accompany these cuts. They are, in effect, hoping that someone else's tax money will be used to support the programs that they benefit from. What they are hoping for amounts to a free lunch. And if you ask people whether they want a free lunch, they will say yes—even if some know, in their heart of hearts, that there is no such thing.

This explanation sheds some light on the otherwise puzzling fact that support for tax cuts is sometimes inversely related to income. A study conducted in Ontario during the Harris tax-cut frenzy showed that support for tax cuts was highest among people earning less than $30,000. This is kind of absurd—bordering on the pathetic—because once the Child Tax Benefit is factored in, most families in Canada earning less than $30,000 wind up paying no income tax.

So tax cuts in Ontario, even though they benefited the rich disproportionately, enjoyed greater support among the poor. In Canada, almost 70 per cent of the money collected through the income tax system comes from the richest 30 per cent of the population. This means that, unless you happen to belong to this group, you are getting a good deal out of the tax system. Someone else is subsidizing the schools your kids go to, the roads you drive on, the water you drink, and the heart bypass you will someday need. So why would anyone in the middle class want taxes reduced? It's like cutting off your nose to spite your face.

It is tempting to speculate that the correlation between education and income level has something to do with these preferences. But there are other factors at play. One of the key forces driving the growth of the state is increased sensitivity to risk. There are lots of risks that we can avoid, so long as we are willing to pay. This means that as people's disposable income rises, the amount they are willing to invest in risk avoidance increases as well. Most people, for instance, are willing to eat regular supermarket vegetables, despite the slight chance of getting sick from the pesticides or preservatives. It's possible to avoid these risks by purchasing organic produce, but this comes at a price. Organic vegetables cost two or three times more. This is enough to deter most people, except those who are either quite wealthy or extremely risk-averse. But as the overall level of wealth in the society increases, it is natural that the demand for organic produce will increase as well.

The most common way to reduce risks, however, is through insur-ance. And since insurance markets are so prone to failure, the demand for risk reduction usually translates into a demand for government intervention. Similarly, once people have all the material goods that they need, they start to focus their attention on more "immaterial" goods. Since markets are notoriously bad at delivering such goods, it again translates into increased demands on government.

But because increased affluence often translates into new demands on government, it means that people who are not quite as affluent have much less of a stake in the success of government initiatives. People who are struggling just to put food on the table don't really care that much about these sorts of marginal risks. This is why many Third World countries still tolerate widespread use of asbestos, DDT, leaded gasoline, and other clearly dangerous substances.

Thus it is plausible to think that rich people have a stronger prefer-ence for public goods than poor people. This would explain why the state plays such a large role in the economies of developed nations, and also why taxes tend to be as unpopular among the poor as among the wealthy (despite the fact that their tax *burden* is so much lighter).

Some people think that government is inherently inefficient. Certainly it will always be inefficient when compared to ideal markets. But when compared to real markets, it often turns out to be more efficient.

States, like corporations, are giant bureaucracies. They get things done by assigning people tasks and then holding them accountable for the proper execution of the job. This is the oldest form of economic organization, and it still has enormous virtues. Markets are really nice when they work. But sometimes it is just not possible to design a mar-ket that works right. Often this is because it's impossible to keep a competition going (e.g., with natural monopolies), or because it's impossible to enforce the rules (e.g., when there are significant exter-nalities). When a market isn't going to work right, a bureaucracy can often do a better job.

Bureaucracy is never popular. But people tend to be partial in their condemnation. The left has no complaints about big government but has big problems with multinational corporations. The right loves the big companies but lives in constant fear of government. Of course, there are problems with both "big government" and "big business," but there are also very good reasons we have big companies and a big state. And the reason is exactly the same—both these institutions are more efficient at satisfying certain needs that we have, as consumers and as citizens.

The most important point is that all these institutions are just alternative delivery mechanisms for goods and services that we want. There is no hard-and-fast distinction between private goods and public goods. Much of it depends upon the current state of technology, communications, and the law. For example, highways are a traditional public good. The reason for this is fairly simple. Charging people for use of a road is prohibitively inconvenient. It used to be that the only way to charge people was to set up tolls. This creates huge traffic jams and incredible annoyances for drivers. So it's much easier just to levy a tax on vehicles or gasoline and use that to supply "free" roads for everyone.

This has had a number of perverse consequences. Public infrastructure is one of the major factors driving urban sprawl. The lower the population density, the more it costs per capita to supply people with roads, sewage, water, and so on. But because these goods have traditionally been provided "free" to all taxpayers, there is no disincentive against building very low-density housing developments, even though this imposes very high costs on society.

The development of technology, however, has made it much easier to charge people for their use of infrastructure. Instead of installing toll booths, people can be charged for access to roads through transponders and electronic billing. This means that private roads are now much more feasible than before (although maintaining competition is still a problem, and so there are good reasons for wanting either strict regulation or Crown ownership).

Charging people tolls for use of roads has a number of attractive consequences. It means that people who live in the suburbs will have to pay something much closer to the true cost that their lifestyle imposes upon society. It also eliminates one of the major disadvantages that public-transit users have faced (since people who drive cars often don't pay for infrastructure, whereas transit users do).

The case for toll roads is in fact identical to the case for water meters. In the same way that charging people for the water they use encourages conservation, charging people for their use of roads promotes moderation in the use of private vehicles.

In both cases, we have witnessed a change over time in the technologies that are available for creating markets. When such changes occur, it may become possible to deliver goods through the market that were once best delivered by government. But this cuts both ways. Changes in technology can also undermine markets, creating new opportunities for government to intervene and improve the overall efficiency of the economy. The only way to take advantage of these changes is to maintain a healthy pragmatism about the role of the private and public sectors, and a willingness to reassign roles in the face of change.

Part III. Challenges

One of the great merits of increasing efficiency is that it allows us to defer a lot of social conflict. This is why a growing economy is the best guarantee of political stability. As long as everyone is getting more, they tend not to worry so much about exactly how much they are getting relative to everyone else. It's only when the growth stops that trouble begins. Without growth, one person's gain is another's loss. This encourages people to cast a much more serious eye on their neighbours' possessions.

How do we resolve this problem? We don't really. We just scramble about trying to get the growth going again so that we won't have to deal with the problem.

But can we keep doing this forever? Many environmentalists say we cannot. The "limits to growth" movement argues that unlimited growth is unsustainable—eventually we will exhaust our resources. This means that we will have to get used to living in a zero-growth economy. But once this happens, a lot of problems that we have been trying to avoid will reassert themselves. In particular, the question of social inequality will become increasingly pressing.

The "limits to growth" issue is closely tied to the future of the efficient society. Are there limits to how efficient we can become? Many people think the answer to this question is yes. In the same way that increased economic growth puts strain on the natural environment, increased efficiency seems to place enormous demands upon *people*. The pressure to do everything more economically leads to constant acceleration in the pace of life, both at work and at home. The saturation of our environment with media and advertising threatens to overwhelm our ability to think critically about our world. And social inequality—that persistent scourge of human history—appears to be making a comeback.

All these problems represent fundamental challenges to the future of the efficient society. Unless we can respond effectively, our civilization will be nothing but another dead end, a mere curiosity to be recorded in the great book of human social experimentation. Efficiency has been very good to us so far. But how long can we keep riding the wave?

Inequality

St. Matthew had a number of good lines. My favourite is his somewhat infamous principle of justice: "To everyone who has will be given, and he will have abundance, but from him who has not, even that which he has will be taken away. Throw out the unprofitable servant into the outer darkness, where there will be weeping and gnashing of teeth."

This passage occurs in the so-called "parable of the talents," in which Jesus appears to endorse a number of very dubious moral principles. It's hard to imagine the son of God saying, with a straight face, "You should have deposited my money with the bankers, and on my return I would have recovered my capital with interest." But according to Matthew, that's how the story goes.

In any case, many people feel that we live in a society governed by "justice according to St. Matthew." The rich get richer; the poor get poorer. And a lot of people are far less comfortable with this idea than Matthew was.

Much of this inequality seems to stem directly from our commitment to efficiency. According to popular wisdom, the best way to create wealth is to put resources into the hands of those who are best at creating wealth. One of the most reliable ways of determining who is best at creating wealth is to look at their track record. As a result, resources will tend to flow to those who are already wealthy (hence the old catch-22 of borrowing—the best way to get a loan approved is to convince the bank manager that you don't need one).

This raises serious doubts about the long-term viability of our society and our economic system. If economic growth can be achieved only by increasing the level of inequality, it seems inevitable that the have-nots will eventually become frustrated. There must come a point at which the distance between rich and poor will become so great that the poor will simply lose whatever stake they may have in the existing economic order and demand redistribution.

If this is true, then the overriding emphasis on efficiency that currently exists in our society is, at best, just a phase. Eventually, we will have to put emphasis on other values, like equality, because efficiency alone fails to generate a stable social order.

But is the fundamental premise correct? Must increases in efficiency always be tied to increased levels of inequality?

We hear a lot of talk about the "big tradeoff" between equality and efficiency. In its crudest formulation, the choice seems to be one between free-market capitalism, which is very efficient but generates appalling inequalities, and bureaucratic socialism, which promotes equality but at the expense of grotesque inefficiency. The modern welfare state is often viewed as a half-hearted compromise between these two options. The market generates the wealth, then the state gets in and does some redistributing. This state intervention supposedly imposes efficiency losses on the economy, but it also makes the distributive consequences less unpalatable.

This picture is, for the most part, shared by both the left and the right in Canada. The primary differences of opinion then coalesce around how big a tradeoff people are willing to accept. The left is willing to tolerate a lot of inefficiency in return for increased equality, and therefore wants an expanded role for the state. The right accuses the left of killing the goose that lays the golden eggs, and so demands deregulation of the economy and a rollback of the welfare state.

The problem with both views is that their underlying assumption is totally mistaken. Far from serving as a drag on the economy, the state makes a huge contribution to the efficiency of the economy. It does so not only indirectly, by providing the background conditions needed for a flourishing market economy, but also directly, as we have seen, by providing goods and services that are not available in the private sector. The state lays just as many golden eggs as the market.

This is significant because whenever the state is involved in providing goods directly to citizens—such as providing insurance products that private markets fail to provide—there is no particular reason to think that a trade-off between equality and efficiency must be made.

In fact, in the rarefied atmosphere of mathematical economics, it is quite normal to assume that efficiency and equality are completely independent of one another, and that there is no reason we cannot have both. One of the most celebrated theorems in welfare economics shows that there is no necessary trade-off between equality and efficiency. Furthermore, there is no reason, in principle, that a market economy cannot produce a perfectly equal division of wealth.

Of course, like so much of what economists have discovered, this is just the opposite of what common sense tells us. So it's worth taking a slightly closer look at the assumptions underlying this theorem.

The first thing to notice is that the concept of efficiency places no constraints at all on the level of inequality. In other words, an outrageously unequal division of wealth can be just as efficient as a scrupulously equal division of wealth.

To see why, consider the following. Suppose that the Parliament of Canada passes a new law that specifies that from this day forward all the property in the country will belong to one person. Let's say this person is me. The next day we all wake up. Very little has changed, except that I am now fabulously wealthy, and everyone else is totally poor. Naturally, this is great for me and bad for everyone else. But is this distribution inefficient? No. In fact, it is perfectly efficient.

In order to show that my having everything is inefficient, you would have to find some other distribution that makes one person happier without making anyone else unhappy. But since I own everything, any other distribution of wealth that you might propose will have to involve taking something away from *me* and giving it to someone *else*. This will make me unhappy. So there is no way that you can increase the efficiency of this arrangement.

Of course, the fact that I am the one who got everything is irrelevant to the efficiency of the arrangement. It could just as easily have all gone to someone else, in which case any proposed redistribution would have made that person unhappy and so would not have been efficient. The general point is that the principle of efficiency—taken by itself—is compatible with completely arbitrary distributions of wealth. If we took everything and divided it up so that everyone got exactly the same amount, then this would also be completely efficient—in order to make one person happier, we would have to take something away from someone else. So efficiency is compatible with both perfect equality and outrageous inequality.

The example used to illustrate this point may seem implausible, but that's precisely the point. It is very important to recognize that efficiency—in the strict sense—does not preclude these sorts of wild scenarios. It is, as we say in the business, a weak normative constraint. Because it ignores issues of distribution entirely, efficiency could never be the only criterion we use to decide how our social institutions should be organized.

It should also be noted that the examples given involve only static distributions. Nothing at all has been said about how these distributions would affect productivity and hence efficiency over time. Adding in these other variables creates a far more complicated picture. The point is simply that wanting a society that is both efficient and equal is not like wanting to have your cake and eat it too. There is no *a priori* conflict between the two principles; the problems are totally pragmatic.

To say that the problems are pragmatic is not to minimize them. Pragmatic problems can be very large problems indeed. And there are in fact very good reasons to be quite depressed about the levels of equality that we can feasibly hope to achieve. But again, this is due to the perversity of human nature, not to any problems with the ideal of efficiency.

One of the most influential Marxist scholars of the twentieth century is a Canadian by the name of Jerry Cohen. He was born in 1941 in Montreal, where his mother was an official in the Communist Party of Canada. He was, as they say, raised in red diapers. His early education was intensely political. In 1949, at the tender age of eight, he came home from school with an "A" in his "History of Class Struggle" class.

Nowadays, Cohen is, for all intents and purposes, no longer a Marxist. The change in his views was the culmination of a very long process. But the event that most seriously damaged his faith in Marxism was not the Khruschev revelations, or the killing fields of Cambodia, or the collapse of the Berlin Wall. What shook Cohen's faith in Marxism was the "Wilt Chamberlain argument."

It started only as a rumour back in the late 1960s. A young graduate student at Harvard named Robert Nozick was reported to have come up with the ultimate refutation of Marxism. Nobody had seen the actual text of it, but informal summaries spread like wildfire throughout the academy, largely by word of mouth. When Nozick finally did publish, in 1974, leftist scholars throughout the Western world went into full-scale damage control mode. But there was little that could be done. The Wilt Chamberlain argument proved irresistible.

What is this argument? How could it have such a powerful effect? And what does Marxism have to do with Wilt Chamberlain?

Nozick asks us to consider the following scenario: Imagine a society in which the extremes of poverty and wealth have been eliminated. Everyone lives a comfortable, middle-class existence and enjoys approximately the same amount of wealth. Suppose that in this society many people like to watch basketball, and so the skills of talented basketball players such as Wilt Chamberlain are in high demand. Now suppose that Wilt makes the following deal: he agrees to play only if a twenty-five-cent surcharge is added to the cost of tickets at home games, with all of the extra revenue going straight to him.

Here comes the punch line: "Let us suppose that in one season one million people attend his home games, and Wilt Chamberlain winds up with $250,000, a much larger sum than the average income and larger even than anyone else has. Is he entitled to this income? Is this new distribution unjust?"

Remember that this was the '70s, a time when it seemed quite outrageous for an athlete to earn as much as $250,000. (We could update the example by talking about Michael Jordan earning $33 million for his final season with the Bulls.) The point is that Chamberlain's salary completely disrupts the previously equal division of wealth. We now have one person who is very much richer than everyone else.

But it is very difficult to see anything wrong with this new distribution. Each of the fans who comes to a Chamberlain game voluntarily gives up twenty-five cents in order to see Wilt play. For them, it's a good deal. They are *willing* to pay a bit more in order to see a great player. Like all exchanges, it generates an efficiency gain. The fans are happier, and Chamberlain is happier. So what's not to like? Or more specifically— what harm is there in allowing this exchange to occur?

Here we see the tension between efficiency and equality in its starkest form. Chamberlain's arrangement leads to a violation of the principle of equality, but no one is actually harmed in the process. Everyone is better off—the difference is just that each of the fans is a little bit better off, while Chamberlain as an individual is a *lot* better off. But still, everyone is happier. So in order to maintain an equal division of wealth, one would have to prevent people from making even mutually advantageous exchanges. Or as Nozick put it, "Society would have to forbid capitalist acts among consenting adults."

Nozick's argument sparked a huge controversy, most of which is not worth getting into. Marxists were particularly vulnerable, because one of Marx's core assumptions was that workers were entitled to the full product of their labour (capitalism exploits workers by skimming off some portion of this product in the form of profit). According to these assumptions, Chamberlain is entitled to the full product of his own labour and so is entitled to whatever proceeds he can get from the door.

Some people tried to counter Nozick's argument by saying that Chamberlain was just lucky to be born with the right set of skills for basketball playing, and so he is not really entitled to charge extra for his performances. But this isn't much help. Whether or not he got lucky (and as we know from his biography, he got lucky a lot), the fact is that Chamberlain must still *choose* to play. If the ticket-surcharge arrangement is not implemented and so Chamberlain refuses to play, it is everyone's loss. The fans are unhappy and Chamberlain is unhappy. This is a Pyrrhic victory for the champions of equality.

The only alternative is for society to force Chamberlain to play. Many people think this sort of coercion is unacceptable. So as long as we are committed to the basic idea of a liberal society—that people should be left alone to do whatever they like so long as they don't harm anyone else—it is very difficult to prohibit exchanges like the one between Chamberlain and his fans. And as long as we are unwilling to prohibit such exchanges, there is often not much we can do to prevent extremely unequal divisions of wealth.

As a society, we often put efficiency ahead of fairness or equality. What the Wilt Chamberlain argument shows is that our reasons for doing this are not always bad. We are not just callow egoists. There are in fact serious moral considerations that weigh in on the side of efficiency.

Back in the 1970s, there was a board game that my brother and I loved called Land Grab. It taught us a lot more about life than the so-called *Game of Life*. The board was nothing but a map containing empty subdivisions. In the initial rounds, players could buy up unowned land for a relatively small sum. As the game progressed, they could build developments on their land, as well as auction off a portion of their holdings to other players. The goal was to use revenue from your developments to buy adjacent land, build larger developments, and so on.

The game was fun. But now imagine what it would be like trying to join this game *after* the initial land grab was over. Even though you would start out with some money, you wouldn't really have a fair chance. The people who got their fingers in the pie in the initial allocation would have a head start, and latecomers would never be able to catch up with them. The game would be no fun.

But this is exactly what life is like for the vast majority of people in our society. In this country, the "land grab" ended more than a hundred years ago. Some people got in on it, some didn't. The people who did get in, along with all their heirs, have a running head start in life. The people who got shut out, and all of their heirs, begin life at a disadvantage. They have their own labour to sell, and so they are not locked out entirely. But they are at a disadvantage.

What could possibly justify this? I'm inclined to say that *nothing* does. It's simply unfair. The problem is that it's very hard to do anything about it, because it's hard to redistribute wealth without creating inefficiencies. Sometimes these inefficiencies are so serious that we're all *better off* letting the inequalities stand.

This doesn't mean that we need to sit around helpless. But it does mean that when we try to achieve particular distributive goals, we need to be extremely careful about the mechanism we choose to use. For instance, one of the most obvious ways to "level the playing field" and give everyone a fair chance in life is to place restrictions on inheritance. One popular way of doing this is through estate taxes.

Unfortunately, restrictions on inheritance can have all sorts of perverse consequences. In order to give them any teeth, it is necessary to place significant limitations on gift-giving. Without such restrictions, there is no way to prevent people from simply giving everything they own to their children sometime before dying. But this means that a lot of perfectly innocent gifts also get prohibited. Furthermore, it just encourages people to transfer wealth in ways that cannot be taxed—e.g., by sending their children to very expensive private schools.

Even when such taxes can be enforced, they generate strange incentives. One of the major reasons that people save money is to secure their children's future. But savings also generate benefits for society as a whole. If we always consumed everything that we produced, the economy would never grow, because we would not be setting aside anything for investment in capital (e.g., to improve the machinery in a factory). It is only because some people save that funds become available for these purposes. So we want to do whatever we can to encourage reasonable savings. Limiting inheritance unfortunately eliminates one of the major incentives to save. So by preventing people from passing along benefits to their own children, we also discourage them from passing along benefits to future generations in general.

When push comes to shove, people are quite attached to their money, regardless of whether they have done much to deserve it. Redistribution involves taking money away from some people and giving it to others. This means that the people who are going to lose out in the redistribution will spend a lot of time and energy trying to avoid these losses. All of this activity is wasteful.

Given the problems with straightforward redistribution, there is often a temptation to pursue distributive goals more indirectly by mucking around with prices. When people are homeless, for example, it is generally because they cannot afford housing. This can be looked at in one of two ways—either their income is too low or the price of housing is too high. The immediate problem could be addressed by either raising their incomes or lowering the price of housing. Unfortunately, to implement income supports, the government must actually raise funds. Price controls, on the other hand, can be imposed by legislative fiat, and the cost does not show up on government books. It is entirely externalized. As a result, rent control is usually the path of least resistance in addressing housing issues.

The problem with rent control is that it generates all sorts of perverse consequences. The standard objection is that when the price of housing is kept down, it sends a signal to suppliers that there is "too much" housing. Developers having to choose between investing in apartment buildings downtown or tract houses in the suburbs will all choose the tract houses. Similarly, landlords will choose not to invest in maintaining or improving their buildings, because they cannot recover their investment. As a result, both the quantity and quality of rental housing will decline.

Of course, there are various ways around these problems, and most rent-control regimes have special incentives built in that are designed to mitigate them. There is, however, one problem that is inescapable. The basic goal of every rent-control regime is to push prices below market levels in order to making housing more affordable. The problem is that lowering prices makes housing more affordable for everyone, not just the poor. As a result, more people will enter the rental housing market in every income bracket, not just the lower. People who could easily afford to buy their own houses will continue to rent, because it is cheaper. And if a landlord has to choose between renting to a young professional and renting to someone on welfare, he will invariably choose the young professional. This means that the poor are just as likely to get squeezed out of the housing market as before.

This dynamic is clearly visible in Montreal, where the rent-control regime often makes it more attractive to rent than to own. The most extreme scenario is played out in New York, where rent-controlled apartments have basically disappeared from the market. Rich people from around the world have been known to keep rent-controlled apartments vacant in New York just to stay in when they visit town. This is because it is often cheaper to keep an apartment for a year than to stay in a hotel for a week. Thus New York rent control is not only inefficient—it causes desperately needed housing to sit vacant—it has manifestly exacerbated the problem of homelessness.

The moral of the story is that changing relative prices is an iffy way to pursue social policy. When the underlying market is reasonably competitive, this intervention will not only impose efficiency losses, it may even fail to achieve the distributive goals that formed the initial motivation for the intervention.

Faced with these problems, there may be a temptation to throw up one's hands and accept inequality as simply the price we must pay for prosperity. The best way to achieve efficiency is to leave people free to manage their own affairs. This freedom will include the freedom to buy and sell in private markets. As long as initial endowments differ—either natural endowments like talent, or artificial endowments like property—these private exchanges will generate inequality. And the market will stubbornly resist any attempt to correct this inequality. Hence the "big trade-off"—we can have equality or we can have efficiency, but not both.

But things are not quite so simple. While the zealous pursuit of equality will generate inefficiencies, too much inequality can also generate inefficiencies. In an ideal market, this would not be the case. In the real world, however, extreme inequalities in the division of wealth can exacerbate market failure and therefore create inefficiencies in the economy.

Consider the simple case of a corporation that is trying to decide whether or not to instal some new anti-pollution filters in its smoke-stacks. Installing the filters costs money, and therefore decreases the profits of the firm. But *not* installing the filters also generates a cost. The cost is not born by the firm, however. It takes the form of air pollution—a negative externality or "public bad." So will the firm instal filters?

Figuring this out actually requires a bit more information. To simplify somewhat, let us say that the firm will instal filters if the owners of the firm consider it to be in their interest to instal these filters. As citizens, they will suffer just as much from the public bad generated by the firm as everyone else. We all breathe the same air. But as owners, they stand to gain from an increase in the profitability of the firm. In order to decide what to do, they must decide which they prefer: the increased profits or the clean air.

This is where inequality comes in. Suppose that ownership of the firm is extremely diffuse—there are thousands of small shareholders. This means that the monetary value of the profit increase that each shareholder gets is going to be quite small. It may be so small that it is outweighed by the negative value of the public bad generated by the firm. Under such circumstances, the owners will find that it is in their interest to instal the filters. If, on the other hand, ownership is extremely concentrated, then the benefits that come from increased profitability will easily outweigh the negative value of the public bad. And so the filters will not be installed.

Incidentally, this is why small-time investors are far more likely to invest in "ethical" mutual funds than rich people. Business writers often express abhorrence at the thought that these funds may earn one or two percentage points less than their rivals (as though no one in their right mind would choose to earn less money when they could be earning more). They generally fail to note that the significance of these percentages depends upon the amount that is being invested. To a small investor, it may translate into an annual loss of a hundred dollars or so. Lots of people are willing to sacrifice one hundred dollars in order to preserve their moral integrity (not to mention the environment). But to a large investor, the annual loss could be very much larger. At this point, moral integrity may become too expensive.

Thus the problem with social inequality is that it generates a class of people who stand to benefit from the production of social bads. Environmental degradation, production of nuisance goods (such as cigarettes), erosion of health and safety standards, lengthening of the work day—all these practices generate welfare losses for society as a whole, but increased profitability for particular firms. When the ownership class is small, the income that they earn from the increased profitability outweighs the direct welfare losses that they suffer from these activities. Not only does this lead corporations to produce high levels of "profit-inducing public bads," but it also creates a class of people who will actively resist any government intervention that is aimed at the elimination of these bads.

This is why the business lobby consistently opposes government regulation, even when such regulation is clearly efficiency-promoting. Both automakers and gas companies, for example, opposed the introduction of unleaded fuel. But why should they have been opposed? If the government told just one gas company that it could only manufacture unleaded fuel, this would clearly put that company at a competitive disadvantage. The same would be true if only one automaker were forced to instal catalytic converters. But if *every* company is being forced to comply, then why should they care? The increased costs are simply passed along to the consumer, and the companies should be unaffected.

So in a properly structured market, firms should be indifferent to environmental regulation. The problem is that markets are often not properly structured. As long as oil companies were making leaded fuel, they were not paying the true cost that the manufacture of their product imposed upon society. This is because of the negative externality—the airborne lead emissions. As a result, society was consuming "too much" gas. Eliminating the externality should therefore reduce total demand for gasoline and increase the demand for other fuel sources. This is why the oil companies and refiners were opposed. They were profiting from the public bad. Thus opposition from business to a regulation is often a sign that the regulation is a good idea and is likely to improve the overall efficiency of the economy.

The more general point is that the concentration of ownership has a lot to do with the behaviour of these firms. When a small group of people owns most of the assets, it gives them an incentive to externalize costs—to subvert the market mechanism—whenever possible. A society in which ownership is more widely distributed is one in which firms are far less likely to behave so obnoxiously.

In the end, we find ourselves in a bit of a bind. It's very difficult to promote equality without making some serious compromises in other departments. At the same time, we can't just accept whatever extremes of inequality the market happens to generate. The concentration of wealth in a few hands can create its own inefficiencies. So when it comes to promoting equality, we seem to be damned if we do and damned if we don't.

As a result, any plan that we do come up with is going to involve some trade-offs. People around the world have experimented with different ways of controlling inequality, with varying degrees of success. From all these attempts, the most popular solution to have emerged is the progressive income tax. Although it is still the object of controversy in some circles, every advanced industrial nation uses an income tax as an instrument to redress social inequality.

The basic idea is simple. Some goods will not be supplied by markets because of insuperable free-rider problems. Private corporations simply do not have the power to force those who benefit to pay for the benefits. Government steps in, provides the benefits to everyone, then forces everyone to pay for them through some type of tax. But as long as the government is collecting taxes, why not use this as an opportunity to make some corrections in the distribution of wealth? Just make the rich contribute a bit more than the poor. That way we kill two birds with one stone.

This solution has universal appeal. Despite the appearance of controversy, there is in fact a widespread consensus over the use of the income tax to redistribute wealth. Mainstream and left-wing political parties tend to favour progressive income taxes—in which the marginal tax rate increases as earnings increase—while the extreme right often favours flat taxes—where everyone pays the same tax rate, regardless of his or her income. It is seldom noted that *both* of these tax structures are redistributive. Progressive incomes taxes are just *more* redistributive than flat taxes.

At the time of birth, each Canadian citizen gets access to a bundle of public goods. The average Canadian receives, over his or her lifetime, $120,000 worth of free education, $125,000 of free health care, police and judicial services worth more than $65,000, and $40,000 worth of access to transportation and communication networks. These are just the big-ticket items. Naturally, *someone* is going to have to pay for all this. But while every Canadian gets roughly the same package (although not everyone takes advantage of all the opportunities that they are offered), not everyone pays the same amount for it. This is true even with a flat tax. If everyone pays exactly the same tax rate on their earnings, people who earn an average of $10,000 a year are not going to pay very much, certainly not enough to cover the cost of the benefits they receive. Meanwhile, people who earn $100,000 are going to pay for more than the cost of the benefits they receive (although the *value* of the benefits they receive may still be higher than the taxes paid). So even a flat tax has redistributive consequences.

This redistribution often goes unnoticed for the same reason that the contributions of the public sector to the economy go unnoticed. Most government benefits are received in kind, not in cash. They take the form of public goods. A person who pays no tax still receives all these benefits. So, for example, a person who stays at home to raise his or her children still enjoys the protection of the Canadian Armed Forces, still has access to information collected by Statistics Canada, still has the right to ride public transit, and so on. But by using these services, this person is, in effect, receiving a transfer from other taxpayers. It is just not a *cash* transfer, and so it is not treated as a redistribution.

Introducing "progressivity" is one way to amplify the redistributive quality of income taxes. A progressive income tax is one in which there are a number of tax "brackets." The *portion* of the person's income that falls in each bracket is taxed at a different rate. The Canadian federal tax system, for example, has four brackets (provincial tax is then calculated, in most cases, as a percentage of federal tax). At the time of writing, individuals pay zero tax on the first $7,000 of income, 16 per cent on the next $23,000, 22 per cent on the next $30,000, 26 per cent on the next $40,000, and 29 per cent on anything above. (I am belabouring this point a bit because a surprising number of Canadians do not understand the principle of marginal taxation, and so believe that when they move into a higher tax bracket, the new rate applies retroactively, as it were, to their entire income. This is what gives rise to the urban myth about the person who gets a raise and winds up with less take-home pay. It would be interesting to see how much of the popular support for a "flatter" tax structure stems from this widespread fallacy.)

The usual argument for progressivity stems from the decreasing marginal utility of money. Just to be clear: proponents of a flat tax and proponents of a progressive tax both accept the principle that the income tax system should be used to redistribute wealth. (A non-redistributive tax would be something like the flat "poll tax" that Margaret Thatcher tried to implement in the U.K., which led to a breakdown in social order and was eventually repealed). The question of how redistributive the tax should be is the only issue. Proponents of a progressive tax point to the fact that paying twenty or thirty cents in taxes off every dollar is a greater sacrifice for someone who earns $20,000 than it is for someone who earns $200,000. Thus a flat tax, while guaranteeing that everyone pays the same monetary rate, actually imposes a greater hardship on the lower and middle classes. A progressive income tax, on the other hand, is able to ensure that everyone suffers approximately equal hardship.

The standard objection to income taxes is that they act as a drag on the economy by discouraging people from working. According to this view, people will decide how much to work by weighing the value of their earnings against the value of foregone leisure. Taxation diminishes the value of these earnings, and so encourages people to work less (the same way a tax on alcohol encourages people to drink less).

This argument is actually more dubious than it seems, and the empirical data are mixed. Increased income taxes can generate a "substitution effect," in which people work *harder* in order to make up lost income. Furthermore, most people do not choose their hours of work. Most obviously, for people who are paid on salary, there is no direct connection between compensation and the number of hours worked. So tax rates should have no impact at all on their work effort. Also, people who earn high incomes have a much stronger propensity to *like* the work they do than people with low incomes. This may offset the disincentive effect of increasing marginal rates of taxation. Finally, the fact most Canadians use tax-exempt RRSPs as their primary savings vehicle means that the progressivity of the income tax system has little effect on those who want to work harder in order to increase their savings. It is really the person who wants to consume more who is affected.

One popular argument against income taxes is that they generate inefficiencies in the form of tax-avoidance behaviour. People will hire lawyers and accountants in order to find ways to wriggle out of paying their taxes. This creates a classic race to the bottom. One way or another, government services have to be paid for. If everyone hires a crafty accountant and succeeds in paying less tax, then the base tax rate will simply have to go up in order to maintain government services. People then go out and spend even more money on clever accountants, etc. All the time and energy invested here is a complete waste.

But this would be a good argument against taxation only if the sole function of taxation were redistribution. The primary function of taxation, however, is not to redistribute wealth, but to compensate for market failures and provide public goods. Private markets, for example, will not provide certain types of information. We can sit around until the cows come home, and still no private company in its right mind is going to go out and conduct a census. It would simply not be able to recover its costs. At the same time, a census provides incredibly valuable information. It's impossible to develop a marketing plan, for example, without some idea of how many customers you might have and where they might live. So the government hires people to conduct the census. Government is able to do this because government is able to force everyone to pay through taxation. This taxation clearly generates some efficiency losses—people will waste time, energy, and resources trying to avoid these taxes. But when the value of the public good that is financed through taxation—in this case, the census—outweighs the losses incurred through tax avoidance, then the net result will be a gain in efficiency.

As a result, the fact that some people will waste resources trying to avoid paying their taxes is no more an argument against taxation than the fact that people will waste resources trying to steal is an argument against private property. In both cases, a law is passed that is designed to eliminate a collective action problem. Despite the law, some people still try to free-ride. In doing so, they waste resources. But is that a reason to scrap the law? Of course not. It shows why the law is needed in the first place.

So when we examine the efficiency losses that redistribution imposes on the economy, we should not start out with a hypothetical world in which there are no taxes. The basic efficiency losses that come from taxation are already "paid for" by the efficiency gains that are realized through government provision of public goods. The only question is whether these efficiency losses are exacerbated when the existing tax system is made more progressive. As long as the taxes fall reasonably short of confiscatory, it is difficult to imagine that progressivity alone could induce very serious deadweight losses. Again, the reason has to do with the diminishing marginal utility of money. Speaking personally, I am happy to admit that whether I pay 35 per cent or 45 per cent on the last $10,000 of my income makes no discernible difference in my quality of life and makes absolutely no difference in the amount of work that I do.

There are few countries in the world that have made a more serious attempt to minimize social inequality than Sweden. Even after a series of "conservative" administrations, the income tax system remains extremely progressive, with an average top rate of 56 per cent kicking in at around $55,000 of income. There is something commendable about this effort. At the same time, it must be acknowledged that taxes like this have all sorts of weird effects.

Take Ikea. Their furniture is often touted as an example of "Swedish ingenuity." But it could just as easily be held up as a consequence of Swedish taxes. Most people are not very good at building things. As a result, they usually pay someone else to build their furniture. High income taxes, however, increase the price of labour, and so make it more expensive to hire someone. Ikea came along with furniture designs that the customer could assemble at home, in effect transferring a portion of the labour cost from the market into the household—where it cannot be taxed. This has mixed results. We have all had the experience of puzzling for hours over incomprehensible assembly instructions, trying to put together a piece of furniture that an expert could have finished in less than two minutes.

Income tax "renders the value of a dollar not spent increasingly more valuable than a dollar earned." Thus high taxes are a boon for the do-it-yourself industry, even when doing it yourself is not really the most efficient way to get something done. This may seem trivial, until one stops to think about some of the things that people are tempted to do themselves. One of the biggest ways to save money is to look after your own children instead of paying someone else to do it. Higher taxes make it more expensive to hire professional care, thereby encouraging people to stay home with their kids. If the people staying at home are disproportionately women, this means that high taxes can exacerbate gender inequality.

This is just the beginning. The most perverse consequence of the Swedish experiment began to show up only in the long term. Economists noted that, over time, the level of *pretax* income inequality in Sweden had a tendency to increase. As a result, the progressivity of the income tax system had to be continually increased just to keep the distribution of income constant.

Lots of people have offered all sorts of different explanations for this phenomenon. The most persuasive theory, however, is that the rise in pretax inequality is a direct consequence of the tax system itself. A highly progressive income tax, when combined with income supports at the lower end, acts just like an insurance policy against career failure. In the same way that car insurance protects you in case you have an accident, the welfare state protects you in case you can't find a job. Both insurance schemes generate a moral hazard problem. In the case of car insurance, it means that people drive more recklessly. In the case of the welfare state, it means that people choose higher-risk career strategies. Instead of pursuing a safe professional degree in preparation for a modest career in middle management, they are more likely to choose high-risk degrees and enter fields with a "winner-take-all" reward structure. They do this simply because the price of failure is much lower.

When people start taking bigger risks, the number of big winners increases, but so does the number of big losers. So even if *average* rewards remain constant, the distribution of these rewards will become increasingly unequal. However, if one responds to this by confiscating some of the winnings and transferring them to the losers, this will just encourage people to take even greater risks—hence the perverse out-come that progressive taxation may promote social inequality.

At this point, I would like say a few things about the movie *Demolition Man*. This was an especially bad movie, so allow me to preface my remarks with a brief apology. What a lot of people don't understand about science fiction is that it's not really about the future. What science fiction does is present plausible future scenarios as a way of commenting on the present. By changing a few variables and then exploring the broader social consequences, it gives us a way of thinking about what we're doing right and what we're doing wrong. Science fiction of this type is a form of social criticism—hence my interest in the genre.

Demolition Man, while not a good movie, did have a cute premise. The story is set in 2032 in the city of Los Angeles. Sylvester Stallone plays a twentieth-century cop who is revived from cryostasis in order to track down a crazed criminal. When he awakens, however, he discovers to his dismay that California is governed by a sort of benevolent fascism. The difficulties he has adapting to these new arrangements form a sort of running joke throughout the film.

One of the most intrusive features of this new "kinder, gentler" California is that people are no longer allowed to swear in public places. Every time Stallone utters an expletive, a small machine mounted on the wall beeps loudly and issues him a ticket. These machines are meant to symbolize everything that is wrong with the new arrangement and are instrumental in motivating Stallone to eventually align himself with the forces of resistance.

Personally, I found myself unsympathetic to this plotline. Getting a ticket for swearing was intended by the filmmakers to represent an intolerable violation of one's personal liberty, but it struck me as not such a bad idea. Vulgarity was not being banned—it was just being taxed. Stallone's character was basically a cretin, and I have always thought that cretins ought to shoulder more of the burden that their behaviour imposes upon society. Imposing taxes on actions that are burdensome for others is one way to achieve this.

Now consider another example, this one drawn from real life. In Singapore, every car is equipped with a stored-value smart card and a microwave transponder. If you enter or exit the central zone of downtown Singapore during the morning or afternoon rush hour, you will automatically be charged for the trip. Pricing is variable, depending on the exact time that you go through. At peak hours, it will cost you about three dollars.

The logic of the Singapore traffic system is quite straightforward. Driving your car around imposes all sorts of costs on people around you—negative externalities. One of the most important externalities is congestion. Your presence on the road slows everybody else down, making it just that much harder for them to get where they are going. But because the system of markets is incomplete, they are unable to charge you for getting in their way. As a result, the "free market" will always produce traffic congestion, because people don't have to pay the full cost of their decision to drive.

The Singapore traffic control system imposes a slight "tax" on driving during rush hour. This forces drivers to pay something closer to the true cost of their activities, and therefore "internalizes" the negative externality. In this respect, it is no different from the little machines that penalized Stallone for swearing. Uttering vulgarities diminishes the quality of life of those around you (if you don't believe this, go into a crowded subway, start talking up a blue streak, and observe the discomfort of the people around you). A little tax on swearing internalizes that externality.

In the business, these are known as Pigovian taxes (after the British economist Cecil Pigou). What makes them so interesting is that, unlike income taxes, Pigovian taxes *themselves* make the economy more efficient, regardless of how the revenue they generate is spent. In fact, it's a little odd to call them taxes in the first place, since they serve exactly the same function as property rights. One might easily think of them as a sort of "negative" property right. When you create some "good," the system of property rights allows you to recapture some of the benefits that flow to others. When you create some "bad," Pigovian taxes ensure that some of that bad sticks to you, so that you are unable to pass it on to others.

At the moment, our government does not impose many Pigovian taxes. Some of the so-called "sin" taxes are Pigovian. The tax on gasoline is also Pigovian. Such taxes generate efficiency gains on two fronts. First, the tax itself discourages people from engaging in actions that have negative externalities. Thus the gas tax generates efficiency gains simply by decreasing the amount of gasoline that people consume. The second efficiency gain comes after the tax is collected. The money raised goes into general government funds and can be used to supply all sorts of public goods. So, for example, money from the gas tax can be used to subsidize public transit. This generates a second efficiency gain, as consumers get access to goods and services that markets are failing to provide.

Note that the function of Pigovian taxes is not to eliminate the activity being regulated. It is simply to reduce the incidence. People sometimes criticize liquor taxes on the grounds that they make the government dependent upon revenues from sales of alcohol and therefore give government an interest in promoting alcoholism. This is a bit mixed up. The goal of taxes on alcohol is not to eliminate drinking, but rather to achieve a socially optimal level of drinking. Similarly, taxing pollution is not intended to eliminate all pollution, since without *some* pollution we would have no economy. And without unhealthy food and dangerous sports, life would hardly be worth living. What we need to do is simply find the right level. Some people like to drink, or drive fast, or do a little backwoods snowboarding so much that they are willing to pay the full price that this activity imposes upon society. In this case, the right thing to do is to let them do it, but then charge them. Thus Pigovian taxes should generate a stable revenue stream.

Both the *Demolition Man* scenario and the Singapore traffic system show that the capacity of the government to levy such taxes depends upon the level of technology. Just as electronic monitoring and billing enables us to enforce property rights that might once have been unenforceable, they also enable us to collect taxes on activities that might once have escaped scrutiny. So in the same way we can use technology to create markets where none existed before, we can also use it to impose taxes where none existed before. The move to use Pigovian taxes to reduce traffic congestion is already underway. Several European nations are starting to implement variations on the Singaporean system. Charging people for the volume of trash they produce is similar, and has been implemented in many municipalities across North America. The same strategy could be used to reduce a variety of common urban nuisances, such as excessive noise or light pollution, littering, even dangerous driving. We have barely begun to scratch the surface of possibilities. We can be confident, though, that if we continue the drive towards increased efficiency, this will mean not only expanded markets, but also a far more extensive system of Pigovian taxes.

As we have seen, there is often no need to choose between efficiency and equality. We can have both, and Pigovian taxes represent a clear instance where the two objectives can be harmonized.

Nevertheless, it is inevitable that *some* circumstances will arise in which we are forced to choose between the two. The question is then which of the two principles should be assigned greater importance. This can be an extremely difficult choice to make. And unfortunately, as a society, we are generally not very good at thinking about these sorts of situations or making these sorts of choices.

The typical conflict arises when we want to impose some rule that will promote greater fairness, but where doing so will cause some people to take costly evasive action. (For example, we might want to increase income taxes at the top end, while realizing that doing so will prompt some people to pack up and move to the United States.) We are unable to eliminate the free-rider strategy as an option, and so the rule will create some efficiency losses. What do we do?

There is an enormous temptation on the left to simply ignore the efficiency losses. After all, people *shouldn't* be free-riding. They are behaving immorally. And if we refuse to implement the rule just because of them, this will appear to be tacitly condoning their behaviour. Thus making any concessions in the name of efficiency begins to look like a sell-out.

This is clearly what motivates a lot of the hardline opposition on the left to considering efficiency effects. But when taken to its logical extreme, the position quickly falls apart. After all, principles alone have no intrinsic value. The only thing that has intrinsic value is human welfare. Principles derive their value, ultimately, from their effects on people. Imagine two scenarios: one in which everyone is exactly equal; and one in which people are very unequal, but the welfare level of the poorest person is higher than the average welfare level in the first scenario. Which is better? The temptation is to say that since *everyone* is happier in the second scenario, it is better. The only way the first scenario could be better would be if we valued equality for its own sake, regardless of its effects on human well-being. But then what would be the point of such a principle? It would be more of a fetish than a plausible principle of justice.

Of course, this is not a hypothetical example. These two scenarios correspond roughly to the choice that confronted citizens of the former Communist bloc in the late twentieth century. They had to decide between a society in which everyone was relatively equal, but where most people were quite poor, and a society in which there would be much greater disparities of wealth, but where everyone might eventually enjoy a superior quality of life. They overwhelmingly chose the latter. Of course, things have not worked out quite the way they expected. The point is simply that people care more about their own quality of life than they do about abstract principles. They are often willing to tolerate others becoming much richer than themselves as long as they themselves get at least *some* portion of the gain. Thus even the poor may exhibit a preference for greater material inequality.

Considerations such as these have led some people to think that fairness can simply be ignored. One of the most common reasons given for ignoring fairness is that while efficiency is an "objective" standard, fairness is entirely "subjective." As my undergraduate economics textbook put it, "it is possible to talk about *efficient* and *inefficient* allocations, but not about better or worse distribution of income without introducing normative considerations." In this sentence, the authors demonstrate a complete misunderstanding of both efficiency and fairness (and possibly even the word "normative"). Efficiency and fairness are normative standards, and neither is more "objective" or "subjective" than the other. Fairness just tends to be more controversial.

But this does not mean that we can or should ignore fairness. Society is fundamentally a giant system of co-operation. As we have seen, the only way to get out of the state of nature is to establish a set of rules and to convince people to voluntarily refrain from pursuing their self-interest in an overtly individualistic fashion. It is this restraint that establishes the basis for trust, which is the "glue" that holds together all other social institutions, including the market. Because of this reliance on trust, social institutions will function smoothly only if people can be persuaded to play by the rules. If institutions are unfair or if they generate gross inequalities at the end of the day, it becomes that much harder to persuade people to play along. So fairness cannot be ignored. Without it, we cannot establish stable patterns of co-operation.

The moral of the story is that things are complex. We cannot assign unconditional priority to efficiency, nor can we disregard questions of fairness. What we need is a formula that will help us to broker reasonable compromises between the two. What might such a formula look like? That's a more complicated question. That's what we have professional philosophers for—to answer complicated questions like this.

If it's any comfort, please rest assured that we're on the job. We'll get back to you when we have it sorted out.

Efficiency Starts at Home

10 *In the workplace, efficiency* is clearly the dominant value. Employees are constantly bombarded with demands for increased efficiency—increased organizational efficiency, increased productive efficiency, increased personal efficiency. The "gospel of efficiency" has been hammered home so many times that most people experience something close to an allergic reaction whenever they hear the word.

At the same time, many people are willing to tolerate this sort of pressure at work. After all, when you're at work, you're not there to relax and have fun. You're there to get the job done. And as long as you're there to do a job, it only makes sense to do that job as efficiently as possible. Furthermore, when the work is done more efficiently, it *should* free up more time for other things. The sooner you finish work, the sooner you can go home. Or so it would seem.

Unfortunately, things seldom work out that way. Increased productivity at work has not led to a reduction in work hours. In fact, the average number of hours worked has gone up in North America over the last twenty years. Even more disturbing is the fact that, far from freeing up our time for other pursuits, the quest for efficiency seems to be creeping into every aspect of daily life. Not only is the workplace becoming more fast-paced, but all of life seems to be speeding up as well. Instead of creating more leisure time so that we can concentrate on the things that really matter to us, efficiency seems to be becoming an end in itself. People no longer seek efficiency in order to achieve their other goals; they pursue it for its own sake.

This transformation shows up most clearly in the organization of the home. Parents often talk about spending "quality time" with their kids. This is essentially an efficiency concept. Whereas parents used to have more time to spend with their children, the modern parent is chronically time-starved and so no longer has the luxury of just whiling away an afternoon with them. To make up for this, parents now try to use the time that they do have more efficiently. Instead of spending a long period of time with their kids, engaged in some low-intensity activity, parents now spend a shorter period of time with them, but fill it with some more concentrated, high-intensity activity. The increased "quality" of this time is supposed to make up for the decreased quantity.

So just as people are constantly trying to become more efficient employees, they are also trying to become more efficient parents. According to sociologist Arlie Hochschild, "A surprising amount of family life has become a matter of efficiently assembling people into prefabricated activity slots." But this seems to be pushing in one direction—towards increased stress and a chronic shortage of time. If this is what our commitment to efficiency leads to, then there can't be much of a future in it. Eventually we are all going to just burn out.

Unfortunately, I don't have much experience in these matters. My job as a philosopher is actually quite leisurely. And I don't have any kids. Running around with a cellphone, laptop, and pager, touching base with clients while driving the kids to soccer practice—all of this is foreign to me. But the problem is obviously an important one for many people and so cannot be ignored. Since I have trouble putting myself in their shoes, I decided to do the next-best thing. I decided to run a computer simulation to see what will happen to my life when I have kids.

The first step in setting up the simulation was to pick up a copy of *The Sims*, the popular "people simulator" from Will Wright, the creator of SimCity. The game, as the manual explains, allows you to create a set of artificial people. "You create the very electronic marrow of these beings, assign subtle personality traits, and set them in a home of your design." This seemed like the right tool for the job.

So I set about the task of creating a Simjoe and a Simalice. After picking out reasonable facsimiles of myself and my wife, I then had to choose personality traits. The simulator offers five characteristics: neat, outgoing, active, playful, and nice. This presented something of a problem, since I am not really any of these things. So I decided to configure both our personalities using the default values for our astrological signs—Libra and Aquarius.

Once I had the basic personality traits fixed, I moved Simjoe and Simalice into a modest starter home and set them up in appropriate career tracks. Simalice went into medicine. Unfortunately, philosophy was not one of the available careers, so I set Simjoe up as a scientist, which I figured was almost as impractical. Then I began the task of benevolently coaxing them into family life:

> Day 1. Things are under control, although somewhat hectic. Both Simjoe and Simalice have to be up at 6:00 a.m. in order to leave for work at 8:00 a.m. Simjoe takes a shower while Simalice eats breakfast, then they switch. They have exactly one minute to chat before both must head off to work. While they are gone, all the flowers in the backyard die. So when they get home, Simjoe has to spend the evening replanting them. Simalice gets bored and switches on the TV.

> Day 2. The morning routine goes a bit more smoothly. Hunger is still a nagging concern though. Neither Simjoe nor Simalice really knows how to cook, so they both snack a lot or pop something quick into the microwave. The sink gets clogged. Simalice spends half the evening plunging it.

Simjoe gives her a backrub when she's done. Things are looking good.

Day 3. Today Simjoe is depressed. His job is going well, but between that and looking after the house, he and Simalice have no time to see their friends. This doesn't bother Simalice so much, but with Simjoe's outgoing nature, he is beginning to suffer. I try to get him to study, to improve his cooking skills a bit, but he refuses. He's too depressed. Instead he watches TV.

Day 4. Simalice gets promoted! The medicine gig is starting to pay off. Not only does she get a raise, but she now gets picked up for work in a fancy car, unlike the old beater that Simjoe's science buddies are driving. Feeling somewhat ebullient, Simalice suggests that they have a baby. Simjoe agrees.

Day 5. The baby arrives! Simjoe and Simalice decide to name him Damian. The house only has one bedroom, so they put the crib in the middle of the kitchen. Little Damian doesn't seem too bothered. Both Simjoe and Simalice take turns feeding him. Simjoe decides to start working night shifts so that he can be at home during the day.

Day 6. All hell breaks loose. Simjoe gets home from work in the morning and spends two hours trying to get the baby to stop crying. Afterwards he naps for an hour until the baby wakes him up again. When Simalice gets home from work, she takes over. But the baby keeps crying. Simjoe sleeps badly and has no chance to eat before heading out for the night shift. He is late for work.

Day 7. Simalice is up half the night looking after little Damian and doesn't get to shower before going to work.

Simjoe returns home in the morning and collapses in exhaustion on the kitchen floor. The baby cries. Simjoe forgot to pay the bills, and so a warning arrives from a collection agency. The flowers in the backyard have died once again from neglect.

Day 8. It's been a long time since Simjoe and Simalice have had a chance to talk to each other. The relationship is beginning to suffer. Simalice needs time to study in order to advance her career. But she never gets a chance. Once the baby is asleep, she is too tired. They consider hiring a nanny, but find that they can't afford it.

Day 9. Simjoe and Simalice hit rock bottom. A worker from social services drops by to issue a warning. The child is being neglected. Both Simjoe and Simalice are miserable. They have their first fight. Simjoe is late for work again. The toilet gets clogged, but Simalice has no time to fix it before dashing off to work. Bladder control becomes an issue.

At this point I halted the simulation. Time to reread the manual. After all, this was supposed to be a game. It was supposed to be simulated *life*, not simulated *hell*.

The manual did in fact contain some useful advice. The key to the simulation, it said, is time management. People have a lot of different needs and seldom enough time to fulfil them all. Thus for the Sims "a good watchword to keep in mind is *efficiency*. You want your Sims to accomplish their goals—whether those goals are getting a raise or getting to the bathroom—in the most efficient manner possible."

With this in mind, I took a look at the way Simalice and Simjoe were organizing their affairs. Clearly something had to give. There simply was not enough time in the day to look after every aspect of the household. Something would have to be done to free up some more time.

The obvious solution was for someone to quit his or her job. And it wasn't too hard to figure out which one that should be. Thanks to her recent promotion, Simalice was making a fair bit more money than Simjoe. So clearly the more efficient arrangement was to have Simjoe stay home and look after the baby.

Day 10. Simjoe decides to sleep straight through his alarm. This gets him fired from his job. He wakes up the next morning and cooks breakfast while Simalice showers. He's not in any hurry, so they have time to chat before Simalice leaves for work. After she is gone, he cleans up, feeds little Damian, then takes a shower. He pays the overdue bills and plants new flowers in the yard.

Day 11. Damian takes a nap in the afternoon, so Simjoe doesn't have much to do. He spends the morning studying cooking. He is starting to get very lonely, so he calls a friend and chats for an hour during the afternoon. Before Simalice gets home, he prepares dinner. That way they can eat early and spend the evening together playing with the baby. Backrubs are exchanged.

Day 12. Simalice used to snack a lot, but now this is unnecessary. Simjoe's cooking skills have gotten good enough that he always has a hearty meal on the table. And what with the crib in the middle of the kitchen, it's an obvious place for him to spend his time. Friends start popping by for dinner as well. They keep Simjoe entertained, so Simalice is able to sneak off and study a bit before going to bed.

Day 13. The baby still wakes up during the night, but Simjoe always gets up to feed him. That way Simalice is well rested when she goes off to work. Simjoe can always take a nap during the afternoon if his energy level gets low. Simjoe spends the afternoon cleaning the bathroom. This is the first time since they moved in that it has been cleaned.

Day 14. Simalice gets promoted again. Thanks to the influence of their new "couple friends," she is quickly climbing the ladder of success at work. And her studying is starting to pay off. Simjoe is thrilled and goes out shopping for new appliances. He buys a nice gas range and a dishwasher. This greatly speeds things up around mealtime.

At this point I stopped the simulation again. The pattern of household organization that was emerging was beginning to look eerily familiar. What had begun as a modern two-career household was slowly metamorphosing into something far more traditional. Under pressure to support the household on a single income, Simalice was investing all her time and energy in her career. Simjoe, meanwhile, was not only looking after the child full-time, but had also taken over all the cooking, cleaning, and gardening. He had even become the one responsible for organizing social activities. To put it bluntly, Simjoe had become a housewife.

How did this happen? Had I decided to condemn Simjoe to a life of domestic servitude? Certainly not. Things just worked out that way.

In fact, Simjoe's domestic servitude arose as a direct consequence of my desire to organize the household more efficiently. The best way to increase overall efficiency was to introduce a division of labour. This may be the oldest move in the book, but that doesn't make it any less effective. When both Sims were pursuing careers, there was considerable duplication of effort around the home. Apart from the fact that both had to go off to work, each one was trying to develop both cooking and job skills. By having Simjoe specialize in cooking, a lot of time was freed up for Simalice to study medicine. So instead of having two people earning moderate salaries and microwaving dinner, I wound up with one person earning a substantial salary and the other cooking hearty meals. In the end, both of them were better off.

The fact that Simjoe also wound up doing all the cleaning and gardening was no accident. There is a cluster of activities around the home that are highly compatible with child care. It is impossible to come home from work every time the baby starts to cry. But if you're cleaning the bathroom, preparing dinner, or chatting on the phone, it's easy to drop what you're doing and care for the child. Once the baby is back to sleep, then you can pick up where you left off.

Needless to say, having Simjoe at home also improved the quality of his relationship with Simalice. Preparing dinner before she got home from work meant that they could eat quickly and then spend the rest of the evening chatting and having fun. In other words, they could spend a lot more "quality time" together.

To anyone with some experience of coupledom, this is all going to sound very familiar. The dynamic that led to Simjoe taking on all the household responsibilities is just as powerful in the real world as it is in the simulated world.

The division of labour within the home used to be determined by a very rigid set of social norms. Cooking and cleaning were designated as women's work, while mowing the lawn and fixing the fence were men's work. This division of labour came under severe criticism starting in the late '60s and has been slowly eroding since. But the breakdown of this traditional "moral economy" has created a vacuum. In most Canadian households, the culture no longer provides a blueprint or operations manual for the organization of the home. Thousands of details must now be actively negotiated.

As a result, modern couples engage in a lot of horse-trading: "I'll clean up the kitchen, as long as you do the laundry." Feminists who led the charge against traditional gender norms had hoped that the principle of equality, or fairness, would help couples decide how to allocate these tasks. What has tended to happen, unfortunately, is that efficiency has become the dominant value in the household, not fairness.

This would be fine, except that there is no guarantee that a fifty-fifty division of labour will be very efficient. And when push comes to shove, people who are forced to choose between efficiency and fairness will tend to choose efficiency.

This preference for efficiency is one of the factors that reinforce the old breadwinner/homemaker division of labour. Despite the fact that we no longer assume that women should stay at home and men should go off to work, a surprising number of families still get organized that way. People are not necessarily committed to a sexual division of labour. But eliminating the sexual division of labour does not necessarily mean eliminating the division of labour.

Take the example of grocery shopping. A lot of couples, when they are young, go grocery shopping together. Once kids come along and they get pressed for time, the inefficiency of this arrangement starts to become a problem. After all, there is no real need for both of them to be there—one person can do the job just as well. But which person will that be? The most efficient arrangement is to have the person who does most of the cooking also do the shopping. The cook is the one who knows what ingredients are needed (and the one who is able to change plans "on the fly" if some particular ingredient turns out to be unavailable).

This is just one example of how household tasks get bundled together. (Another example: if one person is responsible for picking the kids up after school, it might also make sense to have that person run a few errands on the way home—maybe stop by the drugstore or do a bit of banking.) So while a lot of people go into relationships figuring that there will be a fifty-fifty split of domestic responsibilities, this is seldom what they get. The most efficient way to split up household labour is often something more like ninety-ten. An equal division may be stable as long as the couple is childless and carefree. Once the first baby comes along, it disrupts the equilibrium. But rather than disrupting it only slightly, it often displaces the entire burden onto one person. Social scientists refer to this as "tipping."

Of course, the big difference between the real world and the simulated world is that in the real world women are much more likely to get tipped on than men. In the Sims game, there are no gender norms. Each simulated person is functionally bisexual and is equally willing to take on any gender role or domestic chore. This is of course a political choice on the part of the game's creators. The simulation does have some social norms built in. For example, the Sims can be quite picky about having others respect their privacy. So the omission of gender norms is a conspicuous design choice. The game represents a certain sort of gender utopia in which men and women are interchangeable.

It is therefore highly significant that even under such circumstances, the division of labour in the home continues to emerge as a successful strategy. A traditional household is structured by two elements: first, the division of labour into breadwinner and homemaker roles; second, the set of gender norms that assign the breadwinner role to the man, the homemaker role to the woman. The second component is not necessarily efficient, but the first often is. Thus the old-fashion family arrangement was not a complete scam. It may have been unfair to women, but the underlying structure had a sound economic rationale.

In the Sims game, men are just as likely to become househusbands as women are to become housewives. Men do not suffer any extra pain from losing their jobs, and women do not become any more anxious when separated from their children. In the real world, this is often not how things work. This is why eliminating the gender norms, while keeping the division of labour, has proven to be extremely tricky.

All of this helps to explain a little mystery that will be familiar to anyone who moves in broadly left-wing circles. Almost every woman I know of my generation is a self-described feminist. Almost all of them have university degrees. When they enter into relationships, it is invariably with sensitive, enlightened, politically correct men. And yet an alarming number of these women have wound up becoming housewives.

How did *that* happen? What do you say about supposedly "progressive" couples who wind up reproducing the traditional patriarchal division of labour?

People's instinctive reaction to situations like this is to assume that some kind of inauthenticity is at work. Perhaps these women were only talking a good game, but then "sold out" when the first baby arrived. Or perhaps the men were just paying lip service to feminist values—the price to be paid for getting educated women into bed—but over time their true colours emerged. These are all accusations that I have heard made.

Whenever we start ascribing these sorts of lowly motives to decent people, it is usually a sign of desperation. In this case, I think it is a sign that people are genuinely confused by the situation. How could women who swore up and down that they would never get stuck in a situation like their mothers' wind up in a situation so much like, well, their mothers'?

Of course, there are still plenty of people who cling to the old gender roles and believe that women should stay at home with the kids. And there are still a shocking number of men who simply refuse to take on their fair share of work around the house. Others don't want anything to do with a woman who will earn more money or have a more demanding career than they will.

When men adopt this sort of attitude, it is not surprising that the women who marry them wind up taking on the lion's share of domestic responsibilities. But what is harder to understand is how couples who have a strong commitment to equality of the sexes could nevertheless wind up reproducing the traditional division of labour.

The answer has to do with efficiency. Having children puts an incredible demand on people's time and resources. So when they have a baby, couples start looking for ways to economize. Because society in general is still organized around the assumption that women are the primary caregivers, often the easiest or more efficient way to do things is to have the woman take on the homemaker role. People generally do not anticipate this, because they have difficulty imagining just how great the demands of a baby will be. As a result, they make all sorts of unwise choices early on in their lives and in their relationships, because they don't see how it will affect them in the long run. (And their parents are usually unable to advise them, because they have no experience in the matter.)

Take the most obvious example. Child care is extremely expensive. Furthermore, child-care services are always second-rate in the mind of the parent (I've never met anyone who believed that a stranger could raise their kids better than they could). As a result, the temptation for one parent to cut back on work hours or to quit working entirely is often overwhelming. Of course, if one person stops working, this results in a substantial cut in household income. Many people can't afford to cut back on work. Among those who can afford it, the person who earns less will almost invariably be the one who quits.

Within the couple, this may seem like a perfectly non-sexist criterion. In the world of the Sims, it was perfectly neutral, and the result was that Simjoe quit his job. But in the real world, women who work full-time earn less, on average, than men. So it is most often the woman who quits work or starts to cut back. (This becomes a vicious cycle, insofar as it makes companies less likely to offer women advanced training, or promote them, or put them into positions of responsibility, out of fear that they may cut back their hours or quit work entirely when a child comes along.)

What's worse, women may choose to pursue careers in fields that offer flexible work time, precisely because they want to keep their options open in terms of eventual family responsibilities. (For example, they may enter into teaching because it allows them to go home early and take summers off.) But this flexibility often winds up reducing their options once they have a child, because it disadvantages them in their domestic negotiations. If the husband has an inflexible work schedule, he can refuse any of the various child-care demands that might be made—"I'd love to, honey, but I can't possibly make it home by then." If the wife's flexibility allows her to take on some tasks, such as picking up the kids after school, she may find that all the rest get "tipped" onto her as well.

Many of the other mechanisms that displace primary child-care responsibilities onto women are more subtle. For instance, there has been enormous emphasis in recent years on the importance of breast-feeding. While this is all well and good, it tends to entrench a certain pattern of female caregiving that can be very difficult to shake. When the baby starts crying in the middle of the night, it is naturally the breastfeeding mother who has to wake up. Her husband could get up as well, to keep her company and help out. But this is extremely inefficient. Why should both of them lose sleep when only one is needed? Efficiency pulls in the direction of an unequal division of labour.

More intensive early contact with the baby often makes the mother far more expert than the father at attending to the baby's needs. Because of this, it may take the father twice as long as the mother to put the baby to bed. It may take the father an hour to get the baby to stop crying, whereas the mother can do it in a few minutes. So it is not uncommon, even in highly egalitarian couples, to see the father try for a few moments to calm the baby, but then hand it over to the mother once these early efforts prove fruitless.

Even more subtly, mothers have a tendency to be far more risk-averse about the physical security of their children than fathers. How many times have we seen a father tossing his kid up in the air while the mother looks on anxiously, muttering "I wish you wouldn't do that" under her breath? A lot of women simply do not trust their husbands to take proper care of the kids and are not willing to sit around doing nothing while they learn. Forced to choose between the abstract principle of equality and the physical security of their child, most women will set aside their concern for equality.

All of this is a mixed blessing. The mother is usually the first to establish herself as an expert in the care of the child. This expertise can be a source of enormous pride. But the problem with being the expert is that when some problem arises, people turn to you. Thus the woman, in establishing herself as the expert, also puts herself in a position where efficiency concerns constantly push her into the role of primary caregiver. There is, of course, no reason that the man can't catch up with the level of expertise reached by the woman. But this will often require special effort, and it will initially require a willingness to set aside efficiency considerations.

⟡

What can be done?

First, we need to realize that there are two different ways of achieving gender equality in our society. One way is to break down the traditional division of labour in each individual home so that all men and women share domestic responsibilities fifty-fifty. Another way is to preserve the division of labour in each individual home, but ensure that, across society as a whole, the same number of men occupy the domestic role as do women. These are completely different strategies and are usually not adequately distinguished. But it is important to keep them apart, because the former is often in serious tension with our commitment to efficiency, whereas the latter is not.

People who get into a serious time bind usually wind up there because they have chosen the first option—a two-career household. They have chosen to reject the central division of labour in the home and the major efficiency gains that go with it. This makes it very difficult for them to compete, in terms of securing quality of life, with couples who do adopt that division of labour. They wind up being harried because they try to make up for this big efficiency loss by creating efficiency gains in every other area of life: skipping breakfast, persuading the nanny to do the laundry, ordering pizza for dinner, and so on.

The obvious solution is for women to secure the same advantages as men who have a housewife "in their corner." In order to achieve gender equality, a lot more women are going to have to marry house-husbands.

Of course, not many men start out life wanting to be househusbands. What women really need to do is position themselves in their relationships in such a way that when it comes time to negotiate who will take on primary child-care responsibilities, they have a stronger hand than the man. The best way to do this is to make sure that they are better educated than their husbands and that they make more money. But how can this be done, given the persistent gender gap between men and women? Simple. Women can simply choose to marry men with lesser prospects. As feminist author Rhona Mahony put it, women need to "train up and marry down."

This is, unfortunately, much easier said than done. Most people look to marriage as a way of enhancing their social status. The kind of partner you are able to attract says a lot about you. Having a partner who is obviously defective in some way suggests that you are also somewhat defective. Having a partner who is an obvious "catch," on the other hand, suggests that you must have something going on. Typically, for a man, having a beautiful wife or girlfriend earns the respect of other men. And typically, for a woman, having a partner who is witty, intelligent, or wealthy earns the admiration of other women.

The problem with this status system is that it reinforces the division of labour in the home. Intellectuals like to downplay it, but the hard fact remains that many women still look for a man who will be able to "provide" for them. Men, on the other hand, are not entirely averse to marrying women for beauty alone. Drop by any high-end singles bar and you can see this exchange taking place in front of your very eyes. The recent TV show, *Who Wants to Marry a Multimillionaire?*—in which beautiful women competed against each other for an opportunity to marry a troll-like rich man—scandalized people not because the underlying premise rang hollow, but because the spectacle made an obvious display of an arrangement that most people would prefer remain tacit.

Of course, if a woman's goal is really just to marry a rich man, then more power to her. The problem arises when women with career ambitions stick to this pattern and marry men who earn more than they do or who have more "high-powered" careers. For example, a study of Stanford MBA students showed that after graduation men earned an average salary of $144,461, while women earned $101,204. Here one can see a typical "gender gap" in earnings. Even more startling, however, is the gap in what their spouses earned. The female MBA's husband earned $120,124 on average, while the average male MBA's wife earned only $30,323. The message is fairly clear: despite making extremely high salaries, most of the female MBAs in this study still managed to marry men who earned more than they did.

The authors of the study reported their findings by suggesting that women with MBAs "marry up," while men with MBAs "marry down." This is very misleading. Having an MBA from Stanford makes you a pretty strong competitor in the marriage market, so all of these people probably had a good chance to "marry up." My suspicion is that many of the men "married up" by choosing beautiful women (regardless of their career aspirations), while women did it by marrying men with "high-powered" careers. Both groups gained status through the exchange. But the men also created a domestic situation that enhanced their ability to compete in the workplace, while the women created a situation that threatened to undermine their ability to focus on career objectives.

A lot of energy has been focused on trying to get men to stop doing this, and with some success. There is now an undercurrent of public opinion that ridicules men for having "trophy wives." Still, there's a pretty solid supply of women who have no particular objection to the idea of marrying a rich man, then staying home and tending the kids. And as long as there are women willing to accept this arrangement, there will be men willing to take them up on the offer. After all, when people have these sorts of preferences, the exchange is mutually advantageous.

Rather than trying to get men to stop, perhaps our energies would be better spent trying to get women to *start* marrying homemakers.

The idea that women who want careers should go out and look for men who are willing to stay home and raise kids runs contrary to the traditional wisdom. The standard feminist line has been that women can manage both career and children as long as they have three things: accessible daycare, flexible work hours, and a partner willing to split domestic responsibilities fifty-fifty. As a result, the pressure these past few decades has been on governments, corporations, and men generally to provide such arrangements.

While there can be no doubt that the realization of these goals would lead to a vast improvement in the quality of life of women in our society, some prominent feminist authors have begun to question whether these changes alone are enough to secure the equality of women. Day-care, for instance, is hardly a magic bullet. As Rhona Mahony writes:

> I'm afraid many women have been kidding themselves. We kidded ourselves when we thought that government subsidies to childcare centers would eliminate the second shift. We kidded ourselves when we thought about our own futures. "Oh, it won't happen to me," we said. "I have lots of energy and my husband will help." Or: "My mother will babysit and I'll be office manager in no time." We were kidding ourselves when we said those things because we weren't facing up to some basic arithmetic. There are 24 hours in the day. There are 7 days in the week. That means that there are 168 hours in a week. If Grandma or the childcare center or a babysitter takes the children for, say, 50 hours a week, that still leaves 118 hours. Our kids need us for a surprising, appalling, delightful number of those 118 hours.

There is always the option of purchasing more than the usual forty to fifty hours of child care. But at a certain point this becomes uneconomical. It is axiomatic that daycare workers and nannies have to earn less than their employers. It they didn't make less, the parents wouldn't be able to hire them—it would be cheaper just to look after the kids themselves. But even at that, child-care workers are usually interested only in working a standard forty-hour week. One surgeon I know gets around this by employing both a "day nanny" and an "evening nanny." But this starts to get ridiculous—employing two people full-time just to raise your kids. In any case, this is an option that can never be available to anyone but the very rich.

If daycare does not provide enough relief, an obvious alternative would be to make work a bit less demanding. However, sociologists such as Arlie Hochschild have raised important doubts about the ability of flex-time or part-time employment to ease the condition of working women. Hochschild's first book, *The Second Shift*, was instrumental in drawing attention to inequalities in the division of household labour between men and women. The overall tone of that book was quite upbeat. Once men start pulling their weight, she figured, everything else would sort itself out. Her latest book, *The Time Bind*, strikes a far more pessimistic note. She is clearly troubled by the ineffectiveness of many traditional remedies. While *The Second Shift* leaves the reader outraged, *The Time Bind* is more likely to leave the reader depressed.

The Time Bind is based upon Hochschild's study of a large American corporation—referred to as "Amerco" to protect the anonymity of her sources—that was trying to create a workplace that would better accommodate employees with child-care responsibilities. The company was clearly taking a leadership role on this issue, and it was consistently ranked as one of the ten most "family friendly" corporations in the United States. But despite making a wide range of such programs available to its employees, rates of participation were abysmally low. Hochschild set out to discover how the following three facts could obtain: "First, Amerco's workers declared on survey after survey that they were strained to the limit. Second, the company offered them policies that would allow them to cut back. Third, almost no one cut back."

This pattern was not unique to Amerco. A 1990 study of 188 Fortune 500 companies showed that when companies did offer "alternative" work arrangements, participation rates were very low among eligible employees: between 3 and 5 per cent for part-time work, 1 per cent for job sharing, 10 per cent for flex-time, and less than 3 per cent for flex-place. At Amerco, participation in 1990 in each of these programs was less than 1 per cent, except for flex-time, "a policy allowing workers to come and go early or late." This program, as Hochschild points out, "rearranged but did not cut back on hours at work." To top it all off, Hochschild discovered that workers with young children put in, on average, more hours at work than those without children; 56 per cent of them regularly worked on weekends.

Upon investigation, Hochschild was able to quickly dismiss the standard explanations for these low participation rates. There was no correlation, for instance, between income level and participation rate, making it difficult to make the case that employees chose not to work part-time because they could not afford it. Hochschild also found that the policies were not just "window-dressing," but that a good-faith effort had been made to implement them. And perhaps more importantly, the majority of employees *believed* that the company was making a good-faith effort.

What Hochschild ultimately found was that most employees did not take advantage of the alternative work arrangements because it was not in their interest to do so. It's one thing to go part-time when your job involves stacking boxes in a warehouse. Here you are clearly being paid an hour's wage for an hour's work. But this "market" model of the labour contract is clearly inapplicable to most jobs. In most corporations, employees do not exchange money for discrete units of time. They are paid to become members of a team. Their salary is paid in exchange for their co-operation—the willingness to place the firm's interest above their own. Once this exchange is made, employees are expected to throw themselves into any project with all the energy and enthusiasm they can muster.

If we think of employment as teamwork—and the corporation as a moral economy—then it is easy to see why part-time work is not a solution. The problem with teamwork is that it doesn't allow for degrees. Either you're in or you're out. Either you're there for the others or you're not. To form a cohesive group, people need to know that they can rely on each other when the crunch comes. When someone chooses to work part-time, it sends all the wrong signals. It suggests that they are not "really" committed to the team, and that when push comes to shove, they can't be relied upon.

The problem is exacerbated by the fact that promotion in large companies is often based on the level of commitment that an employee exhibits. Actual performance can be difficult to evaluate, especially when people are working in groups. Furthermore, once people rise to a certain level in the corporate hierarchy, obvious incompetence becomes increasingly rare. As a result, managers begin to rely on more intangible qualities, such as commitment, as a guide in making promotional decisions.

Unfortunately, an employee's level of commitment is not directly observable. What can be observed is the amount of *time* that the employee spends at the job. Managers therefore often take time as an index of the employee's commitment level and promote people based on the sheer quantity of time that they spend at work. Of course, if the way to get promoted is to put in *more* hours than everyone else, this quickly becomes a race to the bottom. Soon everyone winds up working much longer than anyone would like. No one can change it, though, because in this sort of environment, cutting back on work hours is equivalent to career suicide.

Finally, and perhaps most importantly, many people *like* to work. Modern companies go to great lengths to ensure that good workers are properly rewarded and feel appreciated. At home, there are no professional managers around to make sure that everyone feels good at the end of the shift. As a result, many people—both women and men—feel a lot better about the job they do at work than at home. People also tend to have more friends at work than in their neighbourhoods. All of this is exacerbated when young children are involved. Many people—both men and women—told Hochschild that coming into the office often felt like an "escape" from home.

The picture that emerges is somewhat bleak. Two-career couples give up all the efficiency gains that come from the division of household labour. They try to compensate for it by contracting out household services and by making up time in other areas of life. But only so much can be accomplished in this way. Unless both members of the couple are making a lot of money, they will find themselves falling behind—both at work and at home. Daycare offers only partial relief, and cutting back on work hours is often not an option. The result will be a chronic shortage of time, and they will have trouble competing with couples who do adopt a division of labour. This may lead to stress, overwork, and in many cases, divorce.

If women are going to compete with men who have housewives, the easiest way for them to do this is to secure househusbands of their own.

Unfortunately, this is much easier said than done. While a lot of men express some uneasiness about marrying women who make more money than they do, women's own attitudes can also be a major impediment. The biggest problem is that women with a strong career orientation tend to want men who share this value. Women may say that they want a man who is warm, caring, and nurturing. Whether they will actually *choose* such a man—over one who is bold, ambitious, and successful—is a different matter.

The more general problem is that feminism, despite all protestations to the contrary, has had the effect of devaluing the homemaker role. Young career women often think that becoming a housewife is a sign of failure. It is difficult to avoid projecting the same attitudes onto men. Anyone who thinks that housewives are losers is probably even more likely to think that *househusbands* are losers. As a result, they are unlikely to respect a man whose goal is to stay home and raise kids.

Women with careers have little incentive to marry men for their money. But because they tend to value career achievement, the qualities that they seek in a man also tend to be qualities that are rewarded in the marketplace. As a result, many career women wind up marrying men who will earn more than they do, even if they didn't set out to do so.

The only solution to this problem would seem to be for women to start valuing other qualities in men. It is, unfortunately, not obvious that a simple reversal of the traditional beauty/wealth exchange is going to work out well for women. Some people have looked to marriage patterns among black Americans for inspiration. Studies have shown that black women consider the physical appearance of their partner far more important than do most other American women. Many people think that this is economically driven. While college-educated black men in America earn, on average, substantially less than white men, college-educated black women earn roughly the same amount as white women. As a result, in black couples the woman is more likely to be the one bringing money and earning potential into the relationship. Black men have, on average, less to offer in the way of financial security. This has apparently generated a role-reversal, leading to the development of a cult of physical beauty among black men.

Whether or not this is true, or whether the model can be generalized, is a judgement call. I am not especially optimistic. As things stand currently, it seems to me that the vast majority of men care a lot more about what their partner looks like than do women. As a result, it is not obvious that women stand to gain as much, on a personal level, from a reversal of the beauty/wealth exchange. Whether this can be changed is an open question.

If there is any hope at all on the horizon, I think it may come from an increased propensity among women to marry "creative" men. One of the major attractions of poets, sculptors, writers, painters, and perhaps even philosophers is that while their activities confer enormous cultural status, they have almost no market value. Furthermore, their schedules tend to be extremely flexible. This makes them very attractive marriage material for aspiring career women. Their lack of earning potential makes them the obvious choice for primary caregiver. And the prestige associated with art and culture means that women who do hook up with such men will not suffer any loss of status. Granted, there are not currently enough of such men to go around, but this may change if the general level of affluence continues to increase as it has done.

Men may be catching on to this too. One of the most memorable characters in Guy Vanderhaeghe's *Man Descending* is the man who admits that "after being unemployed for a full twelve months I had to invent a plausible occupation. People were always asking me what I did. I didn't do anything. I was simply unemployed. . . . So one day, in answer to the inevitable question as to what I did, I replied that I was a writer. It just popped into my head. I noted a cessation of embarrassing questions."

So maybe artists will become the trophy husbands of the future.

Many people are disturbed by the changes that have been going on in the family. Home has become a lot more like work, as chronically time-starved parents manage a small army of subcontractors, then try to squeeze in an hour of quality time in the late evening. In the end, the parents feel guilty, and the kids—well, who knows what happens to the kids? It depends who you ask.

Amidst all this anxiety, there has been a tendency to blame our commitment to efficiency for the situation that has developed. Hochschild, for instance, draws a comparison between modern parents and the "time-and-motion" experts of the early twentieth century, suggesting that parents are trying to squeeze more performance out of their kids in the same way that a factory manager would. She claims that we are living in the era of the "Taylorized family."

The problem with this attack is that it mistakes the symptoms for the cause. The core problem with the modern family comes from the rejection of the division of labour and the efficiency loss that this entails. All the other things that parents do—the "Taylorian" organizational strategies—are simply an attempt to make up for this loss. It is these attempts to fix the problem that are mistakenly identified as the source of it.

Of course, nowhere is it written in stone that parents must make up for this efficiency loss. If people's goals were just to keep their families in food and secure a roof over their heads, then this could be accomplished with fairly minimal demands on their time. But this is generally not all that people want. Instead, they try to maximize household income or household consumption. Once this choice has been made, then efficiency becomes a dominant concern in the organization of the home, and it begins to create pressure to reintroduce the traditional division of labour.

Shop to Live, Live to Shop

In 1988, *I made a special trip* to Toronto to attend what was jokingly referred to as "the anarchist convention." One of the largest of its kind in North America, the "survival gathering"—as it was more officially known—brought together radicals and agitators from around the world. Central issues on the agenda included the abolition of property rights and the overthrow of the state. A good time was had by all.

The organizers were thoughtful enough to hold the conference across the street from a beer store. This would have been convenient, except that the police decided to camp out in the parking lot and arrest anyone who jaywalked. Canadians were fined, but anyone from outside the country who got stopped was hauled off to the police station, handed over to immigration authorities, and promptly deported.

So over the course of the convention, anyone who happened to pass by could see gangs of thirsty anarchists dutifully tromping down the street to the nearest intersection, then sullenly waiting for the light to change. A dramatic illustration of Rousseau's dictum that "man is born free, but everywhere is in chains."

Flash forward to 1998. The anarchist gathering convenes once again. Three things have changed. First, the police don't seem to care very much about anarchists any more. Second, mass media outlets all provide fawning coverage. Third, the conference is dominated by a new set of concerns. Most of the talk is now about advertising and consumerism. The anarchist movement is dominated by a new bunch of radicals who call themselves "culture jammers."

The flagship publication of the culture jamming movement is the Vancouver magazine *Adbusters*. Their goal is to undermine capitalism by blocking or subverting advertising messages. According to Kalle Lasn, the founder of *Adbusters*, culture jamming "will become to our era what civil rights was to the '60s, what feminism was to the '70s, what environmental activism was to the '80s."

This is pretty big talk. But many of us from the old school have our doubts. Is consumerism really that important? Will capitalism grind to a halt just because some punks spray "subversive" messages on billboards? What exactly is wrong with companies "branding" their products?

Seeking answers to this question, I decided to drop by the *Adbusters* web site. There I discovered to my surprise an entire section of *Adbusters* merchandise. Get your *Adbusters* T-shirts! your *Adbusters* calendar! your *Adbusters* postcards and posters! your *Adbusters* culture jammers how-to video! I noticed that Lasn has even begun leveraging the *Adbusters* brand into book publishing with his latest title, suitably named *Culture Jam*.

Obviously I had underestimated the *Adbusters* phenomenon. Buying the magazine is just the beginning. You can also purchase the entire line of *Adbusters* lifestyle products. You can *become* a culture jammer.

This is a nice example of what we used to refer to, back in the old days, as the "cultural contradictions of late capitalism."

The incoherence of the *Adbusters* message is so close to the surface that it may seem a little mean-spirited to point it out. And besides, there is a serious point underlying it. We live in a society that enjoys an unprecedented level of material comfort, and yet none of it seems to have made us much happier. This naturally invites us to wonder what the point of it all is. We are busy despoiling the planet and consuming natural resources at an unsustainable rate, but to what end? The cost of our activities is apparent, but the benefits are less than obvious.

The reason that there has been so little increase in overall happiness is not hard to figure out. No matter how much people have, they always seem to want more. Human desire has so far proven to be insatiable. Each new product makes us happier for a while—I genuinely like my new dishwasher, and it does a better job than the old one—but within a short time the novelty fades, leaving us wanting more.

Back in the 1920s, Joseph Schumpeter pointed out that if a 2 per cent annual growth rate were maintained for only fifty years, even with a sizable increase in the population, average income would still double. This explosion of prosperity would create such a vast abundance of resources that we could easily eliminate poverty with just spare change. He speculated that "if capitalism repeated its past performance for another half century starting with 1928, this would do away with anything that according to present standards could be called poverty, even in the lowest strata of the population, pathological cases excepted."

Sixty years earlier, Karl Marx had made roughly the same prediction. Economic growth was creating such a preposterous excess of wealth that he could scarcely imagine the persistence of poverty. The fact that people fought tooth and nail to defend their little hoard was assumed by both authors to be a product of ongoing scarcity. Once people became richer, they couldn't possibly begrudge their neighbour at least a share of these riches.

What an epochal miscalculation. If one thing has been proven over the course of the twentieth century, it is that the level of possessiveness and greed exhibited by the average person has nothing to do with his or her absolute level of wealth. Walk into any casino in Canada and you can find hordes of senior citizens with so much money on their hands that they can't even think of ways to spend it. They wind up frittering it away on the slots. But suggest to them that they should perhaps pay more taxes in order to help the poor, and things may get ugly.

The mistake that both Marx and Schumpeter made was to assume that people's needs would remain roughly constant. It is certainly true that if we had continued to eat the same sort of food, live in the same sort of houses, and wear the same sort of clothes as our great-grandparents, then we would all have so much money left over at the end of the day that we wouldn't know what to do with it. But of course as we got richer, our desires changed as well. We don't like eating the same thing day after day. We like to put on a fresh set of clothes every morning, instead of wearing the same ones for a week. We like to have bathrooms in our houses. As a result, we have no more "left over" at the end of the day than people did fifty or one hundred years ago. The huge surplus that was supposed to eliminate poverty simply never materialized.

If all the needs and desires that we have now had been there from the beginning, then none of this would be a problem. People one hundred years ago would have been desperately unhappy, and the growth of the economy since then would have slowly reduced this misery. But this is clearly not how things have worked. Many of the needs that our economy currently satisfies are of much more recent vintage. The process of economic growth has been accompanied by the creation of new wants. People didn't start to want electric toothbrushes, automatic garage door openers, or video games until *after* someone started to manufacture them.

This represents a profound challenge to the ideal of an efficient society. If the creation of new products leads to the development of new needs, then the net effect is not a gain in efficiency. People were just as happy when they had no video games and no need for video games as they are today when they have both the games and the need for them. And since the production of these goods generates negative externalities, in the form of environmental degradation and resource depletion, the net effect is actually negative. The introduction of new products would appear to generate an efficiency loss.

Even worse, when a new product is introduced, it is not always available to everyone. The latest electronic gadget may be affordable only to a small segment of the population. The introduction of that gadget may, however, create a *need* among a much broader stratum. Once one kid at school gets a Game Boy, every other kid has to have one as well. But not every kid's parents can afford it. Thus our ability to create new desires may outstrip our capacity to satisfy them. The result is that new products, by creating new desires, actually lead to *unhappiness*. The kid who gets the Game Boy winds up being no happier than he was before he had even heard of Game Boys, and all the other kids who didn't get one are miserable. As a result, no one benefits, and the welfare of some is reduced. It is a lose-lose transformation, a textbook case of Pareto-inefficiency.

Our economic system, however, encourages people to make this happen. The creation of new products, and with them new desires, is richly rewarded by the marketplace. As a result, the minds and energies of our brightest, most ambitious citizens are absorbed into activities that ultimately produce goods for which, in some sense, we have no need.

The core problem is what we in the business call "the proliferation of desire." Desires are like rabbits, or cockroaches, or tribbles. If you feed them, they reproduce. Then you just have more to feed.

In case you didn't know, that's why you can't get no satisfaction.

The big question is whether this problem is universal. If it were simply the human predicament, then not much could be done. It would just be one more reason not to place too much emphasis on production, or wealth, as an index of human well-being. But critics of consumerism are making a more radical claim. They argue that something specific to our society encourages the proliferation of desire. The cycle of increased production followed by expanded need is, if not unique to our culture, then at least exacerbated by aspects of our economic system.

The major culprit is supposed to be advertising. If there is one feature of our society that is most obviously involved in the manufacture of desire, it is advertising. (Furthermore, advertising is a very characteristic component of our way of life. One of the symptoms of Westernization in many parts of the world is the appearance of billboards and commercials.)

Every day, the average North American is bombarded with more than three thousand advertising messages, each one encouraging us to believe that life will be unbearable without the purchase of some new product.

It's not hard to imagine that this massive assault has a seriously distorting effect upon our desires and expectations, that we are being manipulated by these ads, persuaded to want things we don't really need.

One can find examples of this view everywhere. It is the line Mark Kingwell takes, for instance, in his recent book on happiness:

> What makes a good advertiser good is precisely his or her ability to make us want something we did not previously feel any need for. . . . Advertisers are therefore the contemporary world's leading experts at instilling desire and manufacturing longing—injecting us with images, humour and state-of-the-art graphics, as a virus might be injected via a finely tuned hypodermic needle.

Kalle Lasn expresses much the same concern:

> The commercial mass media are rearranging our neurons, manipulating our emotions, making powerful connections between deep immaterial needs and material products. So virtual is the hypodermic needle that we don't feel it. So gradually is the dosage increased that we're not aware of the toxicity.

I don't know what the fixation on needles is about, but the point is pretty clear. Increased production is obviously of no value if the goods are being produced to satisfy needs that are themselves the product of advertising. More radically, the efficiency gains achieved are of no value if the desires that are being satisfied are themselves manufactured. People would be just as happy not having either the desires *or* the goods.

But this criticism moves a bit too quickly. No one wants to claim that all production is useless or that all desires are manufactured. Clearly our need for food on the table and a roof over our heads is perfectly authentic, and a society that provides these things for its members is better than one that does not. Thus critics of consumerism like

Kingwell and Lasn must draw some kind of distinction between natural or authentic needs (those that society has an interest in satisfying) and artificial or inauthentic ones (those that are of no particular value).

The secret to avoiding consumerism, according to Kingwell, is to get rid of all those artifical needs. When searching for happines, we need to ask ourselves, "How do we dig beneath the layers of manipulation and distortion that blanket our ideas of happiness? Is there a residue of happiness, a substratum of genuine meaning uninfected by the viruses of technology, advertising, pathologization, narcissism and popular culture?"

As far as I'm concerned, the answers to these two questions are "we don't" and "no" respectively. The idea that we have some sort of natural self, hidden deep beneath all the artificial layers added on by society or "popular culture" is nothing but a Romantic article of faith. In its modern form, the idea comes from Jean-Jacques Rousseau's *Discourse on the Origin of Inequality*. Here, Rousseau draws an invidious contrast between our "natural" desires, which are all good and pure, and the "corrupt" desires, which are a product of the so-called progress of civilization.

This distinction is dubious in the extreme. Every desire we have is a product of our cultural environment, and all culture is, in an important sense, artificial. The kind of food we want to eat, the housing we expect, the clothing we feel comfortable wearing, all of these desires are formed by looking around us at the sort of things that other people have. Some people acquire these desires through exposure to advertising, others acquire them simply by seeing an object or hearing other people talk about it, or by being given a sample at a friend's house, or by being forced to consume it by their mother. Which of these processes is the more "natural"? It is difficult to imagine that any clear distinction can be drawn here.

Besides, even if we could dig down into the farthest reaches of our psyche to find desires that are uncontaminated by any external influences, it is wishful thinking to believe that we would actually *like* anything that we found. One of the major functions of socialization is to help us suppress some of the more extreme antisocial impulses that we all seem to experience at one time or another. Thus there is no particular reason to believe that the secret to happiness lies in digging down and discovering our inner selves.

This is not the biggest problem with the standard criticism of consumerism. Even if it were possible to filter out all the "artificial" desires instilled in us through advertising and find some respectable set of innate needs, it is not clear what we could do about it. Unlike feminism and environmentalism, both movements with a clear legislative agenda, the standard critique of consumerism could never serve as a suitable basis for political action.

Critics of consumerism often describe our society as one that is dominated by shallow, materialistic values. This may in fact be true. But in a pluralistic society, government is not in the business of deciding whose values are important and whose are shallow. Bad taste is not a crime, nor should it be. We can use the critique of consumerism as grounds to harangue our fellow citizens and try to get them to improve their consumption choices, but we cannot use it as a basis for public policy.

The problem, ultimately, is that the standard critique of consumerism is a more-or-less disguised form of perfectionism. Like Aristotle and his medieval interpreters, these critics assume that we are capable of sorting out some appropriate conception of the good that all should share. The critics of consumerism may not use the terminology, but what they are really doing is separating virtue from vice—defending the Jerusalem of our inner self against the Sodom and Gomorrah of the marketplace. But while the lure of perfection may be great, politically it is a non-starter. We may believe that frugality and thrift are important virtues, but that doesn't entitle us to use state power to enforce them. Some people's consumption habits may indeed be excessive. But who are we to tell them to stop?

The major attraction of efficiency as an organizing principle of society is that it does not require us to make judgements about the relative importance of different people's life projects. This is what allows us to achieve social order despite deep differences in cultural tradition and religious doctrine. If a particular change makes some people happier from their own point of view and doesn't harm anyone else, then we are inclined to go for it. Hence the deep connection between the principle of efficiency and the ideal of a society ruled by agreement or contract.

The perfectionist critics of consumerism are tempted to turn back the clock on these developments and re-establish a social order based on a consensus about the good. This isn't a problem so long as they are only interested in caviling about the overall decline of good taste. They are free to use whatever techniques of persuasion they can muster. But what they are not entitled to do, within the framework of a liberal political order, is use state power to force people's hands, or even to discourage them from their choices. We cannot legislate desire. Nor is it appropriate to even sanction desire if our only reason for doing so is that we consider some desires to be less important than our own.

So even if we don't like consumerism and consumerist values, it may still be wiser for us to take people's expressed needs at face value and to judge a social arrangement preferable if it provides more adequately for these needs. If people say that they need Prada handbags and Gucci loafers, we are better off letting them have them. Denying such requests gets us into political territory that our ancestors wisely chose to abandon.

If life were simple, that would be the final word on consumerism. Life, however, is not simple. There is another strain of criticism in the anti-consumerism literature that is actually quite different from the perfectionist line, although the two are seldom adequately distinguished. This has to do with competitive consumption.

We do not buy things just to satisfy our physical needs. Our consumption choices send very important signals to others about what kind of people we are. We express ourselves through our clothes, our houses, our cars, and our lifestyles. (This is true of everyone, not just those who are into shopping. Often among those who are hostile to consumerism, it takes the form of negative preferences—*not* driving a Pontiac, *not* drinking Budweiser, or *not* wearing a tie. These sorts of negative choices are just as important as positive ones in constructing one's personal identity.)

The problem arises because these sorts of choices also have important consequences for one's social status, and social status has an intrinsically competitive structure. Whether it be Armani suits or body piercings, you get status by having *more* of them than most people. As a result, status competitions often turn into little arms races. People wind up acquiring far more of the fetish objects than they initially intended to acquire, because they come under pressure to "keep up" with others.

Critics of consumerism often allude to this by identifying "envy" as one of the negative consequences of advertising. According to this view, advertisers encourage these sorts of status competitions by making people envious of each other's possessions. Once this is done, people will begin competing with one another to buy more and more. Thus envy is held to be the root cause of the typical "keeping up with the Joneses" consumption pattern.

This is basically correct, but the identification of envy as the root cause is misleading and betrays the moralistic core of the standard perfectionist critique. Envy, as we all know, is one of the seven deadly sins. This can easily make it seem as if what is wrong with keeping up with the Joneses is that it is motivated by "bad" values. But the problem is not with people's motives. It is with the *outcome* that they get. Competitive consumption is a prisoner's dilemma. The real problem with consumerism is that it is *inefficient*.

The focus on envy helps to conceal the fact that any comparative preference can generate a prisoner's dilemma for consumers. In the movie *American Beauty*, for instance, Annette Bening's character considers it important to project an "image of success." The problem, of course, with projecting an image of success is that success is entirely relative. What were considered sure signs of prosperity and success thirty years ago are now just rudimentary components of a middle-class lifestyle. The only way to project success is to appear more successful than one's neighbours—to drive a nicer car, have a larger house, and so on. Thus comparative consumption can easily become competitive consumption. And in many circumstances, this competition becomes a race to the bottom.

Suppose that two neighbours are working a standard week and driving modest Honda sedans. However, by putting in a bit of overtime, it is possible for each to buy a more expensive car, say a BMW. Suppose further that the extra status associated with being the only one to own such a vehicle is of greater value than the foregone leisure time, and that the humiliation associated with being the only one *not* to own such a vehicle is worse than the loss of leisure. The interaction then has the structure of a classic prisoner's dilemma. Here are each neighbour's preferences, in order of desirability:

1. You get the BMW; your neighbour keeps the Honda. Success level: high. Work load: high.
2. You both keep the Hondas. Success level: average. Work load: low.
3. You both get BMWs. Success level: average. Work load: high.
4. You keep the Honda; your neighbour buys a BMW. Success level: low. Work load: low.

Both neighbours will decide to work harder and buy the BMWs, either to get the extra status or just to avoid looking like losers. As a result, they will wind up with outcome three, making their own lives worse. They will still be driving the same type of car—and so neither will gain status—but now they will be paying $79.95 for an oil change. Thus the outcome produced through status competition is inferior, from both the participants' perspectives, to the situation that initially obtained.

The problem of consumerism, according to this view, is not a challenge to the ideal of an efficient society. The fact that people are the victims of consumerism is not a reason to ignore the significance of efficiency gains in the economy. Instead, consumerism is diagnosed as a source of inefficiency. Abolishing competitive consumption is seen as a way to increase the overall level of consumer satisfaction. Thus increased efficiency is the solution, not the problem.

Focusing critical attention on competitive consumption—on the grounds that it leads to inefficient outcomes—has a number of attractions. It helps to explain how we can have such enormous material prosperity and yet not be happy. It also provides a diagnosis that could be useful in formulating public policy. The problem of consumerism, according to this view, has nothing to do with people having "bad" desires. And so there is no need to come in from the outside and start telling people what they should and should not want. One need only point out that because of the competition that the quest for certain consumer goods generates, everyone winds up in worse condition—from the standpoint of their own preferences—at the end of the day.

For example, it is perhaps not surprising that the resurgence of consumerist spending habits that occurred during the 1980s coincided with a "flattening" of the U.S. income tax system. Once basic material needs are taken care of, almost all consumption consists of buying "nice" things. Whether or not something is "nice" is completely comparative—it depends upon how nice *other* people's things are. Thus people in higher income brackets are natural suckers for competitive consumption.

This contributes to the cycle of overwork and overspending that has recently become the subject of much discussion in the United States. People put in a bit more time at work in order to increase their consumption. This leads their nearest competitors to ratchet up their own work hours and consumption level in order to stay even. The only way to make gains at this point is to put even more time into work and to consume even more. This is what creates the infamous rat race. The result is that everyone winds up working more and consuming more than they actually want.

A progressive income tax helps to discourage this by imposing an increased cost on those who adopt the free-rider strategy of working more. In a situation in which people are both overworked and overspent, income taxes may increase the efficiency of the economy, even if they reduce both work effort and overall output. This may sound strange, but it must be kept in mind that the efficiency of the economy is not judged by the sheer volume of material goods that it produces. The economy is efficient if and only if it produces goods that satisfy people's *needs*. When people get into competitive consumption, the goods that they purchase fail to satisfy their needs. So while eliminating these competitions will lead to a decline in the production of certain goods, the result will be an improvement in everyone's overall level of satisfaction. Thus a contraction in the economy will coincide with a gain in efficiency.

There is nothing wrong with recommending changes in the tax structure based on considerations such as these. It is not like the situation in which one group in society would simply impose on others its own view of what should and should not be consumed. Deterring competitive consumption is something that, in principle, everyone should be able to agree to, because the race to the bottom frustrates everyone's desires.

The "keeping up with the Joneses" model is helpful because it shows how people can get stuck in cycles of ever-expanding consumption. Unfortunately, it also serves to perpetuate a somewhat antiquated view of how competitive consumption works in our society. When we think of consumerism, we tend to think of classic 1950s-style status competition. We think of acres of identical tract homes in the suburbs, people driving big cars, tending their perfect lawns, rearing 2.3 kids, and so on. In this status system, everyone strives to be respectable and has a compulsive need to conform to the expectations of their neighbours and peers.

The problem with this picture is that it identifies consumerism with conformity. Thus the individualist or the rebel, the one who lashes out against the staid conformity of suburban living, becomes a cultural hero, someone who strikes a blow against the shallow materialism of our age. The re-enactment of this narrative has become so dominant in our culture that it is almost never subjected to critical scrutiny. (Think again of the movie *American Beauty*, which provided one of the most formulaic versions in recent memory.)

But it only takes a moment of reflection to see that the desire to conform could not possibly be among the forces driving consumerism. If all that people wanted to do was fit in, then there would be nothing to generate competition or escalate the level of consumption. In a society of compulsive conformists, everyone would run out and buy the same stuff, but once that was finished, the spending spree would come to an end. The system would quickly reach an equilibrium in which everyone had the same things, and everyone was perfectly satisfied.

Status competition is not about fitting in or conforming. Quite the opposite. Social status is obtained by achieving some form of *distinction*—doing something that sets you apart from others. And status comparisons are always invidious. The only way to acquire status is to acquire *more* of it than someone else.

In the typical suburban scene, it may look as though everyone is a conformist. But this is to mistake the outcome for the cause. In fact, people are all striving for distinction. The first BMW showed up because someone wanted a more luxurious car than his neighbours. This initiated the prisoner's dilemma, forcing everyone else to follow suit in order to retain position. Then someone else got the bright idea of installing a private swimming pool, and so everyone had to get one of those. Things degenerated from there. Lately people have been ripping out their lawns and installing expensive "English gardens."

The important point is that it is the individualist—the one who tries to achieve distinction through consumption—who sets the whole thing off. Marketing agencies have understood this for a long time, which is why the image of the "rebel consumer" has been assiduously cultivated by advertisers since the early 1960s. The style of "better living" advertising of the '50s, which encouraged people to consume in order to impress their neighbours and project an image of domestic harmony, became moribund a long time ago. Since the '60s, advertising agencies have been encouraging consumers *not* to fit in, but to rebel, to express their individuality through their consumption choices. And far from being an attempt to co-opt a rebellious and individualistic counter-culture, this movement in advertising often predated the formation of the relevant subcultures.

The clearest example of this is the first Volkswagen Bug, which became one of the most prominent symbols of the hippie counterculture of the late '60s. This was entirely a product of effective advertising. At the end of the 1950s, most Americans thought the Bug was ugly and associated it primarily with the Nazis. The car's fortunes in America were turned around by a now-famous advertising campaign, which began in 1961, that encouraged consumers to buy Bugs precisely because they were ugly, unglamorous, and square. Buying a Bug was a way of rebelling against the big three automakers and their programs of planned obsolescence. It was a way of taking a stand against consumerism.

In this way, the classic critique of consumerism was itself used as a way to sell cars, and with enormous success. Wanting to be a rebel, an individual, to stand out from the crowd, is an *intrinsically positional good*—it derives most of its value from a comparison with others. If everyone else is going to be wearing a suit and tie, then showing up in casual dress is a way to appear more relaxed, personable, and fun than everyone else. If everyone else is driving an Oldsmobile, then driving a Bug makes you stand out; it seems fresh, hip, cool (or as we would now say, irreverent, quirky, edgy). Of course, when everyone else joins in the rebellion, the effect is lost. So the individualist has to come up with some new way to stand out from the crowd. Often enough, this will involve buying something new. Thus individualism generates its own cycles of obsolescence.

There was a time when a man could get along fine with just three good suits. But the need to express one's individuality through clothing demands a much larger wardrobe. The man in the sensible suit is now labelled a conformist, an object of contempt and derision. The individualist, or the rebel, is smarter. He can break all the rules and still get ahead. (After all, the man who breaks the company dress code must be really hot stuff, otherwise they would have fired him long ago.) Thus the classic critique of consumerism becomes the primary mechanism through which cultural élites express distinction and assign low status to the consumption choices of the majority. In other words, the critique of consumerism is one of the major forces *driving* consumerism today.

So when we look around for someone to blame for consumerism, we should point our finger at the rebels, not the sheep.

What is cool? A surprising amount of ink has been spilled on the subject. We can all think of examples of people or things that are cool. But what is cool itself? What is it about these people or things that makes them cool?

The answer is quite simple. Cool is the central status hierarchy in contemporary urban society. Cool things are the objects that satisfy the consumer preferences of cool people.

This is why cool is the central ideology of consumerism in our times.

Cool is first and foremost a form of distinction. People cannot be cool unless the majority of other people are uncool. The other central component in the ideology of cool is what social critic Thomas Frank has called the "countercultural idea." According to this story, mainstream culture is monolithic, homogeneous, and hierarchical. It projects these values onto society both directly—by dominating sectors of the market—and indirectly—through advertising. Squaring off against the mainstream are the life-affirming, Dionysian cultural rebels. These people are able to elude the mesmerizing effects of consumerism and create their own spontaneous, vibrant, authentic—cool—cultural communities. These pocket subcultures are profoundly subversive of the established order, yet are somehow always in danger of being absorbed into the mainstream. Thus there is a constant struggle between the two, as the counterculture subverts the mainstream, while the mainstream attempts to co-opt the subculture (by adopting its images for use in advertising, mass-producing its clothing styles, etc.).

Of course, none of this is true. The myth that subcultures are co-opted stems from a failure to recognize the positional nature of the goods that are being sought. The problem is not that corporations co-opt countercultures, it is that rebelling through style or consumption is collectively self-defeating (in the same way that conspicuous consumption is). Owning a Mercedes twenty years ago in North America conveyed enormous status. Now that they can be purchased through any Chrysler dealership, they aren't such a big deal. Similarly, being a fan of REM or the Red Hot Chili Peppers fifteen years ago conferred enormous status upon the listener, whereas now it means nothing.

Originally, the cachet lay in being one of a small number of people who knew about a good band (which showed that one had the right sort of connections or was part of the right scene). The problem was that as more people achieved this, the status associated with it declined. So eventually the band came to be seen as a "sell-out," even though their sound did not change one bit. Thus co-optation is not something that corporations do from the outside; it is an endogenous effect produced by consumers, a logical consequence of many people seeking to obtain the same positional good.

It would be nice if we could always drive down uncongested freeways, or hike through untouched wilderness, or enjoy the work of fantastic "underground" artists. In the same way, it would be nice if, like the children of Lake Wobegon, we could all be above average. Unfortunately, everyone wanting it precludes everyone getting it.

This is why "cool" has proven so elusive to many theorists. It is a positional good. As soon as other people find out about what is cool, then one has to move on. For example, seriously cool people in New York City are always dismayed when their favourite new bar or club gets a write-up in the *Village Voice*. Those on the inside track initially would have gotten to know about the place through word of mouth, and so their presence there conferred status. However, once it appears in the *Voice*, then a predictable flood of yuppies begins to arrive, ruining it for everyone else. (This is often why unadvertised goods have high cachet. One has to be in the know in order to know whether or where to buy them. Purchasing and displaying them is a sign of having desirable social connections.)

The fact that cool people display an ironic attitude towards consumption and are sometimes even vocal critics of it does not mean that they are not engaged in consumerist behaviour. Often this is concealed by the fact that their consumer taste is dominated by negative preferences—things that one wouldn't be caught dead reading, wearing, or driving. But whenever such a comparative preference structure is in place, it has the potential to generate the type of collectively self-defeating behaviour that is the core component of consumerism.

This is why so much popular criticism of consumerism is pointless. More often than not, the critics are themselves using these denunciations as a way to establish their own distinction. They are also engaged in status competition—usually trying to up their "coolness" factor. But whether you spend your money on a fancy car or go off backpacking for six months in Thailand, you are still engaging in conspicuous consumption (as Thai peasants will no doubt attest—after all, *not* working is the oldest and most ostentatious way to display wealth).

The fact that certain consumption choices reflect supposedly "post-materialist" values is irrelevant. The whole "new simplicity" movement, for instance, far from being an escape from consumerism, is just one more formula for achieving distinction through consumption choices. What matters is whether the goods or the lifestyle are *positional*. As long as some portion of the value of goods is derived from a comparison to others, then their acquisition contributes to the consumerism of our culture.

Only when we learn to feel comfortable once again wearing uniforms will consumerism be vanquished. If we persist in valuing individuality and non-conformity, then we must learn to stop complaining about the consequences of this decision—one of which will be that we live in a consumerist society.

What I have been arguing so far is that consumerism is first and foremost a product of consumer behaviour rather than external pressures, and that most popular denunciations of consumerism are simply an expression of the critic's irritation over the loss of distinction that occurs when exclusive goods become objects of mass consumption.

While this may be true, it still seems to let corporations off the hook a bit too easily. Advertising is, after all, genuinely objectionable. The contamination of our environment by advertising messages is probably the most conspicuous defect in our economic system.

Consider the following definition of pollution, which comes from a standard textbook on government regulation:

> [Pollution] is the result of (1) the production of a product with no commercial value because it is technologically tied to the production of a product that has economic value, (2) the dumping of the unwanted by-product into the environment to dispose of it, and (3) the consumption of the by-product, with a negative value to anyone forced to consume it, simply by being exposed to it.

If we take this definition at face value, then advertising is clearly a form of pollution. We generally do not like ads, and we do not choose to consume them. They are fed to us at times when we are a captive audience—sandwiched between segments of a TV show, displayed on billboards as we drive down the road, or plastered over the walls in elevators and washrooms. If advertising had positive value for consumers, none of this would be necessary. You could charge people for the privilege of viewing advertisements. So even though some ads are entertaining, the fact that no one will pay for the privilege of viewing them shows that they have, at best, zero value to consumers.

But there is one big difference between advertising and standard pollution. While most pollution is "technologically tied" to the production of certain goods—so there is no way to get the goods without getting the by-products—nowhere is it written in stone that companies have to advertise. Advertising is something that they choose to do. In many ways, this makes it even more obnoxious. It means that the welfare loss created when we are forced to consume unwanted advertising messages is unnecessary.

This observation has long fuelled the suspicion that advertising is a source of inefficiency in the economy. More than US$200 billion is spent on advertising every year in the United States. Of course, advertising agencies contribute to the GDP as though they were productive enterprises, even though most of the goods they create have negative value to consumers. The efficiency loss only comes into view when one thinks about other ways that these resources could have been spent, and how much better off we would all be if the clever people in the advertising business spent their time producing something that we *want* to consume.

Of course, some advertising has the simple function of providing information to consumers. Announcing that there is a sale going on or informing consumers about a new product being introduced has obvious social value. It can also be argued that "branding" creates value in a product by building up positive mental associations that heighten the consumer's enjoyment. But these are clearly marginal cases. Most advertising has the structure of a race to the bottom. Take the example of a heavily advertised product such as beer. The overall level of beer consumption has been flat for the last thirty years. Since the size of the market has remained fixed, breweries compete with one another only for market share. They do not create new customers, they only take customers away from each other. Thus a gain for one firm is a loss for some other. (This is actually a common feature of many industries in which there is heavy advertising. Advertising seldom increases the overall size of a market; it only increases relative market share.)

In Canada, the beer market is dominated by two major breweries—Molson and Labatt. Despite a steep decline in market share over the past few years, these two companies still control 74 per cent of the Canadian market. Suppose that in the beginning neither company spends much on advertising. If either company starts to advertise, it will be able to steal some customers away from the other. But if the other company responds with its own advertising campaign, the effect will be neutralized. So in the end, the number of customers will be the same, and the relative market share of both firms will be the same. The only difference will be that both firms are sustaining expensive advertising campaigns.

Thus competition through advertising is like price competition: it is not in either firm's interest to do it, but because they are stuck in a prisoner's dilemma, they have no choice but to do it. The difference is that price competition drives prices down and therefore benefits consumers. Advertising competition, on the other hand, drives prices up, produces nuisance goods, and generates wasteful investment in unproductive activities.

Naturally, if companies begin spending too much money on advertising, they will begin to attract "discounters" into the industry, who will compete by offering substantially cheaper unadvertised products (as with the introduction of "no name" brands into grocery stores). Thus the most heavily advertised products are in areas where there are substantial barriers to entry. In the beer industry, for example, there are major economies of scale, which make it difficult for new firms to compete on price, even if they do not advertise. Thus microbrewery beer is usually more expensive than "macrobrew," even though the two big Canadian breweries spend more than $200 million every year on advertising.

So advertising is a source of enormous waste. The whole point—the only point—of having an economy dominated by profit-maximizing private firms is that these firms will engage in price competition, and this competition will generate increased efficiency. This means that whenever firms are not engaged in price competition, then the entire rationale for their existence disappears.

If this were all there was to it, then it would be possible to make a compelling case against advertising. People are usually scandalized to discover that a significant fraction of the money they give to charity does not find its way into the hands of the needy, but is used to finance further solicitation. We should be just as scandalized that a significant fraction of the money we spend on beer is used not to produce beer, but to finance solicitation. Both represent a waste of resources that could have been used to improve human welfare.

Certain professional associations have rules that prevent their members from advertising. Doctors and lawyers are a case in point. There is no reason other industries could not follow suit or governments could not legislate similar arrangements. (For example, direct-to-consumer advertisements for prescription pharmaceuticals are pernicious on every possible level—the fact that they remain legal is extraordinary.) Similarly, governments could—and probably should—stop treating the money spent by companies on advertising as a tax-deductible business expense.

It will often be in the interest of corporations to accept such regulations simply because advertising, like price competition, is an inter-firm prisoner's dilemma. Many cartelized industries ban advertising by member firms for precisely this reason. (This is what explains the curious fact that in Canada we have ads for "eggs" in general or "butter" in general, but not for specific dairy producers.)

The attempt to ban tobacco advertising has shown, however, that there are some problems associated with this strategy. Advertising may be a waste of resources, but it also has the function of sustaining a wide range of economically marginal yet socially beneficial activities. Many people supported the ban on tobacco advertising until they discovered that such a ban might mean the cancellation of their favourite jazz festival, car race, or tennis championship. As it turns out, beer companies were willing to step in and take up the slack. But if *all* advertising were restricted, this option would no longer be available. Many of these events would then no longer be economically viable.

Anyone who uses the internet regularly must have mixed feelings about advertising. In the last five years, the most significant improvements in my personal productivity, along with my overall quality of life, have all been delivered courtesy of the internet. And I have not paid a cent for any of it. Whether sending mp3 files to my friends by e-mail or sitting around at home running Unreal Tournament, ICQ, and Battlechat simultaneously, I am using up a huge chunk of bandwidth. Someone has been thoughtful enough to lay down miles of fibre-optic cable, all of which I am able to use at no cost. Where does the money for all this come from? Most of it is financed through advertising.

When used in this way, advertising is basically a non-market mechanism that corporations can use to recover some of the costs associated with the provision of goods and services. Some websites are restricted to members only. In order to get access, you need to pull out a credit card and pay a fee. This is a standard market transaction. Along with it come all the transaction costs associated with the market mechanism—the cost of tracking payments, the risk of fraud, concern about the quality of goods purchased, and so on. Because these costs can be relatively high, a lot of mutually beneficial exchanges will not occur if the market is the only mechanism through which the transaction can be organized.

In cases where these transaction costs are too high—where people would not be willing to pay for the content—an alternative is to finance delivery through advertising. In this case, value is extracted from consumers, not in the form of an immediate cash payment, but in the form of an increased average propensity to purchase the goods being advertised. Thus the people who eventually purchase the advertised goods because they have seen them advertised are the ones who wind up paying for the content.

Because it represents an alternative to the standard market transaction, advertising is able to correct certain types of market failure—and thus to create efficiency gains. In particular, it is able to finance the provision of goods that are poorly protected by standard property rights, but not important enough to warrant state provision. A perfect example of this is information.

As we have seen, it is very hard to exercise property rights on information. If the only way you could find out what happened yesterday was to buy your own copy of the newspaper, then you would be willing to pay a fair amount for it. But the company that publishes the newspaper is not able to exercise effective control over the information that it provides. Once one person has read the paper, there is no way to prevent her from passing it on. So instead of buying a copy of the newspaper, you have the option of getting the news "for free," by asking someone else what happened or by borrowing a copy of the paper. As a result, newspapers are unable to charge consumers for the full value of the information that they provide, because it is too easy for people to free-ride.

As a result, private markets for information have a tendency to fail. It is possible for the state to step in and correct this market failure. In the former Soviet Union, the state newspaper was posted in public squares for everyone to read. Similar practices prevail in contemporary China. This type of arrangement treats the information as a standard sort of public good, paid for through taxation and provided free to all by the state.

But there are clear disadvantages to this public-goods model as an alternative to the private market solution. For one thing, it lends a tone of great seriousness to all publications, since the only information that will get produced is information that people are willing to pay to receive or that the state considers important enough to tax people in order to provide. The transaction costs are very high in either case, and anything that is merely entertaining, or diversionary, is unlikely to make it through.

Advertising provides a perfect middle road between the private market and the public provision models. With advertising, consumers pay fees that cover only a portion of the cost of the information they receive. The rest is recovered through advertising. These ads can be thought of as a minor "fee" that is levied on each consumer—you get the information, but you also agree to expose yourself to commercial messages.

The ratio of advertising to end-user fees in many media is a direct function of the ease with which people can free-ride on the information source. To take just one example, magazines with no ads are very expensive. As a result, they tend to go out of business, even if there is a decent market for them. For instance, *Cook's Illustrated* is one of my favourite magazines. It does not carry any advertisements, and so it is a lot more expensive than other magazines. As a result, I don't buy it unless it has several recipes in it that interest me. Instead, I leaf through it in the grocery store. If it contains only one or two good recipes, I often just memorize them and write them down when I get home. This is a classic free-rider strategy. If I weren't able to copy the information this way, I would probably get a subscription. And if the magazine carried ads, I would probably buy it every month because it would cost half as much.

Thus advertising may eliminate market failures and thereby produce efficiency gains. Entire segments of the economy currently sustained through advertising might simply cease to exist were this practice to be eliminated. The internet is a case in point. If I had to pay a download fee for every packet I received from the net, I would almost completely stop using it. So would most other people. But the alternative of direct state provision has its problems. Anyone who has used France's disastrous Minitel system will know what I mean.

Advertising may be a nuisance, but it is unfortunately a nuisance that we have come to depend upon in order to organize part of our economy. In many cases, it functions as an alternative to the price mechanism, enabling transactions that might otherwise not occur. One can imagine an arrangement under which government would provide something like a *Consumer Reports* database, freely accessible to all citizens, which would list and evaluate all major consumer products on the market. With an information source like this available, it would then be possible to place restrictions on the amount of advertising that companies could purchase (the same way election spending is currently capped). But in the process, we would undermine a number of different sectors of the economy that depend upon advertising for their survival.

So we cannot without hypocrisy blame advertising for all the ills of our civilization. Or even for a majority of them. And as far as consumerism goes, it is not obvious that advertising has much to do with it. The underlying problem is the competition for status or distinction. The best way to avoid consumerism is to get out of this competition.

Thinking back to the anarchist gathering, it occurs to me that one other thing changed between 1988 and 1998. There was a dramatic increase in the average number of body piercings and tattoos. Back in

1988, my five earrings, a nose ring, and a tattoo were enough to attract some attention. At school, they even caused a minor sensation. But the 1990s saw some serious escalation in the piercing/tattooing competition. Nowadays six piercings won't get you any attention and are certainly not enough to qualify as cool.

I realized that I had no chance of keeping up in this race on the day that I first picked up RE/Search's *Modern Primitives* volume. Flipping through it once was enough to persuade me that I didn't have the makings of a contender. I was playing a game that I could not win. So I dropped out. (I think it might have been the photos of the ampallung that pushed me over the edge.) Dropping out meant learning to live with the fact that, as far as being cool was concerned, I had plateaued at the tender age of twenty.

As consumers, we are in exactly the same position. In order to escape from overwork and overspending, we need to drop out of the competitive consumption race. One way to do this is to avoid positional goods and comparative preferences. By avoiding buying things just because they are cool, or distinctive, or popular, you can avoid many of the pitfalls of consumerism. Other people's consumption choices will then no longer affect the level of satisfaction that you get from your purchases.

However, there is only so much that can be accomplished on an individual level. Because consumerism is a collective action problem, the only effective solutions to it must also be collective. When it comes to influencing consumer decisions, the most powerful instrument in the hands of government is its power of taxation. Thus reform of the tax system is the more promising vehicle.

It is sometimes suggested, by those innocent of all economic learning, that taxing consumption is the best way to discourage consumerism (the same way that taxing alcohol discourages alcoholism). In the background is often the view that consumption taxes are better than income taxes, because consumption is bad while working is good. The mistake here comes from a failure to realize that consumption and income are just the same thing, seen from two different perspectives. Your consumption is someone else's income, just as your income comes from someone else's consumption. This is why you can calculate the GDP by adding up either the total of goods and services purchased, or the amount of income earned. The sums will come out the same. (Thus the annual "buy nothing day" sponsored by *Adbusters* could just as easily be called "earn nothing day.")

The way to discourage consumerism is therefore not to have a consumption tax, but rather to have a progressive consumption tax. It is the progressivity that counts, because competitive consumption tends to occur in the so-called "disposable" income range. Implementing such a tax is not as hard as it sounds. Since all income is either saved or consumed, the easiest way to create a progressive consumption tax is simply to have a progressive income tax, with a special exemption for savings. And since retirement savings in Canada are already, for the most part, tax-exempt, this is not so different from what we already have. The best thing to do now is simply make the system more progressive. In so doing, it is important to keep in mind that such actions will not promote economic growth as measured by GDP, but they will make the economy more efficient. Efficiency, after all, is not about goods; it's about the level of satisfaction that goods create. If it is possible to achieve the same levels of satisfaction with fewer goods, then the most efficient economy is the one that produces fewer goods.

Infotopia

12 *The year is 2020.* Economic globalization has run its full course. The logic of comparative advantage now dominates all economic activity. Every country in the world has become narrowly specialized, producing only the one or two things that it does best. As a result, the entire American economy has become focused on the provision of four goods: music, movies, software, and high-speed pizza delivery.

This is the future imagined by Neal Stephenson in his hugely influential novel *Snow Crash*. In Stephenson's future, the logic of economic globalization has overwhelmed all other forms of social organization. Even nationality—the modern seat of ancient tribal loyalties—has become commercialized and, in the process, deterritorialized. For a modest fee, people can become members of any Franchise-Organized Quasi-National Entity, such as Mr. Lee's Greater Hong Kong, which offers a variety of judicial, political, and security services at locations throughout North America.

In this world, information is currency. Anyone who wants to know anything logs on to the Central Intelligence Corporation's database, which is a giant clearing house for information of every type. Millions of freelance "stringers" collect every bit of information that might be useful to anyone and upload it to the database. Whenever it is accessed, they are paid a small royalty.

A different vision of the future prevails in Bruce Sterling's *Distraction*. In Sterling's future, the American economy has collapsed entirely. As part of a more general strategy of economic warfare against the United States, China has taken every piece of intellectual property held by Americans—every piece of music, every movie, every software package—and made it freely available to anyone over the internet. Overnight most of the privately held wealth in America has become valueless.

In Sterling's world, people have been forced to revert to a form of moral economy. Trust is secured in some communities through a central computer database that tracks reputation. Responsible behaviour earns you a high "trust rating" and increases the chances that people will cooperate with you in the future. In this way, people are able to control free-rider problems without relying upon the increasingly useless system of private property rights.

Both of these scenarios are, in their own way, plausible. Stephenson remains optimistic that the market economy will adapt to technological change. He may not be optimistic about the *consequences* this will have for our society, but he does not think there is any tension between modern technology and the logic of the market.

This is perhaps too sanguine. Even in North America, where intellectual property rights regulations are highly detailed and vigorously enforced, more than a quarter of all software in use is pirated. In Eastern Europe, the figure is more like 75 per cent, while in China an amazing 96 per cent of the software in circulation is pirated. In 1997, worldwide losses to piracy in the software industry alone were estimated at $11.4 billion. Losses in the music and video industry were equally impressive. In 1995, 88 per cent of the forty million CDs bought in China were pirated. Several times as many pirated CDs were manufactured in China for *export*.

This will hardly be surprising to anyone who has spent some time in Asia. The first time I rented a video in Taipei, I was surprised to discover that I was free to return it any time I liked, and that there was no late fee. The moment I popped it into the VCR I discovered why. It was a copy. Actually, it looked more like a copy of a copy of a copy. I'm sure the moment I walked out of the store with it, the clerk just ran off another one to replenish the shelves. No wonder they didn't care when I brought it back.

The challenge that piracy presents to intellectual property has become increasingly urgent. Greater efficiency in production has generated a steady decline in the amount of time and effort that we must spend producing material goods. According to some estimates, more than 25 per cent of exports from the United States now consist of intellectual property. The problem with this increased dependence on the "knowledge economy" is that it rests upon an extremely fragile system of rights. These rights have always been difficult to enforce, but the development of information technology—in particular the internet—has made this even more problematic.

This is certainly not something that Neal Stephenson is unaware of. His recent interest in cryptography may be a reflection of some doubts in this regard. He recognizes—presciently—that the possibility of exercising property rights over information will soon depend entirely on the availability of secure encryption. After all, unless you can secure privacy—and thereby eliminate free-riders—you have no intellectual property.

But even with strong cryptography, it is not certain that the enforcement of property rights over information is viable in the long term. After all, what prevents people from leaking or reselling information after it has been decoded? But if the system of property rights fails, that means we will need to find some other way to organize the production and exchange of goods. Capitalism may prove unsuitable as a foundation for the information economy.

❧

So far I have been speaking in relatively vague terms about "intellectual property." It would be helpful to be more precise. Every manufactured good contains both material and—for lack of a better word—ideational content. A standard kitchen chair, for instance, is made out of some material—plastic, wood, or metal. People spent a lot of time and energy harvesting the relevant resources and transforming them into something usable. But the chair also contains an ideational component—its design. Someone had to sit down and think about what the chair would look like, how to ensure that it wouldn't collapse, how it could be constructed most economically, and so on. Both of these components contribute to the value that the chair has for consumers.

When it comes to your basic chair, the physical resources make up the preponderance of its value. With some goods, however, the ideational component makes up a much larger fraction of its value. The value of a book, for instance, is in part constituted by the value of the "paper, print, and bind," but the intellectual content—what it says—makes up a far greater share. That's what makes people willing to pay for it. In some cases, the value of a good is made up entirely of its ideational content. The value of a weather forecast, for instance, consists entirely of the information it contains.

One of the most easily observable facts about economic development is that with increased affluence, ideational content begins to make up an ever-increasing share of the value of goods that we consume. The progress of industrialization makes material goods cheaper and cheaper. You can buy a simple, perfectly functional plastic chair for five dollars, just as you can buy a decent pair of pants for ten dollars. This leaves people with more and more disposable income, and so they become more willing to spend money on "extras," such as design.

The most basic problem with the so-called information economy is that it is very difficult to control this ideational content. When it comes to chairs, it's fairly easy to prevent people from making unauthorized use of the materials. You can put them in a locked room. But controlling the ideational component is much more difficult. Hence the appearance of knock-offs of almost every successful design. Ideas are extraordinarily easy to reproduce. They have an almost viral quality.

There are a lot of examples of this in the history of architecture. Take, for instance, the arch. An arch is something that when sketched out on paper, looks as though it will not work. Our everyday experience with stacking things suggests that the keystone will cause the whole arch to collapse. As a result, arches are not an obvious architectural innovation. But despite this implausibility, they do actually work quite well.

The first arch is thought to have been constructed in ancient Egypt. Once it was built, the innovation began to spread. Anyone who looks at an arch can see how it works, and that it represents a useful innovation (especially if you are trying to build a roof out of stone). So travellers from Greece saw arches, and when they returned home, they started to build their own. From there the idea travelled to Rome, where architects began to make large-scale use of them. In this way, the arch was propagated through the ancient world the same way a computer virus spreads through a network.

In a sense, our minds are like incredibly active copying machines. Seeing an arch (or a bow, or a stirrup, or a plough, or what have you) and understanding how it works amounts to making a copy of the idea in your own mind. Reading a book amounts to constructing a copy of the plotline or the characters in your mind—leaving you free to reveal its contents to the next person you meet. Hearing the weather forecast enables you to tell everyone else you know whether it is going to rain.

All of this makes it very difficult to exercise property rights over ideas. Almost anyone who comes into contact with an idea has the capacity to reproduce it at little or no cost. When someone sees a chair that you have built, he is going to have to do a bit of work to get access to the materials needed to reproduce it. But when it comes to reproducing the idea, his brain already provides all the resources necessary. As a result, if the ideational component makes up a larger share of the value of a good, it will be harder for the original owner to capture all the benefits that the good produces.

There would be no problem if good ideas just appeared out of the blue. The difficulties arise because producing good ideas requires time, effort, and resources. Scientists work just as hard in their labs producing information as woodworkers do in the shop creating chairs. The woodworkers, however, are able to recover their investment by charging the eventual users the full value of the goods produced. If scientists are unable to charge the full value of the information they produce, they will be unable to recover their costs. As a result, society will tend to produce less scientific research than it wants. We will have more chairs than we really need and not enough science, simply because it is easier to charge people for chairs. This is inefficient.

Given all the hype we have been hearing about the information economy, it is worth keeping in mind that it is not actually possible, in our society, to exercise property rights over either ideas or information. There is simply no such category of ownership. The two major categories of intellectual property rights that we have—patents and copyrights—do not protect ideas directly. Patents are intended to protect only the practical application of an idea, while copyrights protect only particular expressions of ideas. Allowing people to exercise rights over ideas would lead to obvious absurdity. Imagine if Isaac Newton had "patented" his law of gravity so that anyone using it in their calculations would be forced to pay him a fee. The results would be not only grotesquely inefficient, but positively unworkable. The transaction costs alone would be staggering.

Naturally, the shift towards increased ideational value has created considerable pressure to extend the patent system from practical applications of ideas to the ideas themselves. In the later Reagan years, a gung-ho U.S. Patent and Trademark office began issuing patents on all sorts of claims that would previously have been rejected out of hand. But a flood of court challenges to these patents, combined with opposition from pretty much every segment of the affected industries, has led to the annulment of many of them.

Some of the patents issued in the United States in the 1990s illustrate quite effectively the absurdity of trying to use private markets to coordinate the production and distribution of knowledge. In the late '80s, the American government began issuing patents on medical procedures and surgical techniques (most countries in the world, Canada included, specifically prohibit such patents). A researcher in San Diego, Mark Bogart, observed a connection between the level of human chorionic gonadotrophin in pregnant women and the incidence of Down's syndrome in the foetus. This information could easily be used to develop a diagnostic test for Down's syndrome. But instead of developing some specific test, Bogart applied for a patent that would cover this entire *method* of detecting Down's. The patent office went along with this, making Bogart one of the first people in the world to own a fact.

Even greater absurdities followed. In 1993, a software company named Compton managed to persuade the U.S. Patent office to give it proprietary ownership over the concept of multimedia software. Henceforth, any company that wanted to produce a searchable database containing sound, graphics, and text would have to pay Compton a royalty of between 1 and 3 per cent. Another firm managed to patent the idea of e-commerce, so that any firm conducting a financial transaction over the internet would be forced to pay them a fee. It is not clear that officials at the patent office really understood what they were doing when they issued either of these patents.

Eventually, people began to wonder just how far the patent office was willing to go. Roger Schlafly, a mathematician in California, succeeded in taking out a patent on two large prime numbers. Anyone who wanted to use these numbers would henceforth have to secure his consent.

These gaffes led to a significant deterioration in the credibility and reputation of the U.S. Patent and Trademark office, along with a chorus of protest from other countries. Many of these patents were ultimately disallowed or overturned in court. Significantly, it is often the private sector that has taken the initiative in contesting these patents. The American Medical Association took the lead in pressuring Congress to enact legislation restricting the imposition of patents on medical procedures, and Bogart's patent was challenged in court by Kaiser Permanente. The only group that has consistently supported the patent office is the American Association of Trial Attorneys. This alone speaks volumes about the anticipated efficiency effects of these patents on the economy.

All of this suggests that patenting ideas is ultimately unworkable. Markets are simply not an efficient way to organize the production and distribution of knowledge. But this leaves us with our old problem. Research still requires resources. It's one thing to be opposed to patents on the grounds that they create an effective monopoly. It's easy to forget that an invention might not have occurred in the first place without the promise of profits (in the same way that a carrot might never have been planted without some promise to the farmer that he could sell it once it was harvested). If markets fail to supply the right incentives, then some other institutional arrangement will have to be devised.

Copyrights are, in principle, easier to deal with than patents. It is not illegal to *tell* someone what a book says or to give away the ending of a movie. It is only illegal to photocopy the book or make a videotape of the movie. This narrow scope should make copyrights easier to interpret and to enforce. But even here, significant problems have developed.

Most copyrights function somewhat indirectly by controlling the physical medium through which the idea is reproduced. This indirect strategy is becoming increasingly ineffective as developments in technology continue to make reproduction easier and easier. The internet, in particular, has the effect of "dematerializing" all intellectual property. This has made enforcement much more difficult.

The internet functions in much the same way that our brains do. When you view anything on the net, it is downloaded to your computer. In other words, it makes you a personal copy (in much the same way that, when you read a news article, a copy of it is made in your mind). Once a person has her own copy, it is very hard to control what she does with it. All of this poses a very serious challenge to the possibility of using copyrights to organize the buying and selling of information.

The first industry in North America to encounter real problems on a large scale was the music industry. From a corporate perspective, the one saving grace of the internet to date has been that it is slow. Plain text can be transmitted with reasonable speed, but rich media—anything containing images, audio, or video—can experience prohibitively slow transmission speeds. In the case of recorded music, much of this changed with the invention of the mp3 file format. Mp3 converters take a sound file, strip off anything that is outside the normal range of human hearing, then run it through a compression algorithm. The resulting file is about one-tenth the size of the original CD track.

The development of the mp3 format permitted the easy transmission of music files over the internet. It became possible for users to download music or even e-mail songs to each other. Once someone acquires these files, it takes only an inexpensive "burner" to transfer them back onto a CD. As a result, the mp3 innovation made it extremely difficult to exercise property rights over music.

The early reaction of the music industry came in the form of a court case launched against the Napster corporation. Napster itself was not involved in the distribution of music. The original version of their software created a small index of all the music on the user's hard drive. When the user logged on to a Napster server, all these files became available to all other users currently logged on, and in return the user got access to all the files on the hard drives of all other users. Thus Napster itself was just an indexing service—the files were exchanged directly by users.

This is precisely how Napster chose to defend itself. Informed observers could see, however, that the outcome of the Napster court case was irrelevant. A new batch of user-to-user exchange programs provides exactly the same file-swapping capabilities, but without the use of central servers. People can open up the contents of their hard drives to anyone else in a distributed network and can, in return, poke around the hard drives of all other users, looking for interesting files to copy. Searches are conducted by propagating a request through the network, not by querying a central server. This makes the system all but impossible to control. These distributed systems, like the internet itself, are designed to withstand a nuclear war.

In short, people can now locate and copy pretty much anything that can be stored in digital format. The music industry was hit first only because its product requires less bandwidth to transmit. (Although some smaller industries have voiced similar complaints. It seems, for instance, that instead of buying patterns, many needlepoint aficionados have been swapping patterns over the net, leading to a decline in sales.) It is only a matter of time before the movie industry confronts a similar challenge—the growing popularity of DVD format movies makes this an inevitability.

Many Napster users consider themselves to be outlaws on the digital frontier, taking a stand against the giant corporations that control and profit from the production of music. This is all fine, as far as it goes. The real concern is that such free-riding will lead to a decline in the amount of content produced. Destroying the market for a particular good does not mean that some other institutional arrangement will immediately spring up to manage delivery of the good. Society may simply fail to produce any more. We are so accustomed to the performance of the market—and the efficient outcomes that it promotes—that we lose sight of the possibility of a reversion to the state of nature, in which nothing gets produced at all.

This is why many musicians have aligned themselves with the record companies in attacking internet piracy. Most of the money in the music industry is still made from the sale of CDs. If it becomes impossible to make money this way, then private markets will generate less and less music. This may not be such a bad thing in the short term, since the "winner-take-all" structure of the music market undoubtedly attracts too many entrants. But it becomes a more serious concern if people can no longer make a living recording music, or creating software, or writing magazine articles. This is not inevitable, but it is a serious danger.

The managers of Nike Town in Seattle must have known they were in trouble. In late November 1999, tens of thousands of protesters started filing into the city, preparing to disrupt the annual meeting of the World Trade Association. Nike had already been catching flak for working conditions in its overseas factories, and now protesters could be seen milling about with signs reading "Better naked than Nike" or "Lefties of the world unite, you have nothing to lose but your Nikes." Nike had become a lightning rod for much of the discontent with the new global economy.

When the dust and tear-gas settled, Nike Town Seattle had been trashed. Protesters had smashed the windows, spray-painted the exterior. One was even photographed making off with the T from the Nike Town sign. The damage would have been worse if it hadn't been for the last-minute intervention of a group of pacifists who formed a human chain out front to keep the store from being looted.

If the managers of Nike Town felt that they had been unfairly singled out, they were not entirely mistaken. There is no question that workers in the Third World sweatshops that manufacture Nikes are poorly paid and toil in unsafe, inhumane conditions. But if you pick up any pair of no-name sneakers at Wal-Mart, they are almost certainly manufactured under identical conditions. And if you buy sneakers in the actual Third World countries where they are produced, this much is guaranteed. So why pick on Nike?

The difference is that the no-name shoes cost around $20, while high-end Nikes sell for more than $150. So Nike appears to be making outrageous, obscene profits on the backs of its workers, while the no-name company is just paying the bills. But this is an illusion. Nike is not an especially profitable company—its stock has been in decline since sometime in 1997. The reason Nike shoes cost so much is that the company employs not only cheap Third World labour but also a lot of extremely expensive First World labour. Thousands of highly educated, highly paid Americans spend their days designing the shoes, coming up with catchy slogans and otherwise cultivating the Nike brand.

Nike shoes provide the perfect illustration of how, with increased affluence, the balance of material versus ideational value shifts towards the ideational. The value of Nike shoes does not come from the rubber, cloth, and who-knows-what-else that goes into them. The value comes from the cultural symbols associated with the brand. A lot of this is simple status— the shoes are cool, and so wearing them makes you cooler than anyone else. People from all walks of life are willing to pay good money to be cool. They buy Nike shoes for the same reason that other people buy Gucci shoes, despite the availability of cheap knock-offs. (Of course, nobody cares what rich white people do with their money, and so nobody smashes up a Gucci store for encouraging this sort of competitive consumption. Nike customers, on the other hand, are often people who— according to critics—should really be spending their money on other things. One cannot help but wonder how much this paternalistic attitude towards Nike's *customers* has to do with hostility towards the firm.)

The other important thing that people are buying when they pick up a pair of Nikes is motivation. Exercise is hard work. Nobody feels like getting up at 6:00 a.m. to go for a jog. Rich people hire personal trainers whose primary job it is to motivate their charges. But not everyone can afford a personal trainer. So instead they buy a nice pair of running shoes. And when they look at their shoes at 6:00 a.m., they think, "Just do it." Or they think about Michael Jordan and how much they want to "be like Mike" (actually a Gatorade slogan, but you see my point). If this is psychologically effective and if people are willing to pay for it, then it's difficult to see anything wrong with it. In this respect, Nike's only crime is to have made available to the masses a set of cultural goods that have traditionally been reserved for the élite.

Personally, I don't care much for running shoes. But I understand the psychology of the typical Nike customer from my experience with computers. This book could easily have been written on any old piece of junk. Instead it is being written on a very slick bondi blue iMac. Needless to say, the iMac cost a fair bit more than other computers, because the sale price covers not only the cost of the factory workers who assembled it but also the more expensive services of people such as British designer Jonathan Ive, who made it look so pretty. I was willing to pay the extra price for the simple reason that I like the iMac. When I sit down in front of it, I experience a pleasurable sensation. This makes me more likely to sit down and write, and when I do sit down, I generally get more written. Given the amount of time I spend writing and the amount of time I spend trying to get myself to write, anything that improves the experience and makes me more productive is worth a lot of money to me.

Here we see the typical shift away from material towards ideational value. We often do not realize, however, just how precarious this sort of value is. Within a couple of months of the iMac launch, several cheaper Windows-based knock-offs had appeared. This has been a persistent problem for Apple (the company once tried unsuccessfully to sue Microsoft for having cribbed the "look and feel" of its graphical user interface). This is the major reason why the high-tech sector is so notoriously fast-paced. Because firms are unable to secure adequate protection of their intellectual property, they respond by increasing the pace of innovation. That way, by the time their competitors get a knock-off onto the market, they will already have a new improved version ready to unveil.

The case is similar for companies that rely heavily upon brand identity. The ideational value in Nike products is all freighted onto the company's trademark "swoosh." It's not hard for some other company to stick a swoosh on a piece of clothing and appropriate all the value Nike has invested. Of course, many customers want only genuine Nike products— for exactly the same reason that art collectors want real Gauguins, not clever forgeries. But in the case of shoes, it is much easier to make the forgery undetectable. Thus the only thing that protects the ideational value is the somewhat fragile legal apparatus that enforces the trademark.

The United States has been especially aggressive in pushing for international agreements to protect copyrights, trademarks, and other intellectual property. But the case is extremely difficult to make. Increased consumption of intellectual goods and ideational value is largely a product of increased affluence. People's primary concern is to achieve material satisfaction—food on their plates and roofs over their heads. It is only after they have these things that they start to develop a taste for gourmet cuisine or designer homes. Thus the protection of intellectual property is almost entirely a First World concern. Third World nations have almost no incentive to respect these rights. As a result, the only way that the United States can get them respected is by strong-arming its trading partners.

The problem with doing this, in a global context, is that there is no agency with the power to actually enforce agreements. This places fairly dramatic limits on the protection that can be achieved. Without the rule of law, there is no way to eliminate all free-riders.

Most countries, for instance, will allow ships to be registered under their flag only if they meet fairly strict standards. This creates a huge opportunity. The tiny African country of Liberia discovered it could earn valuable foreign currency by agreeing to flag anything—for a price. Under the so-called "open registry" system, firms need only register their corporations in Liberia, pay the appropriate fees, and they will receive their licence. (The system is not even run by the Liberian government, but is subcontracted out to an American firm.) Unwilling to see all this cash flowing to Liberia, other countries such as Panama and Honduras soon followed suit. The result, of course, is a complete inability to enforce any maritime safety standards in an international context.

One can easily imagine, if some concerted effort were made to control intellectual property rights, the creation of an internet Liberia. If one country simply refused to enforce international property rights, the benefits could easily outweigh whatever sanctions the international community would be likely to muster. (Already, internet casinos have opened up in the Caribbean in order to circumvent American and Canadian laws restricting gambling. When the transactions are processed through credit cards, it is impossible for governments to control.) Thus Bruce Sterling's scenario, in which one rogue country decides to "give away" all the intellectual property in the United States, is not so far-fetched.

In the case of intellectual property rights, this may not seem like such a problem. After all, given the dramatic disparities in wealth between the First World and the Third, it may not be a bad thing that Third World countries are able to catch a free-ride every now and again. But in other areas, the problems can be much more severe. This is most noticeable in the case of labour and environmental legislation. One of the legitimate grievances expressed by the protesters in Seattle was that international trade with nations that have a poor regulatory regime or weak public infrastructure can easily set off a race to the bottom. A country with strict environmental regulations is, in effect, forcing its corporations to "internalize" more of their costs of production. As a result, the goods produced will be more expensive and uncompetitive in the global market. Of course, the proper solution—the one that guarantees an efficient outcome—is for all nations to adopt stricter regulations. But since citizens of one country have no control over what their neighbours do, they may instead choose to scale back their own regulations in order to avoid being suckered. The resulting outcome is inefficient.

When such a situation develops, trade liberalization can actually damage the overall efficiency of the economy. But this will only occur if countries give in and agree to weaken their regulatory regime or scale back on the public goods provided by the welfare state. Weak environmental regulation and lower wages in Mexico may mean that certain goods produced there are cheaper than the same good produced in the United States. But the reason they are cheaper is that the Mexican people in general—not the people who buy the good—are shouldering part of the costs of production in the form of negative externalities. It is ultimately not in their interest to do this. The only solution is to improve regulation inside Mexico, not weaken it elsewhere.

I'm dwelling on this point because Canada is in very much the same situation with respect to the United States that the United States is in with respect to Mexico. Lower taxes in the United States, both corporate and personal, mean that the cost of production is generally lower than in many parts of Canada. This has led to considerable domestic pressure to reduce Canadian taxes in order to bring them into line with American ones. But all that would accomplish would be to escalate the race to the bottom. Many Americans suffer from genuine hardship because of the inadequacy of their public sector. To respond by cutting back our own taxes would only lead to a competition in which there are no winners.

Globalization of commerce is often seen as a threat to the power of the state. If anything, the opposite is true. Economic globalization may be eroding the power of individual nation states, but it is also leading us, inexorably, towards the creation of world government.

The first thing to notice about globalization is that even though it is often presented as some kind of relentless, impersonal force, it is actually a direct consequence of a choice that we have made. Our commitment to globalization is driven entirely by our commitment to efficiency. We participate in the global economy because we want the benefits of trade. We could choose to manufacture our own sneakers, our own clothes, or our own camcorders. Unfortunately, Canadians are not very good at making these things. We are much better off just buying them from people who are good at making them in exchange for stuff that we are better at making—such as paper, or movies, or financial services.

We could choose to stop this trade at any time and become completely autarkic. But then we would have to start doing all the jobs that we're not very good at doing. The result would be a huge decline in our standard of living, for both the rich and the poor.

Canada participates in global trade because Canadians want the efficiency gains that come from it. (In fact, the obvious efficiency gains available *within* the domestic economy have already been exhausted, and so we must turn to international trade for new sources of growth.) But participating in the system also requires playing by the rules. We sometimes chafe under the restrictions that international trade bodies place on us—as when we are told that our dairy supply management system is unfair. But this is a simple *quid pro quo*. The Canadian govern-ment is just as active on the international front, pressuring other coun-tries to eliminate their internal subsidies. If we want the benefits of trade, we must accommodate the demands of other countries, just as they must accommodate ours.

So even though trade liberalization imposes constraints on what nation states can and cannot do, all these restrictions are driven by a choice that we make—the choice to pursue efficiency gains through international trade. This means that the forces of globalization are only as powerful as the size of the efficiency gains that global trade offers. If glob-alization stops producing efficiency gains, then all the nations involved lose whatever incentive they may have had to abide by restrictions.

This is significant, because at the same time that globalization creates gains from trade, it also creates a whole new set of collective action problems. All sorts of prisoner's dilemmas that we thought were taken care of once and for all by the welfare state have now been revisited upon us on the international stage. Environmental regulation is just one example. Inside a country, the state has the power to make polluters pay. But if the pollution is coming from across an international border, then one country lacks the power to make the polluters pay, while the other country lacks the incentive. The conflict between Canada and the United States over sulphur dioxide emissions or between Canada and Spain over fishing are straightforward prisoner's dilemmas. These would never be tolerated within a nation state (this is precisely why we have emission controls and fishing quotas). But because there is no global state, these problems can only be addressed through seemingly endless, and often ineffectual, negotiations.

So part of the loss of sovereignty associated with globalization comes when national regulations are undermined by collective action problems that appear on the international level. But this hardly makes govern-ment obsolete. There is no effective substitute for the rule of law. Mar-kets achieve efficiency gains through trade. Governments achieve efficiency gains by exercising powers of compulsion—collecting taxes and imposing regulations. National economies are efficient precisely when the right balance is struck between the two. The global economy will be efficient only when the same balance is struck. If the development of international law begins to lag too far behind the development of trade, then the efficiency gains associated with globalization will begin to recede, and nations will lose the incentives that they have to participate in the system.

The rule of law requires credible enforcement, and this requires the creation of a supra-national state. Exactly the same forces that led to the growth of the national welfare state—the need to enforce rights, to correct market failure, to limit negative externalities, and so forth—are leading to the growth of international agencies. Thus global capitalism will breed a global welfare state just as surely as national capitalism bred the national welfare state.

This is why the anti-WTO protests are half-baked. Many of the people there seemed more upset by the cure than by the disease. If there is any way to rein in global capitalism, it will be through transnational agencies, such as the World Trade Organization, the European parliament, and someday perhaps the United Nations. People may not like the way these organizations are currently run or some of the policies they have adopted. But opposing policies is not the same thing as opposing the organizations themselves. International agencies may be impersonal and bureaucratic, and people may find this alienating, but the alternative to bureaucracy is simply unfettered capitalism. And unfettered capitalism—what the French call *le capitalisme sauvage*—will certainly do a lot more harm than good.

Living under world government will of course lead to a decline in the sovereignty of national governments. More and more decisions will be taken at an international rather than a national level. But if global organizations exercise power responsibly, the only freedom lost by individual nations will be the freedom to free-ride.

These reflections suggest that government—the state—still has a brilliant future ahead of it. While the specific services that governments provide may change, and while the balance of power between national and supranational authorities may shift, there is simply no effective substitute for the organizational achievements that government alone is able to provide.

Even in the freewheeling world of high tech, where private fortunes are built and lost over the course of an afternoon, it is the slow, steady hand of government-subsidized research that has generated the big technological innovations. The free-rider problems associated with information technology are simply too great. Private firms lack the incentive to invest in the kind of fundamental research that generates technological revolutions.

The most obvious example is the internet itself, which began as a project of the American military and was incubated in the universities. To this day all the heavy-duty software technology that keeps the internet running—such as UNIX, TCP/IP, or Apache—was either produced in the public sector or is now in the public domain. Private firms such as Microsoft have been very successful in delivering shrink-wrapped software to end-users. But the people who need to keep servers running don't care much for Windows. More than half of them have switched to non-proprietary alternatives such as Linux. Even Apple, one of the companies that has most jealously guarded its intellectual property, has given in, incorporating significant segments of the "open-source" FreeBSD into its new Mac OS X. In so doing, Apple is tacitly admitting that the private sector cannot outperform the public sector in this domain.

Consider the billions and billions of dollars in private funds that have been pumped into internet firms in the last five years. What has this produced? What has been the return to society on this investment? Compare that to the mere millions of dollars of government funds that have been channelled into the computer science department at Berkeley or the media lab at MIT (or the student loan program in Finland, for that matter). The returns here have been immeasurably greater. Because they take the form of public goods, their value is much more difficult to quantify. But this does not make the benefits any less real.

The reason that public (or quasi-public) agencies have taken the leading role in high tech is simple. Private firms are often unwilling to pay people to sit around and think up good ideas, because they have no guarantee that they will be able to capture more than a small fraction of the value these ideas create. Hence the opportunity for the public sector. Since the benefits are enjoyed by the public at large, the government can use some fraction of its tax revenues to hire the right sort of people and give them the time they need to exercise their talents. The results, once produced, can be made freely available to everyone.

Thus the information economy is still fundamentally a moral economy. This is certainly a more attractive, and more efficient, model. Universities, however, have been moving in the opposite direction in recent years. There has been enormous pressure within the academy to develop partnerships with the private sector and to conduct research that will lead to the development of proprietary technologies. Universities are increasingly trying to acquire patents and use them as a revenue stream to fund future research. They have also begun to defend their patents more aggressively through the courts.

Part of the motivation for these changes stems from the pressures of globalization. While Canadian taxpayers subsidize the Canadian university system, the benefits of this system are increasingly spilling over into other countries. Research produced in Canadian universities is often commercialized by foreign companies. Students who receive a taxpayer-subsidized education often pick up and move to the United States.

This is a typical example of "bad" globalization reintroducing collective action problems that were once resolved by the welfare state. Knowledge is a public good. In order to provide it, the state taxes all citizens and then makes that good freely available. But the state is only able to tax its own citizens. This creates an opportunity for countries that invest less in education to free-ride off the Canadian system— snapping up ideas and people, but not contributing to tax revenues.

But what are the alternatives here? Cutting back on the public contribution in order to stave off the free-riders is not an attractive option. The private sector simply lacks the tools needed to organize the production and diffusion of knowledge. The only way we can generate anything close to an efficient level of knowledge-production is through a robust public sector. If international free-rider problems threaten this arrangement, then the only solution is to develop international agreements and give international authorities the power to mitigate these effects.

Thus the pressure towards increased private/public collaboration in the universities is at best a stop-gap measure. It has no future, as far as the production and diffusion of research is concerned. The most efficient way to handle knowledge is to treat it as a classic public good.

The last twenty years have not been kind to the left.

Here is how the story is usually told: In the '80s, neoconservative governments in England, the United States, and Canada initiated a wave of privatizations, creating a significant rollback of the welfare state. The fall of the Berlin Wall and the collapse of the Soviet Union undermined the credibility of communism as an alternative to capitalism. Centre-left governments took power in the '90s, only to find that their hands were tied, both by electorates hostile to taxation and by the forces of globalization. At the end of the century, government was in a state of full-scale retreat. Laissez-faire capitalism had triumphed.

But this triumph is completely illusory. While the specific tasks that government performs may have changed, the fundamental rationale for having government involved in the economy is still rock-solid. The welfare state exists to correct market failure. Changes in technology have changed the structure of our markets. Sometimes this has had the effect of eliminating market failures, but sometimes it has created new ones. The welfare state has adapted accordingly, getting out of sectors where its services are no longer needed, but also establishing a greater presence in areas where its organizational achievements have come into demand. These changes, far from being a symptom of decline, have actually been instrumental in securing the ongoing viability of the welfare state.

If you walk around any older city in North America, you often come across buildings that used to be public baths. Most of them have been closed down now. Governments have generally gotten out of the bath-house business. Why is this?

A hundred years ago, many people could not afford indoor plumbing, much less hot water. This made bathing a very time-consuming and expensive business. Unfortunately, most of the benefits of bathing take the form of positive externalities. People tend to get used to their own smell. If they choose not to bathe, the cost of this decision is borne pri-marily by their neighbours. So when the cost of bathing is high, private markets will tend to produce an inefficient level of personal hygiene.

This created a perfect opportunity for governments to intervene. By providing subsidized bathing facilities, the state was able to induce people to bathe somewhat more often than they otherwise would. The result was a public benefit enjoyed by all. (Not to mention the obvious efficiency gains associated with having many people share the same bath water.)

What changed all this was a dramatic decline in the cost of plumb-ing and hot water. Eventually, private bathing facilities became a stan-dard feature of every home. This eliminated the rationale for taxpayer-subsidized bathhouses.

Is anyone upset about the decline of public bathing? Perhaps at one time people were, but by now the issue has completely disappeared from the public agenda. The reason is that people are perfectly satisfied with the performance of the market in this sector. We have even begun to appreciate some of the benefits that privatization has brought, such as being able to bathe in the privacy of one's own home.

Thus the privatization of baths, far from being a "rollback" of public services, was simply a change in the way government chose to invest its resources. The state got out of a business in which its services were no longer needed in order to concentrate on other areas.

Many of the privatizations that have taken place in the last twenty years are of exactly the same type. This is not to deny that *some* privati-zations were driven by right-wing ideology and carried out without any attention to their efficiency effects. The privatization of the water sup-ply in England is a case in point (or of water-testing in Ontario). But these privatizations usually turn out to be unpopular and so are often reversed when it becomes clear that the private sector is less efficient than the public sector in these domains.

In any case, these ideological privatizations were more the exception than the norm. In most cases, privatization occurred because technology made it possible to create competitive markets where none had existed before. And a hundred years from now, many of these privatizations will be as uncontroversial as the privatization of bathing is today.

Electricity supply provides a good example. Hooking up electrical cables to people's houses is a natural monopoly. Once you've hooked up one person's house, it costs almost nothing to hook up their neighbours'. As a result, no competitor could offer rival service at a competitive price. It makes sense to have this monopoly owned by the state, or at least heavily regulated, in order to prevent it from adopting inefficient pricing policies. However, once the lines are installed, there is no reason that the electricity that flows through them cannot be supplied by different companies. Twenty years ago, trying to keep track of how much power each company fed into the grid and trying to keep track of which firm each different customer was contracting with would have been a logistical nightmare. But information technology changes all this, providing a massive reduction in the transaction costs. As a result, it becomes possible to organize a competitive market for electricity, even if the distribution system remains a Crown monopoly.

Thus there is nothing especially "right-wing" about the privatization of the major electrical utilities. In fact, many environmentalists are quite pleased by this development, since it will give consumers the opportunity to choose "green" suppliers and avoid nuclear or coal. There is even a growing movement among alternative-energy users in the United States to arrange for two-way transactions with the electrical companies. Someone with their own facilities for generating solar power would be able to feed excess power into the grid on very sunny days and then draw from it when it is cloudy. They would only pay for their net consumption. The technology for this is already in place, since a standard electricity meter will run forwards or backwards, depending upon which way the current is flowing. The major barriers are all institutional. As long as the state exercises a monopoly on the provision of electricity, no one else is allowed to feed the grid. Privatization changes all this, not just for corporations but also for individuals.

Characterizing privatizations of this type as a "downsizing" of government or as a scale-back of the welfare state is highly misleading. The frontier between the state and the market is simply shifting. The state is taking on a different role, not a reduced one.

At the same time that government has been getting out of some sectors, it has also begun to invest more heavily in new ones. In particular, forward-looking governments throughout the Western world have made heavy investments in the knowledge sector. In the United States, government agencies have made information sources such as the Human Genome Project and Medline freely available to all through the internet. In Canada, the federal government has committed more than $5 billion to create endowed research chairs at universities across the country. These investments are likely to continue as technological change makes intellectual property rights increasingly difficult to enforce.

Tax resistance has certainly prevented many governments from moving into these sectors as aggressively as they might like. But governments have considerable latitude when it comes to collecting taxes, and technological change creates all kinds of new opportunities. In general, technology makes it easier to keep track of things. This makes it possible to create markets where none existed before, but it also allows us to collect taxes where none had been collected before. Even the ability to tax services and not just goods is made possible in part by technological improvements in accounting systems.

The most exciting opportunities involve the possibility of developing new systems of Pigovian taxes. Governments have only begun to scratch the surface here. Information technology makes it possible for us to control all sorts of socially pernicious activities that were in the past impossible to regulate. The major targets so far have been urban sprawl and pollution. Several European countries have experimented with variants of the Singapore traffic congestion tax. And Pigovian taxes on pollution—including greenhouse gases—are being received with increased favour. The only boundaries here are the limits of human ingenuity.

With all these new opportunities in play, the idea that the welfare state is in retreat is entirely mistaken. The left has a tendency to underestimate the robustness of the state, to assume that it is more vulnerable than it actually is. Much of this stems from the perception that the fundamental role of the welfare state is to promote greater fairness or equality. If this were its primary function, then the assault from the right would be a significant threat. If the welfare state exists to promote equality, and people who don't care much for equality get elected, there isn't much to stop them from tearing it all down. After all, it doesn't really affect them or the affluent voters who supported them.

But this isn't how it works. As we have seen, the welfare state exists first and foremost to promote efficiency. If it gets torn down, this will affect everyone. Starving the public transit system of funds creates traffic congestion that slows everyone down. Rich people can't get to their cottages any more than poor people can get to their dental appointments. Cutting back on environmental protection contaminates the air that we all breathe (and as it becomes more difficult to escape from the city, this begins to affect everyone equally).

Naturally, the rich are able to get around many of these problems. They can hire private security guards, drink bottled water, and fly away to island retreats. So unlike the poor, who have no choice but to rely upon public goods, the rich can switch to private suppliers. But this still imposes a heavy cost upon them. They are not deprived of the good, like some people, but they wind up paying a lot more for it than they would otherwise have to. The decrease in their quality of life is not as dramatic, but it is still tangible.

This is why the welfare state should enjoy a universal constituency. The problem is that we often don't realize how much of its benefits we enjoy. People think it's reasonable to shell out 30 per cent of their income every month to pay for their mortgage. But for some reason, they think it's unreasonable to shell out the same amount every month in taxes to pay for the heart bypass that they are eventually going to need—even though the heart bypass may cost just as much as their house.

The chief danger to the welfare state is not that it will be dismantled out of malice or indifference, but that it will be dismantled through ignorance. If we fail to realize the contribution that the state makes to our quality of life, we may inadvertently destroy what we have built. The most persistent danger is that we will fall into a race to the bottom with the United States. We would be well advised to avoid this. Americans have proven, time and time again, that when it comes to tolerating inefficiency, they will always have the upper hand. We simply don't care enough about liberty to make it worthwhile for us to compete with them.

So how do we steer the course? When it comes to thinking about government and markets, about taxes and trading, we can do no better than to heed Hobbes's warning:

> All men are by nature provided of notable multiplying glasses (that is their passions and self-love), through which, every little payment appeareth a great grievance; but are destitute of those prospective glasses (namely moral and civil science), to see afar off the miseries that hang over them, and cannot without such payments be avoided.

With any luck, there has been enough progress in the "moral and civil" sciences since the seventeenth century that we can act with greater wisdom than Hobbes's contemporaries.

Conclusion
We Have Seen the Future, and It Is . . . Efficient

Naturally, it is an exaggeration to say that Canada is as close to utopia as it gets. Of all the societies that exist in the world today, Canada may well have reached the highest level of "human development," but there is still plenty of room for improvement. The fact that life currently doesn't get much better than this doesn't mean that it couldn't someday.

The point that I want to make is a bit more subtle. Even though the economic and social order in Canada has its flaws, these flaws are for the most part there for a reason. We have already eliminated the easy problems. The ones that remain are a lot harder to fix. This is usually because they cannot be addressed without making some sort of trade-off among the various values that we cherish.

This is most obvious in the case of social inequality. Many of us would like to see significantly less of an income gap between the rich and the poor in our society. But there are many other social objectives that we would like to see achieved. We want to promote equality of the sexes and encourage women to enter the workforce. But this tends to amplify income inequality, since people usually marry within their own social class. Similarly, we want people to save for their children's education and to provide them with greater opportunities. But this inter-generational transfer exacerbates inequality over time.

This doesn't mean that women shouldn't work or that all inheritance should be taxed away. It means that we are forced to make compromises. We simply cannot simultaneously meet all the various social justice concerns that we have. So when it comes to utopia, "as close as it gets" may not turn out to be very close at all.

I think this is worth keeping in mind, because our society suffers from a wide range of extremely obvious defects. Naturally we do not *need* thirty-six different varieties of Crest toothpaste. Of course the average quality of television programming is somewhat low. And yes, it is true that politicians almost never discuss the "real issues." But what are we to make of all this?

The very obviousness of these flaws tempts many social critics into thinking that people must be stupid to tolerate them. This in turn suggests we can solve all these problems just by waking up and smelling the coffee. Once we emerge from our "unconscious" state, or our consumerist stupor, thanks no doubt to the bracing wit and incisive commentary of the social critic, we will shrug off these problems. Someday, years from now, we may look back and ask, "What were we *thinking?*"

This is pure fantasy. A lot of these outstanding problems remain outstanding simply because they represent compromises that we have reached between some set of values that are in genuine conflict. For example, an enormous amount of abuse has been heaped on corporations over the past decade for their fixation on developing brands and brand identities. But one of the major reasons that brand has become so important is that there has been a major intensification of competition in consumer retail markets. Thirty years ago, most of these markets were regional quasi-monopolies—American car companies sold cars in America, European companies sold cars in Europe, and Japanese companies sold cars in Japan. One of the major effects of improved communications technology—above all the internet—and of globalization has been to break down many of these effective monopolies. As a result, there is much less difference now than there used to be between the goods that are available to consumers, in terms of both price and quality. The quality gap between American and Japanese cars, for instance, has been almost entirely closed. So how do companies convince consumers to choose their product rather than someone else's? One way is to build a strong brand.

The point is that the emphasis on brand, rather than being a defect in the capitalist system, is in many ways a sign that capitalism is now functioning better than it used to. In a perfectly competitive market, commodities would be completely indistinguishable—same price, same quality. Such a market is also one in which consumers would have no good reason to choose one manufacturer's product over another's. This is precisely what creates the opportunity to introduce brand as a way of swaying purchasing decisions. Thus the fact that consumers care so much about brand is in part a reflection of the fact that the quality of manufactured goods is relatively uniform and high.

So we can grant that in our society we waste an enormous amount of resources creating and maintaining brands. This may seem like an obvious defect. But upon closer examination, the picture turns out to be much murkier. The power of brands is, quite literally, a problem for happy people.

The same thing applies in most other areas of public life. We all find bureaucracies and hierarchies frustrating. We know that they have their problems. But just try organizing any sort of large-scale co-operative enterprise without the benefits of bureaucratic control. Everyone should be forced to live in a commune for a month as part of their general education, just so they can learn to more fully appreciate the benefits of institutionalized authority structures.

Most importantly, we know that the market system has enormous flaws. We know, for example, that it often fails to bring out the milk of human kindness. In fact, markets tend to encourage inequality, conspicuous consumption, greed, and a wide range of other anti-social attitudes. But markets also allow us to achieve levels of productivity that could not otherwise be obtained. This doesn't all get funnelled into luxury cars and opera tickets. It also gets funnelled into indoor plumbing for the working poor, health care for the aged, reproductive technology for women, and so on.

Whenever we consider the downside of living in a market society, it is always important to keep an eye on this upside. Markets greatly expand our capacity to organize co-operation. As a result, we are able to accomplish something that we would not otherwise be able to do. Human beings simply lack the organizational ability to put together an advanced industrial society without using markets to organize some significant fraction of their affairs. We rely in turn upon this organizational ability to carry out our broader humanistic agenda. Whether it be providing low-income housing for Canadians or sending famine relief halfway across the world, we need to have a lot of resources and a sophisticated ability to deploy them in order to even consider pursuing these objectives.

That having been said, we should not shrink from the observation that markets impose very real constraints on the level of social justice that we can hope to obtain. By adopting an economic system that relies upon decentralized decision-making to organize production, we have in effect forfeited much of our ability to determine the outcome of these decisions. The NHL sets the rules of professional hockey in this country, but it does not determine who wins the Stanley Cup. Similarly, government sets the rules of the market economy, but it exercises very little control over who will end up winning and how wide the margin of victory will be.

Because the market places such clear restrictions on our ability to achieve socially desirable outcomes, there will always be people who think that getting rid of the market will improve our situation. But while this line of thought is tempting, it is ultimately a dead end. Overthrowing capitalism is no longer on the agenda, nor should it be. The reason for this is simple—there are no credible alternatives.

Very few people these days are willing to defend central planning as a form of economic organization. This means that any proposed economy, regardless of how it treats property, will rely upon exchange to organize the distribution of goods. But this is a fateful concession. As soon as you introduce exchange, you decentralize decision-making. Once you decentralize decision-making, you lose the ability to specify outcomes directly. And so the traditional scourges of capitalism—unemployment, inequality, market failure, even consumerism—reappear. And so you need something very much like the welfare state in order to mitigate these effects. In the end, it is not clear how the proposed alternative will differ from what we have now.

There is of course a huge literature on the subject of market socialism, which explores the ways that one might preserve the market mechanism and yet modify ownership structures in such as way as to promote more egalitarian outcomes. This trick turns out to be much harder to pull off than one might initially expect. To take just one example: it is very important to ensure that not all the wealth produced in our economy is consumed, but that some portion of it be saved and invested. This is how we maintain the stock of equipment and machinery that we will use in future years to reproduce this wealth. Thus we want to supply individuals with some incentive not to consume their entire income, but rather to save whatever portion of it they are able. In other words, we want to pay them some interest on their savings. But where will this interest come from? Since the savings will be invested in some productive enterprise—that's the whole point—the interest paid will represent the return on this investment. This all seems fine, and it's hard to think of any other way to organize things. But when people are taking private savings, investing them in productive enterprises, and receiving some portion of the profits as return, that's just *capitalism*.

This is why, when people such as Francis Fukuyama claim that welfare-state capitalism represents the "end of history," we are forced to pay attention. We may not like it much, but the fact is that we have run out of alternatives. Fukuyama was subjected to a lot of abuse, largely because he seemed a bit too content with this state of affairs. But many theorists with more impeccable left-wing credentials have been saying much the same thing. Jürgen Habermas, for instance, in discussing "the exhaustion of utopian energies," comes very close to the same conclusion as Fukuyama.

The only other option, in terms of utopian thinking, is to hold out for some transcendence of material scarcity. It is possible to imagine, as Marx did, that improvements in productivity will eventually make it so easy to produce so many goods that people will cease to guard their own shares as vigilantly.

This may happen. It is also possible that Christ will come again in glory. Personally, I'm not holding my breath.

The reasons that post-scarcity conditions are unlikely to be achieved have become fairly obvious over the course of the twentieth century. Apart from population increases, which have the capacity to absorb any surplus, there is also the simple fact that many of people's preferences are comparative. Thus our concept of what we "need" is subject to constant escalation. There is no way to correct this tendency without taking fairly authoritarian measures.

Finally, it is worth noting that a wide range of goods are intrinsically scarce. Sometimes this is natural—there is only so much beachfront property in the world; the rest of us will just have to settle without. Sometimes scarcity is a product of the social dynamic that generates the good in the first place. Downtown real estate, for example, is always scarce, simply because everyone wants to be where everyone else is. Uncongested roads and untouched wilderness are scarce for the opposite reason, because everyone wants to be where no one else is. Both types of goods will have to be rationed in some way in order to prevent collective action problems. And how better to do this than with a system of prices?

We always have the option of scaling back entirely. If the market is the only way to sustain an industrial society, then maybe an industrial society is not worth the trouble. Maybe we would all be better off going back to the land and trying to recover the lifestyle of eighteenth-century peasants.

This proposal has one thing that sets it apart from the rest. It is coherent. Unfortunately, it is also extremely unattractive. Almost nobody is prepared to sacrifice all the gains that have come from increased economic efficiency. We have become used to having the power that industrial society gives us—the power to cure disease, to alleviate suffering, to feed the hungry, to control reproduction. We are in far too deep to turn around now. We are hooked on efficiency.

As long as efficiency remains a central value in our culture, then the basic institutional blueprint for Canadian society—welfare state capitalism—is unlikely to be improved upon. Despite a million flaws, what we have is simply the best overall arrangement.

So what is left of utopian thinking? The most exciting proposals for social reform currently being generated all come from the field of economics known as "mechanism design." Rather than simply trying to legislate desirable social outcomes, the goal of the mechanism designer is to develop a set of rules that will indirectly constrain the conduct of individuals in such a way that it will be in their interest to promote the desirable outcome. The principle that private interests must be brought into alignment with the public good is known as incentive compatibility. The best-known instance of such a design is the proposal for tradeable pollution permits.

This is the future of utopian thinking: mechanism design, incentive compatibility. Utopianism can no longer consist of sweeping proposals for fundamental reform. We need to put the spectre of the French Revolution behind us once and for all. Any improvement is going to be in the details. Utopian thinking can only consist of workaday attempts to eke out small improvements in human welfare within the broader set of constraints imposed by the market economy. It is going to involve worrying about policy and questions of implementation. This is frustrating and unglamorous work. The only thing it has going for it is that it may turn out to be useful.

Notes on Further Reading

Introduction

The annual Human Development Report is produced by the United Nations Development Programme. It is available both in print form and through the internet (*www.undp.org*). The ranking is based on three measures: life expectancy, education (based on literacy rates and educational enrolment), and real GDP per capita. The system is based on the work of economist Amartya Sen.

Every time Canada gets ranked number one, the reaction in the domestic media is predictably sour. A recent column by Jeffrey Simpson, "How do I measure thee? Let me count the ways," *Globe and Mail* (October 9, 2000), p. A13, provides a typical example. Simpson simply asserts, without argument, that the index "gives less weight than it should to per capita income" and thus represents "a limited and skewered [*sic*] measuring stick."

It is of course possible for reasonable people to disagree over how much of a contribution income makes to overall quality of life. Unlike Simpson, I am not quite as breezy when it comes to dismissing the work of Nobel-prize winning economists. Anyone interested in seriously investigating the issue should start by reading Sudhir Anand and Amartya Sen, "The Income Component in the HDI—Alternative

Formulations" (New York: United Nations Development Programme, Human Development Report Office, 1999). A more general discussion of the underlying issues can be found in Amartya Sen and Martha Nussbaum, eds., *The Quality of Life* (Oxford: Oxford University Press, 1993).

On the subject of inequality, recent data from the World Bank put Canada's Gini coefficient at about .315: *World Development Indicators 2000* (Washington, DC: World Bank, 2000), pp. 66–68. (The Gini coefficient is a standard measure of income inequality—the higher the number, the greater the level of inequality.) This puts Canada slightly above Germany and just below France. The most social-democratic northern European states, along with Japan, have Ginis around .25. In the United States, it is just over .4. While the level of income inequality has risen sharply in the United States in the past two decades, it has remained essentially unchanged in Canada. See M. Wolfson and B. Murphy, "Income inequality in North America: Does the 49th parallel still matter?" *Canadian Economic Observer* (August 2000).

The statistics on government health care spending as a percentage of GDP come from Pat Armstrong and Hugh Armstrong, *Universal Health Care* (New York: New Press, 1998), p. 106. The staffing levels figure is from p. 114. On administrative costs, see Robert Chernomas and Ardeshir Sepehri, *How to Choose? A Comparison of the U.S. and Canadian Health Care Systems* (Amityville, NY: Baywood Publishing, 1998), pp. 33–36, also p. 13. On volume of physician services, see p. 30.

The notion of a "control fallacy" I take from Joseph Stiglitz, *The Economic Role of the State* (Oxford: Blackwell, 1989). This book presents a more detailed account of the general position that I defend in chapter 8. Anyone interested in the reorientation of socialist parties since the 1970s, and in particular the problems surrounding nationalization/privatization, should consider also Joseph Stiglitz, *Whither Socialism?* (Cambridge, MA: MIT Press, 1996).

The statistics on small business failure in Canada come from John Baldwin et. al., *Failure Rates for New Canadian Firms* (Ottawa: Statistics Canada, 2000).

For a more general discussion of the perversity of GDP as an economic indicator, see Clifford Cobb, Ted Halstead, and Jonathan Rowe,
"If the GDP is up, why is America down?" *Atlantic Monthly* (October
1995) pp. 59–78. The quote about the calculating machine that adds
but doesn't subtract is from p. 62 of this article.

Chapter 1

The information on Wal-Mart is drawn from Sandar S. Vance and
Roy V. Scott, *Wal-Mart: A History of Sam Walton's Retail Phenomenon*
(New York: Twayne Publishers, 1994): its advertising budget, p. 72;
overhead costs, p. 89; computer technology, pp. 93–95. For a sample of
the many accusations levelled against Wal-Mart, see Bill Quinn, *How
Wal-Mart Is Destroying America and What You Can Do about It* (Berkeley: Ten Speed Press, 1998).

The statistic on world productivity and inequality in the twentieth
century comes from the International Monetary Fund, *World Economic
Outlook* (Washington, D.C: The Fund, 2000). See also *Critical Trends:
Global Change and Sustainable Development* (New York: United Nations,
1997), p. 66. According to this report, between 1960 and 1993 the
share of world income going to the richest 20 per cent of the population
increased from 70 per cent to 85 per cent. World inequality increased
because rich nations got a whole lot richer, while most others got only a
little bit richer. Income inequality in Canada remained pretty much
unchanged throughout this period.

Anyone with a burning desire to know more about Aristotle's doctrine of the four causes should consult his *Physics Books 1 & 2*, trans. W.
Charlton (Oxford: Clarendon, 1970). My etymology of the word "efficient" is drawn largely from the ever-helpful *Oxford English Dictionary*.

My discussion of the efficiency movement owes a lot to Robert
Kanigel's biography of Frederick Winslow Taylor, *The One Best Way*
(New York: Viking, 1997). The profile of Frank Gilbreth, which
includes some entertaining bricklaying stories, can be found on pp.
414–15. The discussion of Brandeis is on pp. 429–31, and the magazine
cartoon is mentioned on p. 514. The Taylor/Schmidt dialogue is from

Taylor's "The Principles of Scientific Management," reprinted in *Scientific Management* (New York: Harper and Brothers, 1947), pp. 44–46. Finally, the long quote from Kanigel occurs on p. 18.

For an introduction to the evolutionary foundations of altruism, see Elliot Sober and David Sloan Wilson, *Unto Others* (Cambridge, MA: Harvard University Press, 1998).

The "contemporary estimate" of the comparative productivity of workers and steam engines comes from Harrington Emerson, *The Twelve Principles of Efficiency* (New York: The Engineering Magazine, 1913), p. vii. In this book, Emerson quite clearly lays out his ambitions for a new morality grounded in efficiency: "The age of muscular human effort and of the lash is passing away, and the old morality with it; the age of supervision, of co-operative stimulus, is in full advance; and with it comes a new morality, under which the Golden Rule can be extended from the relations between individuals to those between classes, nationalities and races," p. xi. Note that this prediction was not entirely false, although it took a long time to play out.

The instructions on how to improve one's shaving are from Henry Chellew, *Human and Industrial Efficiency* (London: University of London Press, 1919), p. 42. And Emerson's line about sitting around in a tub occurs in *Efficiency as a Basis for Operation and Wages* (New York: The Engineering Magazine, 1914), p. 20. The quote about the nature of the corporation is on p. 236.

The important work by Vilfred Pareto is his *Manual of Political Economy*, trans. Ann S. Schwier and Alfred N. Page (New York: A. M. Kelley, 1971). The definition of "maximum ophilemity" occurs in chap. 6, sect. 33.

Chapter 2

Aristotle's perfectionist views are present throughout his *Politics*, but are even more explicit in his *Nichomachean Ethics*, trans. Martin Ostwald (New York: MacMillan, 1962). Perfectionism is still defended by some philosophers, but the doctrine has largely become toothless. For a good example of this, see Thomas Hurka, *Perfectionism* (New York: Oxford University Press, 1993). The most persistent legacy of perfectionism is the view that society is held together by "shared values" (as opposed to simply institutions or laws). The assumption is especially common among critics of multiculturalism. For the classic challenge to this view, see Michael Mann, "The Social Cohesion of Liberal Democracies," *American Sociological Review*, 35 (1970): 423–39.

The facts about gunpowder, cannons, and churchbells is from David S. Landes, *The Wealth and Poverty of Nations* (New York: W. W. Norton, 1998), p. 53ff. There is also an interesting discussion in Jared Diamond, *Guns, Germs and Steel* (New York: W. W. Norton, 1997), p. 247. Diamond argues that Christianity and Islam were essentially stuck in an arms race for about a thousand years. So by the time they ventured out beyond their borders, they were ridiculously over-equipped.

The core of Thomas Hobbes's social contract theory is presented in *Leviathan*, ed. Richard Tuck (Cambridge: Cambridge University Press, 1991). For John Locke's version, see his *Second Treatise of Government* (Indianapolis: Hackett, 1992). I am soft-pedalling Hobbes a bit here. He was, in fact, an authoritarian, and so he thought the best way for people to escape the state of nature would be for them to give a king absolute power over their lives.

Anyone interested in the Star Trek story can find scripts of the relevant episodes collected in *Becoming Human: The Seven of Nine Scripts* (New York: Pocket Books, 1998). What I call the "cornerstone" of Rawls's philosophy comes from John Rawls, *Political Liberalism* (New York: Columbia University Press, 1993). Serious Rawls fans will no doubt notice that I paraphrased his remark quite significantly. What he actually says is "political liberalism assumes that, for political purposes, a plurality of reasonable yet incompatible comprehensive doctrines is the normal result of the exercise of human reason within the framework of the free institutions of a constitutional democratic regime," p. xvi. But this is just Rawlspeak for what I said.

Chapter 3

The information on the Dutch trucks comes from "Inhalen voor Vrachtauto's Verder aan Banden," *De Telegraaf* (June 7, 1999). Anyone who doesn't like this example can choose from among dozens of other prisoner's dilemmas that impede traffic flow. Here is one example from Thomas Schelling, whose book *Micromotives and Macrobehavior* (New York: W. W. Norton, 1971) is a classic in the field: "Returning from Cape Cod on a Sunday afternoon, motorists were held up for a mile or more, at a creeping pace, by a mattress that had fallen off the top of some return-ing vacationer's station wagon. Nobody knows how many hundreds of cars slowed down a mile in advance, arrived at the mattress five minutes later, waited for the oncoming traffic, and swerved around before resum-ing speed. Somebody may eventually have halted on the shoulder just beyond the mattress and walked back to remove it from the traffic lane. If not, it may still have been there the following Sunday," pp. 125–26.

The study that shows that many drivers pass because of an illusion is by Donald A. Redelmeier and Robert J. Tibshirani, "Why cars in the other lane seem to go faster," *Nature* (Sept. 2, 1999), p. 35. Of course, on a two-lane road with heavy volume and no obstruction, it is neces-sarily the case that most people will wind up in the "slow lane," since the slow lane is usually just the one with the majority of drivers in it.

The term "prisoner's dilemma" and the associated story is due to a RAND Institute consultant named Alfred Tucker. He presented the story in a lecture given in 1950, but never published it. The prisoner's dilemma is often mistakenly attributed to John Nash, who is, in most other respects, the founder of modern game theory.

For a more extensive defence of the view that Hobbes's state of nature is really a prisoner's dilemma and so does not presuppose evil motives, see David Gauthier, *The Logic of Leviathan* (Oxford: Claren-don, 1969). A good example of this is when charities spend a lot of money competing with one another for donations and therefore wind up giving less to the needy. Their altruistic motives are no protection against collectively self-defeating behaviour. Interested readers might also like to consult Gauthier's very important book *Morals by Agreement* (Oxford: Clarendon, 1986).

The hockey helmet story is a bit more complicated than I made it sound, since the rule was grandfathered in. For an analysis of the prisoner's dilemma in this case, see Thomas Schelling, *Micromotives and Macrobehavior* (New York: W. W. Norton, 1971), pp. 211–43.

The survey of SUV safety that I quoted is James L. Gilbert, Stuart A. Ollanik, Paul J. Komyatte, "The trouble with sport utility vehicles," *Trial*, 32:1 (1996). Interested readers might also check out Robert L. Simison, "The Safest Cars on the Road," *The Wall Street Journal* (Nov. 12, 1999). One highlight of this study is their finding that the VW Bug is safer than the Jeep Cherokee.

Chapter 4

On the critique of Hobbes's "solution" to the state of nature, see Michael Taylor, *The Possibility of Cooperation* (Cambridge: Cambridge University Press, 1987). This book should be required reading for anyone who takes anarchism at all seriously.

The whole "what if everyone did that" business has its roots in Immanuel Kant's *Foundations of the Metaphysics of Morals*, trans. Lewis White Beck (New York: Macmillan, 1985). I have simplified Kant's views in my presentation. The supreme principle of morality is actually, "Act only according to the maxim by which you can at the same time will that it should become a universal law," p. 38. Kant later glosses this as a constraint on making an exception of oneself.

The claim that we don't need a "policeman at the elbow" to prevent crime is a standard expression in legal philosophy. I picked it up from Arthur Ripstein, *Equality, Responsibility and the Law* (Cambridge: Cambridge University Press, 1990). The book is an excellent resource for anyone interested in understanding how the central ideas of Kant practical philosophy can be applied to the legal regulation of society.

The factoid about Canadians only carrying garbage for twelve steps before dropping it is from *Shift* magazine, 6:5 (1998), p. 9. The way that I use the expression "trust" is indebted to Francis Fukuyama, *Trust* (London: Penguin, 1995). There he writes, "Trust is the expectation that arises within a community of regular, honest, and cooperative behavior, based on commonly shared norms, on the part of other members of the community," p. 26.

The profile of the Ik that I refer to is Colin Turnbull, *The Mountain People* (New York: Simon and Schuster, 1972). Later generations of ethnographers suggested that Turnbull had simply caught the Ik on a bad day, and that they really weren't so unpleasant. I am clearly in no position to judge this question.

The Jamestown bowling story is drawn from Robert C. Ellickson, "Property in Land," *Yale Law Journal*, 102 (1993): 1315–97. It is a version of the so-called tragedy of the commons. See Garrett Hardin, "Tragedy of the Commons," *Science* (Dec. 13, 1968), pp. 1243–48. The argument that goods held in common tend to be degraded and that collective reward generates shirking is very old. It can be found, for instance, in Aristotle's *Politics*, book 2, sect. 3–5.

The classic discussion of the gift economy is Marcel Mauss, *The Gift*, trans. Ian Cunnison (London: Cohen & West, 1966). See also Karl Polanyi, *The Great Transformation* (Boston: Beacon Press, 1944). For discussion of the insurance functions of gifts among hunters, see Elman R. Service, *The Hunters*, 2nd ed. (Englewood Cliff, NJ: Prentice Hall, 1979), pp. 16–22. It is not quite right to say that nothing obliges people to repay a gift, beyond the force of the moral obligation. Within a status system, failing to repay gifts creates a loss of face, which can in turn restrict opportunities for future satisfaction or rewards. There is also generally a range of spiritual beliefs that motivate compliance. The general point is that, when push comes to shove, no one has the power to compel repayment. Thus the system as a whole cannot function without an enormous amount of voluntary compliance.

The fact about no society in human history having succeeded in constructing a large-scale irrigation system without first creating a state is from Jared Diamond, *Guns, Germs and Steel* (New York: W. W. Norton, 1997), p. 283. For a balanced evaluation of the relative merits of bureaucracy, see James Q. Wilson, *Bureaucracy* (New York: Harper-Collins, 1991). Here one can find a more extensive discussion of the connection between red tape and the need for accountability.

The Marx quote is from the *Communist Manifesto* (Moscow: Progress Publishers, 1986), pp. 38–39. My favourite line comes shortly before.

Capitalism, says Marx, "has drowned the most heavenly ecstasies of religious fervour, of chivalrous enthusiasm, of philistine sentimentalism, in the icy water of egotistical calculation," p. 36. Naturally he approves of this development.

Chapter 5

The complexity of the task that markets perform was first driven home to me by Alec Nove, *The Economics of a Feasible Socialism Revisited* (London: HarperCollins, 1991). Nove gives many examples of things that used to go wrong in the former Soviet Union that I had never even realized *could* go wrong. The example of the airport, along with the information on Soviet planning, is drawn from Nove's discussion on p. 37.

The information on the behaviour of economics students in prisoner's dilemmas is from "How do you mean 'fair'?" *The Economist* (May 29, 1993). In fairness, I should point out that these studies do not show that studying economics *makes* you a bad person. It may just be that bad people are more likely to be attracted to the study of economics. Anyhow, the truth probably lies somewhere in between.

The study on competition cited was issued by the so-called Group of Lisbon, *Limits to Competition* (Cambridge, MA: MIT Press, 1995). The quoted passages are from p. 90.

The observation that an athlete might "break ranks" by training is not implausible. I recently came across the following example: "The Academy Award-winning film *Chariots of Fire* portrays British collegiate track-and-field competitors who have developed an implicit norm that limits their training and practice time. Their apparent understanding is that since the most talented runner will win whether all train arduously or none does, the sensible thing is for no one to train very hard." This little plot synopsis is from Robert H. Frank and Philip J. Cook, *The Winner-Take-All Society* (New York: Penguin, 1995), p. 172.

Facts on Cuba are from Ronald Radosh, ed., *The New Cuba* (New York: William Morrow & Co., 1976), including the quotes from Castro (p. 100) and Guevara (p. 92).

The idea that trade begins as a foreign trade relationship and is then internalized comes from Karl Polanyi, *The Great Transformation* (Boston: Beacon Press, 1944). My point that market economies emerge out of moral economies is a theme that received its most influential articulation in Polanyi's work. However, I think that Polanyi overstates the level of social integration in moral economies. He speaks as if agents in a moral economy lacked free-rider incentives entirely, instead of simply being subject to more informal systems of social control. It is a notorious feature of traditional moral economies that individuals are subject to extremely close scrutiny by their neighbours, for instance.

The Nietzsche quote is from the "flies of the marketplace" section of *Thus Spake Zarathustra.* My favourite translation of this work is by Alexander Tille, *The Work of Frederich Nietzsche, vol.* 8 (New York: Macmillan, 1902).

Chapter 6

The "Rival Chiefs" story was recorded by George Hunt and is printed in *Anthropological Papers: Written in Honor of Franz Boas* (New York: G. E. Stechert, 1906). The other potlatch statistic is from Ruth Benedict, *Patterns of Culture* (Boston: Houghton Mifflin, 1934).

For further discussion of the QWERTY phenomenon, see Paul Krugman, *Peddling Prosperity* (New York: W. W. Norton, 1994), pp. 221–44. A product whose value is in part a function of the number of others who use it is said to generate "network externalities." This term was introduced by Michael L. Katz and Carl Shapiro in "Product Introduction with Network Externalities," *Journal of Industrial Economics* 40 (1992): 55–83. For a more accessible discussion, see Carl Shapiro and Hal Varian, *Information Rules: A Strategic Guide to the Network Economy* (Boston: Harvard Business School Press, 1999).

On Locke's theory of property, see John Locke, *Second Treatise of Government* (Indianapolis: Hackett, 1992), also James Tully, *A Discourse on Property* (Cambridge: Cambridge University Press, 1980).

On Russia, see Chrystia Freeland, *Sale of the Century* (Toronto: Doubleday, 2000). Freeland writes, "Capitalism is often described as heartless;

yet, as Russia discovered, it is remarkably hard to build it out of a society of Tin Men. The impersonal market is actually a sensitive organic system, hugely dependent on trust between its participants," p. 18.

The idea that markets offer freedom from morality is from David Gauthier, *Morals by Agreement* (Oxford: Clarendon, 1986). It is not clear that Gauthier is really talking about markets in the sense that we understand the term. If so, he certainly should have known better, since exchange is obviously compromised by an underlying prisoner's dilemma. See also Bernard Mandeville, *Fable of the Bees* (Harmondsworth, UK: Penguin, 1970).

Some apologists for Ayn Rand try to set aside the rape scenes as merely "rough sex." This is pretty hard to believe. Consider the following, from *The Fountainhead* (New York: Bobbs Merrill, 1943): "He did it as an act of scorn. Not as love, but as defilement. And this made her lie still and submit. One gesture of tenderness from him—and she would have remained cold, untouched by the thing done to her body. But the act of a master taking shameful, contemptuous possession of her was the kind of rapture that she wanted," p. 218. For the source of all this, see Nietzsche, *Beyond Good and Evil*, trans. Walter Kaufman (New York: Vintage Books, 1966).

Incidentally, this is why educated conservatives such as Allan Bloom have such contempt for Ayn Rand. See his *Closing of the American Mind* (New York: Simon and Schuster, 1987). They have read enough books to know that she is a Nietzschean. In the late twentieth century, neoconservative culture critics held Nietzsche responsible for all the deconstructionism and relativism that was, at the time, supposedly undermining Western civilization. So Rand was regarded as very much in bed with the enemy.

On our tendency to overestimate our own abilities, see Thomas Gilovich, *How We Know What Isn't So* (New York: Free Press, 1991). Among the more interesting findings reported by Gilovich is the fact that a whopping 94 per cent of university professors believe that they are better than their colleagues.

Russell Hardin's line about the "backside of the invisible hand" is from his *Collective Action* (Baltimore: Johns Hopkins University Press,

1982). It is not quite right to say that society suffers a "double hit" on the efficiency front when prices do not fully reflect social cost. It is in fact the same hit, seen from different perspectives.

The mosquito-control example is from Joe Stevens, *The Economics of Collective Choice* (Boulder: Westview, 1993).

The literature on futures and insurance markets is somewhat technical. The most important paper on market failure in this sector, and its impact on the economy, is Bruce C. Greenwald and Joseph E. Stiglitz, "Externalities in Economies with Imperfect Information and Incomplete Markets," *Quarterly Journal of Economics* 101 (1986): 229–64. For an introduction to moral hazard and adverse selection, see Eric Rasmusen, *Games and Information*, 2nd ed. (Oxford: Blackwell, 1995), pp. 195–248.

Chapter 7

The pin-factory example occurs in Adam Smith, *An Inquiry in the Nature and Causes of the Wealth of Nations* (Oxford: Oxford University Press, 1976), p. 15. The remark about the division of labour not being an effect of wisdom is on p. 25. My discussion of Smith is a bit uncharitable, since he actually says that the division of labour is not "originally" an effect of human wisdom. Thus he is not actually claiming that markets generate the division of labour, but merely that this is where we originally got the idea from. But this weaker thesis is completely devoid of interest. Who cares where the idea came from?

It is helpful to compare Smith's discussion with another classic analysis, Peter Drucker's *The Corporation* (New York: Mentor, 1972). According to Drucker, mass production depends upon "a conscious, deliberate, and planned order to relations between man and man, and man and mechanical process. The one thing in modern industry therefore that cannot be improvised but must be worked out carefully and beforehand is the social structure of the corporation," p. 34.

The discussion of GM and Fisher Body is drawn from Oliver E. Williamson, *The Economic Institutions of Capitalism* (New York: Free Press, 1985). This is the classic discussion and a founding work in the so-called "transaction cost" theory of the firm. (Along with Ronald Coase, "The Economic Theory of the Firm," *Economica* 4 [1937]: 386–405.) The only weakness in Williamson's account is his failure to notice that transaction costs arise because of an underlying prisoner's dilemma in all economic exchanges. On efficiency wages, see Eric Rasmusen, *Games and Information*, 2nd ed. (Oxford: Blackwell, 1995), pp. 206–7.

The Steelcase ant colony was profiled in "Metaphor of a Corporate Display: 'You Work, and Then You Die,'" *Wall Street Journal* (August 11, 1996), p. B1. The quote from the corporate trainer complaining about Rich's *Survivor* game strategy is from "Survivor's millionaire gives corporate trainers a bad name," *Globe and Mail* (August 28, 2000), p. B9. The point about management literature being indistinguishable from '60s ideology is due to Thomas Frank, "Why Johnny Can't Dissent," in *Commodify Your Dissent* (New York: W. W. Norton, 1997). For the central example of this, see Stephen R. Covey, *The 7 Habits of Highly Effective People* (New York: Simon and Schuster, 1989).

The Brookings Institute data on the ratio of physical to knowledge assets is cited in Seth Shulman, *Owning the Future* (Boston: Houghton Mifflin, 1999), p. 15. Trilogy Software's boot camp is described in "High rollers: How Trilogy Software trains its raw recruits to be risk takers," *The Wall Street Journal* (Sept. 21, 1998), p. A1. "Why your fabulous job sucks," was written by Clive Thompson, *Shift* 7.1 (1999). On Scient's training program, see Noah Hawley, "Do you have the courage to be legendary?" *Shift* 8.3 (2000). Many of these training tactics are sufficiently "cult-like" that Christian management theorists have begun to express concern. For an interesting example of this, see Dave Arnott, *Corporate Cults* (New York: Amacom, 2000).

The data on surplus mammography machines is from Pat Armstrong and Hugh Armstrong, *Universal Health Care* (New York: The New Press, 1998), p. xiii. The discussion of HMOs that follows is necessarily simplified. An enormous number of different packages are sold under the general rubric of "managed care." For a helpful overview of these different arrangements, see Wendy Knight, *Managed Care* (Gaithersburg, MA: Aspen, 1998). On the relative market share of HMOs, see p.

10. It should be noted that not all HMOs are vertically integrated like Kaiser Permanente. It is also worth noting that moral hazard problems are endemic in any fee-for-service physician-payment arrangement, including Canada's. Vertical integration reduces these problems—by eliminating a collective action problem in the domain of physician supervision—but it does not eliminate them entirely. The most aggressive strategy for reducing moral hazard is known as capitation. But there is no intrinsic connection between the HMO model and the use of capitation—similar arrangements have been experimented with in the public system in Canada. My thanks to Peter Nixon from Kaiser Permanente for helpful discussions on this subject.

Chapter 8

On air quality, see Cass Sunstein, *After the Rights Revolution* (Cambridge, MA: Harvard University Press, 1990), p. 77.

The three-cents-per-litre figure is the one used by the World Bank in its campaign to eliminate leaded fuel. The data on Canadian gasoline consumption are from the *Transport Canada Annual Report* (1998), p. 69. Incidentally, it is very important when calculating the efficiency gains associated with the switch to unleaded fuel not to fall into the mistake of counting only indirect gains. For example, it is not unusual for commentators to add up the cost of health care for people with lead-related illnesses as one of the "costs" of leaded fuel. This is invalid, since people who don't die of lead-related illnesses will eventually die of something else, and there is no reason to think that this something else will be cheaper. The efficiency gain comes in the form of clean air. Clean air has no market value, and so it is impossible to do a straightforward cost-benefit analysis. Substituting some other kind of indirect benefit that *does* have a market value just muddies the water.

I adopt the phrase "club goods" from Richard Cornes and Todd Sandler, *The Theory of Externalities, Public Goods and Club Goods*, 2nd ed. (Cambridge: Cambridge University Press, 1996). Whether or not club goods get counted correctly in the GDP is a somewhat tricky question.

Some of the goods provided by corporations, such as the risk-protection that diversification affords, are not counted at all. In other cases, the cost of providing the service will be counted as the benefit.

On the problems with GDP as an economic indicator, see Clifford Cobb, Ted Halstead, and Jonathan Rowe, "If the GDP is up, why is America down?" *Atlantic Monthly* (October 1995). The authors make the following arresting claim about the U.S. economy: "much of what we now call growth of GDP is really just one of three things in disguise: fixing blunders and social decay from the past, borrowing resources from the future, or shifting functions from the traditional realm of household and community to the realm of the monetized economy," p. 72. The statistic on policing levels is from the *Globe and Mail* (May 24, 2000), p. A4.

Statistics on government spending in Canada and the United States as a percentage of GDP are from John C. Strick, *The Public Sector in Canada* (Toronto: Thompson, 1999), p. 65. On the social safety net as a response to market failure in the insurance sector, see Nicholas Barr, *The Economics of the Welfare State*, 3rd ed. (Oxford: Oxford University Press, 1998), pp. 108–27.

The classic discussion of adverse selection is George A. Akerlof, "The Market for 'Lemons': Quality Uncertainty and the Market Mechanism," *Quarterly Journal of Economics* 84 (1970): 488–500. In this paper, one of the things that Akerlof sets out to explain is why the elderly find it so difficult to purchase health insurance. For a more general overview of adverse selection, see Prajit K. Dutta, *Strategies and Games* (Cambridge, MA: MIT Press, 1999), pp. 383–95.

The information on insurance overhead and research expenditures in Canada and the United States is from John Richards, *Retooling the Welfare State* (Toronto: C. D. Howe Institute, 1997), p. 122. A comparison of health outcomes, based on life expectancy and infant mortality, can be found on p. 124. On the ratio of physician fees in Canada and the United States, see Robert Chernomas and Ardeshir Sepehri, *How to Choose? A Comparison of the U.S. and Canadian Health Care Systems* (Amityville, NY: Baywood Publishing, 1998), p. 29. The figures on the price of colonoscopies is from Pat Armstrong and Hugh Armstrong, *Universal Health Care* (New York: The New Press, 1998), p. 107.

The Business Council on National Issues's report, "Winning the Human Race—Developing and Retaining World Class Talent" (May 30, 2000) is available at *www.bnci.com*. The Statistics Canada study on brain drain is "Brain Drain or Brain Gain: The migration of knowledge workers from and to Canada," by Doug Drew, T. Scott Murray, and John Zhao, published in *Education Quarterly Review* 6:3 (2000).

As for the poor supporting tax cuts, see "Poorer voters support Ontario tax cuts, pollsters say," *Globe and Mail* (October 23, 1999), p. A6. The statistics on the distribution of the tax burden are from Joel Ernes and Michael Walker, *Tax Facts 11* (Vancouver: Fraser Institute, 1999).

Chapter 9

The "parable of the talents" occurs in Matthew 25:14–30. The line about giving the money to bankers is not Jesus' own, but belongs rather to the "master" in the parable. Nevertheless, Jesus appears to endorse it. Of course, I'm not a biblical exegete.

The classic work on the tradeoff between equality and efficiency is Arthur M. Okun, *Equality and Efficiency, The Big Tradeoff* (Washington: Brookings Institute, 1975). Personally, I have no idea what people see in this book. The "discovery" that there is no tradeoff between efficiency and equality is a consequence of the Second Fundamental Theory of Welfare Economics. One can find discussions and proofs of this theorem all over the place. I rely upon Gareth D. Myles, *Public Economics* (Cambridge: Cambridge University Press, 1995).

On G. A. Cohen, see his *If You're an Egalitarian, How Come You're So Rich?* (Cambridge, MA: Harvard University Press, 2000). For Robert Nozick, see *Anarchy, State and Utopia* (New York: Basic Books, 1974). The first Nozick quotation, slightly altered, is from p. 161. The line about consenting adults is on p. 163. Cohen's attempts to grapple with Nozick's arguments are collected in a volume of papers *Self-Ownership, Freedom, and Equality* (Cambridge: Cambridge University Press, 1995).

The phrase "profit-inducing public bads" is from John Roemer, *A Future for Socialism* (Cambridge, MA: Harvard University Press, 1994), p. 57. My entire discussion of how inequality can generate inefficiency is enormously indebted to Roemer's analysis. On industry opposition to leaded fuel, see Cass Peterson, "EPA Orders Leading in Gas Cut by 90%," *Washington Post* (March 5, 1985).

The calculation of how much the average Canadian receives in government services is somewhat back-of-the-envelope. It is based on data from 1994–95 and takes no account of past or future changes in government spending. Information on annual government spending is from John C. Strick, *The Public Sector in Canada* (Toronto: Thompson, 1999), p. 32. I then divided this by population and multiplied by average life expectancy. Note that the calculation concerns the cost of supplying these goods and services, not their *value* to the consumer, which may be much higher.

On the effects of the progressivity of income taxes on work effort, see Tibor Scitovsky, *The Joyless Economy*, rev. ed. (New York: Oxford University Press, 1992), p. 100. The quote about a dollar not spent is from this book as well, p. 165.

The theory about progressive taxes generating riskier career strategies can be found in Hans-Werner Sinn, "A Theory of the Welfare State," in Torben M. Andersen, Karl O. Moene, and Agnar Sandmo, eds., *The Future of the Welfare State* (Cambridge, MA: Blackwell, 1996). See also the interesting article in this volume by Mats Persson, "Why are taxes so high in egalitarian societies?"

For an overview of the Singapore traffic congestion tax, along with proposals to implement similar arrangements in Europe, see "Living with the car," *The Economist* (Dec. 6, 1997): 21–23.

For the origin of Pigovian taxes, see A. C. Pigou, *The Economics of Welfare* (London: Macmillan, 1948). These taxes are, of course, not a magic bullet. For a brief overview of the limitations, see Edward E. Zajac, *Political Economy of Fairness* (Cambridge, MA: MIT Press, 1995), pp. 41–42.

The quote comparing fairness and efficiency is from Richard G. Lipsey, Douglas D. Purvis, and Peter O. Steiner, *Economics*, 6th ed.

(New York: Harper & Row, 1988), p. 478. The standard reason for claiming that efficiency judgements are not normative is that they can be made using only subjective preferences. It is often assumed, on the other hand, that judgements of fairness require interpersonal comparisons of utility. This used to be true, given the state of the art in the 1950s, but it is no longer the case. For an overview of these issues, see John Roemer, *Theories of Distributive Justice* (Cambridge, MA: Harvard University Press, 1996). My own preferred conception of equality can be found in William J. Baumol, *Superfairness* (Cambridge, MA: MIT Press, 1986).

Chapter 10

For an accessible survey of work trends in the United States, see Juliet Schor, *The Overworked American* (New York: Basic Books, 1992). According to a recent International Labour Organization study, the average number of hours worked in Canada remained substantially unchanged throughout the last decade (and remained significantly lower than in the United States). See "Key Indicators of the Labour Market 1999" (Geneva: International Labour Office, 1999). The quote from Arlie Hochschild is from *The Time Bind* (New York: Metropolitan, 1997), p. 212.

Special thanks to Jim Preston from Imagine Media/DailyRadar.com for his assistance with the Sim game. I have benefited especially from his Sims strategy guide, *PC Gamer*, 7:4 (April 2000), pp. 150–52. The two quotes from the Sims manual are from pp. 3 and 45 respectively. *The Sims* and *SimCity* © 2000 Electronic Arts Inc.

The classic analysis of the efficiency properties of the division of household labour can be found in Gary S. Becker, *A Treatise on the Family* (Cambridge, MA: Harvard University Press, 1991).

As I mentioned at the outset, I have little direct experience with household management. As my extensive citation shows, much of the discussion in the chapter is drawn from Rhona Mahony's *Kidding Ourselves* (New York: Basic Books, 1995). This book stands head and shoulders above everything else in the field. It is brilliant. Anyone with doubts about the line of argument that I develop should consult Mahony's undoubtedly more compelling presentation. On the expertise gap between fathers and mothers—what Mahony calls the "headstart effect"—see pp. 76–77. On physical risk-tolerance, see p. 108. The long passage quoted occurs on p. 3.

The Stanford MBA study was conducted by Thomas W. Harrell, "Women with MBAs marry up while men with MBAs marry down," *Psychological Reports* 72 (1993): 1178. Of the men, 33.7 per cent were married to housewives. Only 1 per cent of the women had stay-at-home husbands.

The quotes from Hochschild's *The Time Bind* are from pp. 25–26. The study of participation rates in alternative work arrangements at Fortune 500 companies is given on p. 27, with no further source. As for preferring work to home, Hochschild found that 59 per cent of parents rated themselves as "good or unusually good" at home, versus 86 per cent at work.

For a discussion of the beauty/wealth tradeoff in black families, see Robert Staples and Leanor Boulin Johnson, *Black Families at the Crossroads* (San Francisco: Jossey-Bass, 1993), pp. 111–12. See also *Kidding Ourselves*, pp. 21–22. On women showing a disinterest in househusbands, see Kathleen Gerson, *Hard Choices: How women decide about work, career, and motherhood* (Berkeley: University of California Press, 1985). For the career women Gerson talked to, "The great importance they attached to work made it difficult for them to accept the legitimacy of domesticity for male partners as well as for themselves," p. 175.

Finally, the little passage from Guy Vanderhaeghe, *Man Descending* (Toronto: Macmillan, 1982) is from p. 213.

Chapter 11

The quote from Kalle Lasn about the significance of culture jamming for our time is from p. xi of his *Culture Jam* (New York: William Morris, 1999). For all the info on *Adbusters*, along with the full line of *Adbusters* merchandise, see *www.adbusters.org/magazine/*.

The quote from Joseph Schumpter is from *Capitalism, Socialism and Democracy*, 3rd ed. (New York: Harper, 1950), p. 66. The standard critique of consumerism—that the creation of new products creates new desires and so generates no increase in overall satisfaction—is from John Kenneth Galbraith, *The Affluent Society*, 2nd ed. (Boston: Houghton Mifflin, 1969). Just to be clear, this is not a view that I endorse.

The long quote from Mark Kingwell is from *Better Living* (Toronto: Penguin, 1998), pp. 178–79. The second Kingwell quote is from p. 304. Also, Kalle Lasn, *Culture Jam*, p. 12. The needle metaphor is so overused that one critic, James Twitchell, even refers to a certain collection of views as the "hypodermic theory" of advertising, *AdcultUSA* (New York: Columbia University Press, 1996), p. 14.

On inauthentic desires, see Jean-Jacques Rousseau, *A Discourse on the Origins of Inequality*, trans. Franklin Philip (Oxford: Oxford University Press, 1994). I am certainly not the first to point out this connection. Twitchell puts it well: "The idea that advertising creates artificial desires rests upon a profound ignorance of human nature, on the hazy feeling that there exists some halcyon era of noble savages with purely natural needs, on romantic claptrap first promulgated by Rousseau and kept alive in institutions well insulated from the marketplace," *AdcultUSA*, p. 12.

On consumerism as a prisoner's dilemma, see Juliet Schor, *The Overspent American* (New York: Basic Books, 1998), and Robert H. Frank, *Luxury Fever* (New York: Free Press, 1999). Both of these authors recommend a more progressive income tax as a solution to the problem of competitive consumption.

The concept of distinction that I use here is drawn from Pierre Bourdieu, *Distinction*, trans. Richard Nice (Cambridge, MA: Harvard University Press, 1984). The importance of distinction is, in Bourdieu's view, revealed largely through negative preferences. "In matters of taste, more than anywhere else, all determination is negation; and tastes are perhaps first and foremost distastes, disgust provoked by horror or visceral intolerance of the tastes of others," p. 56. Consumerism among upper classes is driven by contempt for popular culture and an attempt to avoid anything associated with it.

The term "rebel consumer," along with the observation that "cool" drives consumerism, is from Thomas Frank, *The Conquest of Cool* (Chicago: University of Chicago Press, 1997). Here is a good example: Naomi Klein starts out her book *No Logo* (Toronto: Alfred A. Knopf, 2000) by lamenting the fact that the old factory buildings in her neighbourhood are being converted and sold off as "loft-living" condominiums. What is the subtext here? Klein makes it quite clear to the reader that her apartment is a *genuine* loft—the kind that only cool people live in. It thus serves as a source of distinction. The condominium projects make this lifestyle—once the exclusive property of cultural élites like Klein—available to people who are merely wealthy. This means that she will have to find another place to live if she wants to maintain her social status.

The "standard textbook" that I cite for a definition of pollution is Giles H. Burgess Jr., *The Economics of Regulation and Anti-Trust* (New York: HarperCollins, 1995), p. 402. The statistics on gross advertising spending in the United States are from Klein, *No Logo*, p. 11. On the effectiveness of advertising on market size/share, see Tibor Scitovsky, *The Joyless Economy*, rev. ed. (New York: Oxford University Press, 1992), pp. 204–5. Twitchell, in *AdcultUSA*, points out that during a recession, ad budgets are the first thing to be cut, p. 75. If advertising actually moved product, this would be very difficult to explain. The statistics on beer are from "Younger Drinkers Snub Molson, Labatt," *National Post* (March 9, 1999). The market share of Molson and Labatt is down from 85 per cent in 1997.

My claim that the level of advertising revenue in a media source is determined by the ease with which people can free-ride seems to me fairly uncontroversial. Consider the following ratios of advertising revenues to end-user fees for different media: newpapers 80:20, magazines 63:37, cable TV 18:82, film 5:95. The data are from Richard Adler, *The Future of Advertising* (Washington, D.C.: Aspen Institute, 1997), p. 17.

The trend-setting book on body modification is *Modern Primitives* (San Francisco: RE/Search, 1989). For further discussion of the proposal for a progressive consumption tax as a cure for consumerism, see Robert H. Frank, *Luxury Fever* (New York: Free Press, 1999). The relationship between income taxes and consumption taxes is also discussed there at greater length.

Chapter 12

Neal Stephenson, *Snow Crash* (New York: Bantam, 1992). True fans will no doubt be aware that the events in this book are not dated. The year 2020 is just my guess. Bruce Sterling, *Distraction* (New York: Bantam, 1998). See also Neal Stephenson, *Cryptonomicon* (New York: Avon, 1999).

The statistics on international software piracy are from "Software piracy," *The Economist* (June 27, 1998), and music, "Stolen melodies," *The Economist* (May 11, 1996). On the importance of intellectual property in the American export economy, see Seth Shulman, *Owning the Future* (Boston: Houghton Mifflin, 1999), p. 18. The examples of dubious patent awards are all from this book. See also Seth Shulman, "Cashing in on medical knowledge," *Technology Review* 101:2 (1998).

I learned a lot about the information economy by hanging around the offices of Organic Online Canada. My thanks to managing director Troy Young for letting me be a fly on the wall, and to Idris Mootee for some interesting suggestions about intellectual property and the high-tech sector. Additional information on the significance of public domain or "open-source" software for the internet is from Peter Wayner, *Free for All* (New York: Harper Business, 2000).

On the subject of Nike's beleaguered stock, see "Investors not running after Nike," *Globe and Mail* (Feb. 11, 2000), p. B15.

The phrase *le capitalisme sauvage* is an extremely apt expression, with no obvious English equivalent. See Michel Albert, *Capitalisme contre capitalisme* (Paris: Éditions du Seuil, 1991). "Unfettered capitalism" is perhaps the closest, but it has odd Marxist resonances.

The final Hobbes quote is from *Leviathan*, ed. Richard Tuck (Cambridge: Cambridge University Press 1991), p. 129. As far as I am concerned, this one sentence says everything that needs to be said on the subject of taxation.

Conclusion

The book by Francis Fukuyama is *The End of History and the Last Man* (New York: Avon, 1992). In the aftermath of the controversy this book provoked, Fukuyama quite astutely pointed out that even though many alternatives to welfare state capitalism had been advanced as counterexamples to his central thesis, none of his critics actually *endorsed* any of these alternatives. The essay by Jürgen Habermas mentioned is "The new obscurity: The crisis of the welfare state and the exhaustion of utopian energies," in *The New Conservativism*, trans. Shierry Weber Nicholsen (Cambridge, MA: MIT Press, 1989).

For further discussion of mechanism design, see Prajit K. Dutta, *Strategies and Games* (Cambridge, MA: MIT Press, 1999), pp. 349–65.

Index